MISSISSIPPI HEROES

MISSISSIPPI
HEROES

EDITORS

Dean Faulkner Wells and Hunter Cole

UNIVERSITY PRESS OF MISSISSIPPI ● *Jackson*

Copyright © 1980 by the
University Press of Mississippi
Manufactured in the United States of America
All rights reserved

Book design by Larry E. Hirst

Library of Congress Cataloging in Publication Data
Main entry under title:
Mississippi heroes.

Includes bibliographies.
1. Mississippi—Biography. I. Wells, Dean
Faulkner. II. Cole, Hunter.
CT243.M57   920'.0762   80-19704
ISBN 0-87805-128-7 (v. 1)

TO THE MEMORY OF

Nannie Pitts McLemore
and
Laura D.S. Sturdivant

Contents

vii

Acknowledgments

The editors thank the following publishers and copyright holders for permission to publish or reprint material used in this book:

To Harcourt Brace Jovanovich for "L.Q.C. Lamar: Artificer of Reconciliation," adapted and reprinted from *South of Appomattox*, © 1959, by Nash K. Burger and John K. Bettersworth.

To *The Journal of Mississippi History* for "Governor Mike Conner and the Sales Tax, 1932," © 1979, and for portions of John Eudy's essay on Thomas Rodney, © 1978.

To Jimmie Rodgers Memorial Festival, Inc., for the photograph of Jimmie Rodgers and for his signature.

To Louise Meadow for the photograph of William Faulkner.

To Mississippi Department of Archives and History for Eudora Welty's photograph of Rodney, Mississippi; for the photographs of Greenwood LeFlore, Jefferson Davis, L.Q.C. Lamar, Martin Sennett Conner, and William Alexander Percy; and for the signatures of Rodney, Davis, Lamar, Conner, and Percy.

To Random House, Inc., for excerpts from *The Civil War: A Narrative: Fort Sumter to Perryville*, vol. 1, by Shelby Foote. Copyright © 1958 by Shelby Foote. Reprinted by permission of Random House, Inc.; from *The Civil War: A Narrative: Red River to Appomattox*, vol. 3, by Shelby Foote. Copyright © 1974 by Shelby Foote. Reprinted by permission of Random House, Inc.

To Yoknapatawpha Press for the signature of William Faulkner.

To Alabama Department of Archives and History for the signature of Sam Dale.

To Doris Allison for the signature of Medgar Evers.

To Cleveland Donald, Jr., for the photograph of Medgar Evers.

For research assistance the editors are grateful to Sarah Portis for her help at Alabama Department of Archives and History, to Forrest O. Lax for research at the National Archives, to Ethelwyn Worden for research on Thomas Rodney at the National Portrait Gallery, Winterthur Museum, and the Historical Society of Delaware, and to A. E. Elmore.

Foreword

Those of us who are of Mississippi—and those of us who are not, but who have felt something of its curious and special nature—know there is something in the very resonance of the name *Mississippi*, and in the place from which the name springs, which makes this state the most *different* among the fifty of the greater American Republic. Foremost, its literary tradition derives from the complexity of a society which still, well into the late 20th Century, retains much of its communal, inward origins. If modern industrialism and the national "values" came to Mississippi later and with greater force and destructiveness than to other areas of the United States, if the traditional federal authority had to exert itself through more oscillations to meet halfway the better instincts of Mississippi, then this had to do in large measure with the direness and beauty of its immemorial past.

William Faulkner, the poet and chronicler of Mississippi, understood how deeply we care for it despite what it was and is—the gulf between its manners and morals, the extraordinary apposition of its violence and kindliness, its nobility, and its haunted and lovely land. He knew that our profound love and despair of our native ground, our desire to embrace it and comprehend it and keep it our own, does not happen everyday in most other American states. Surely there is something that matters in the past of a place which elicits in its sons and daughters wherever they live such emotions of fidelity and rage and passion.

This book, edited by Dean Faulkner Wells and Hunter Cole, is the maiden volume in a continuing series of books to be published by the University Press of Mississippi about individual Mississippians now dead. This first volume begins with Thomas Rodney, President Thomas Jefferson's appointee to the Federal judgeship of the Mississippi Territory, who made judicial decisions which helped keep the rebellious new territory in the mainstream of the American Constitution. The volume ends with Medgar Evers, the modern black leader and native Mississippian who gave his life for the humanity and courage implicit in the finer impulses of Mississippi. In between, there are essays on Sam Dale, pioneer scout of the Old Southwest; Greenwood LeFlore, chief of the Choctaw nation; Jefferson Davis, the secessionist President who said near the end of his life, "Tell the world that I only loved America"; L.Q.C. Lamar, the great pacificator between North and South in the post-Civil War years; William Alexander Percy, the poet and aristocrat of the Delta who wrote after the Flood of 1927: "Whenever you are about to decide that Americans are selfish, unpatriotic, and unintelligent, they prove themselves the most liberal and loveable people in the world," adding: "What a pity they are not disciplined enough to survive!"; Mike Conner, the Governor who saved the state from bankruptcy during the Depression (written by one of his successors to the Governorship); Jimmie Rodgers, the father of country music; and William Faulkner—all part of a narrative rich in irony, sorrow, and understanding. And the thread of this book is the ineluctable link between Mississippi and the America of which it has always been a part.

The editors have not chosen individuals who are "heroes" in the old-fashioned sense, who led troops or who rode on horses with the bands playing. Their criteria of valor were more subtle. They have selected individuals who have contributed to the state's distinctive culture, people from different backgrounds and sections of the state, figures nurtured by Mississippi who in turn nurtured their state and whose influence is still felt—people who have made us what we are as Mississippians.

Terry Southern, the novelist and essayist from Alvarado, Texas, once told me of meeting Faulkner for the first time at a proper dinner in a town house on Central Park West in New York City many years ago. There were twelve or fourteen people at the table, and near the end of the dinner Southern leaned forward:

"Mr. Bill," he whispered, "why are you and I already drinking brandy and everyone else is still drinking wine?"

"Terry," Faulkner playfully replied, "there was a saying in currency in the court of the Emperor Napoleon at the beginning of the last century: Claret is for the ladies and port for the men, but brandy is for the heroes."

Willie Morris
Ole Miss
March, 1980

Introduction

This is the first volume in a series devoted to the study of figures who influenced the course of Mississippi history, beginning with the Territorial period and continuing up to the recent past.

Our view of Mississippi history is in large measure like Carlyle's view of world history, "the essence of innumerable biographies." Like Carlyle we have seen the categories into which heroes—for us, the heroes of Mississippi—may be placed. Included in this volume are a president, a governor, a chieftain, a civil rights leader, a novelist, a poet, a frontiersman, a musician, and two jurists. Patrician and plebeian, varied in their respective callings, controversial in their natures and their public reception, they are, as a group, a mixture which is both unusual and distinctively Mississippian. The assembly of their biographies offers what Carlyle might have called "glimpses into the very marrow" of Mississippi.

Settling the matter of selecting only ten Mississippians was not easy. Initially, we chose ten deceased figures who we thought were significant contributors to the peculiar identity of Mississippi. Then we announced our choices to members of history societies, to members of history departments of Mississippi colleges and universities, and to friends and invited these persons to emend or to add to our list. Our choices also were controlled to some degree by the availability of authors who would write or release essays about the Mississippians included in the list. Throughout the process of making our selections final, we have been guided by the chronology of Mississippi history and by our definition of *hero*.

What is a *hero*? For this book a Mississippi hero is a significant contributor to the state's identity, a person who had a kind of valorous conviction, qualities of leadership, charisma, and an aura that permeates the history of the state. Moreover, each one who exemplifies this definition of hero in this book was nurtured by Mississippi or claimed by Mississippi as a citizen.

With the demise or obsolescence of many feminine words—*prophetess*, *poetess*, and *authoress*—*hero*, for this volume and the ones to follow it, is generic for both genders, and we settled upon the title from the first, continuing to reject suggestions such as *Distinguished Mississippians*, *Eminent Mississippians*, *Mississippians of Worth*, *Mississippi Worthies*, *Mississippi Profiles*.

This book and the succeeding ones will follow the same plan: the presentation of biographical essays about representative men and women whose lives, when arranged in a chronological sequence, outline Mississippi history. Few, if any, of the figures in this series will be accepted with total approbation in a time when even the word *hero* is suspect, but their influence is indisputable. Each is heroic in the leadership he invested in the emerging and developing culture of Mississippi.

Dean Faulkner Wells
Hunter Cole

MISSISSIPPI HEROES

Thomas Rodney
1744–1811

There is no extant portrait of Thomas Rodney. This photograph of the Mississippi river town named for him was made by Eudora Welty in the 1930s.

Thomas Rodney

Patriot in the
Mississippi Territory

ו⌒⊙⌒ו

BY JOHN CARROLL EUDY

Thomas Rodney, a Delaware colonial soldier, born June 4, 1744, traveled to the Mississippi Territory in 1803. In Delaware Rodney lived in the shadow of his older brother, Caesar Rodney, a signer of the Declaration of Independence, but in the Mississippi Territory, Rodney emerged as one of the most interesting commentators upon the lives and the politics of the people of what would become the Magnolia State.[1]

Rodney's transformation from old Delaware soldier into the enthusiastically opinionated judge of the lands west of the Pearl River gave a fillip to his career which had been stymied by political scandal and economic ruin in the midst of the American Revolution. With the unfortunate death of Caesar Rodney in 1783, the cancer which disfigured him also spelled the end to the mercantile and shipping businesses which the two brothers had amassed before the war.[2] A large amount of money had been given to Caesar for his use as brigadier general of the state militia, money which could not be accounted for after his death. Both Delaware and the federal government held the estate liable for the funds. The charges wrecked the financial holdings of both brothers and Thomas Rodney found his postwar prospects ruined.[3] Not until his son became a member of Congress did the old captain of Delaware volunteers regain a

---

[1] Thomas Rodney's career is open to interpretation. William Baskerville Hamilton's *Thomas Rodney: Revolutionary and Builder of the West* and my study of the man offer the reader an opportunity to compare two views of the subject.

[2] Rodney, with his brother deceased, lacked the political power to fend off his brother's enemies.

[3] Thomas Rodney to Speaker of the House of Assembly, October 21, 1790, in Div. of MSS, Historical Society of Delaware; Thomas Rodney Memo Fragment, February 27, 1791, in Div. of MSS, Historical Society of Delaware.

portion of his political power and wealth. Caesar Augustus Rodney, named in his uncle's memory, made Rodney's redemption possible because of his loyal support of Thomas Jefferson's National Republican Party.[4]

Caesar Augustus initially secured his father a position as a Justice of the Supreme Court of Delaware on December 17, 1802.[5] As his powers of patronage increased he arranged for Rodney to receive on June 12, 1803, an appointment as Judge of the Court of the Mississippi West of the Pearl River.[6] The position paid $800.00 a year, and Rodney was also awarded the job of land commissioner for the area, which added $2,000.00 to his annual income.

After accepting the appointment, Rodney gave his colonial tricorn to his son, symbolically surrendering his colonial past to become a man of the western frontier.[7] He commenced his journey to a new life on August 14, 1803.

With him on his trip of discovery were two of the many young men who became a part of his wide circle of friends in the territory. William Shields, a young Delaware lawyer, accompanied Rodney from their home state, and Major Richard Claiborne joined them in Wheeling on the Ohio River.

Wheeling served as an embarkation point for westward travel. Rodney and his traveling companions found many others waiting in the riverside village for the construction of flatboats on which to begin a voyage to the new lands of the West. In Wheeling, Rodney made the acquaintance of Captain Meriwether Lewis. Lewis began his public career as President Jefferson's private secretary and in 1803 was in Wheeling preparing to explore western lands with William Clark in what would become the famous Lewis and Clark Expedition. Both Rodney

---

[4] Caesar Augustus Rodney became the recipient of the majority of his father's letters.

[5] William Baskerville Hamilton, *Thomas Rodney, Revolutionary and Builder of the West* (Durham, 1953), 61, 62.

[6] Clarence E. Carter (ed.), *The Territorial Papers of the United States* (Washington, 1937), V, 218–219.

[7] Thomas Rodney to Caesar Augustus Rodney, September 14, 1803, in Div. of MSS, Historical Society of Pennsylvania.

and Lewis expected the Wheeling boatwrights to launch their crafts within two weeks of beginning construction.[8] With an abundance of work, the riverside carpenters fell behind in production giving Lewis and Rodney an opportunity to become friends. They whiled away their time together in conversation and hosted each other with late night dinners. When Lewis' boat reached completion first, the explorer invited Rodney to begin his journey with him, but Rodney declined for fear he could not rejoin his party further down the river.[9]

Describing his own flatboat, Rodney wrote to his son, "We git it built at a dollar and a qtr. a foot that is 37 dollars, it will have 4 comfortable berths in the stern two on each side . . . covered with painted canvas . . . with curtins . . . like the stages. . . ." The craft, he wrote, "only drew 8 inches of draft to Lewis' 2½ feet."[10]

The voyage down the Ohio and Mississippi Rivers to Natchez and Washington, Mississippi Territory, stimulated Rodney's interest in this new world of nature which the rivers presented to him. He waded in the shallows and rowed about the banks of the rivers in the small skiff attached to his flatboat.[11] He filled his letters with the accounts of ancient Indian burial grounds and recently unearthed archaeological deposits which the ever-changing rivers exposed as they chose new courses. Rodney ruminated about the history of the Indians who had built the grassy burial mounds for their dead, but as for the ancient bones from the age of giant lizards, he dismissed them as particles of bonelike matter—a deception of nature.[12]

Indian mounds and ancient bones piqued the curiosity of the old soldier and his young traveling companions, but the river also provided excitement. Shortly after leaving Wheeling on

[8] "Thomas Rodney," *Dictionary of American Biography*, XVI, 84.

[9] Thomas Rodney to Caesar Augustus Rodney, September 8, 1803, in Div. of MSS, Historical Society of Pennsylvania.

[10] Thomas Rodney to Caesar Augustus Rodney, September 7, 1803, in Div. of MSS, Historical Society of Pennsylvania.

[11] *Ibid.*, October 3, 1803.

[12] *Ibid.*, October 7, 15, 1803.

September 21, 1803, Rodney's flatboat missed the channel and at Anderson Island ran aground. Several holes were gouged in the bottom of the craft. The crew, including two young carpenters who had asked to travel down to Limestone, Ohio, with Rodney's party, quickly repaired the damage.[13] A second sinking soon occurred when a snag speared a six-inch hole in the craft and the swift current capsized it. The tumultuous waters pulled the floating trunks and canvas-bundled stores out of the craft and sent them ripping along the deep channels of the river. Rodney, Shields, and Claiborne followed in agitated pursuit while the remainder of the crew wrestled the boat to a sand bar for extensive repairs.[14] Through these trials of early river travel, Rodney, fortified with drams of whiskey laced with river water, remained serene and at the end of the voyage fondly described the trip as being, "To me all . . . pleasure instead of fatigue."[15] Shields and Claiborne did not remember the voyage with as much happiness. They shared the duties of the deckhands, taking turns at the oars, and much to their indignation, each had to alternate as cook and scullion maid. Indeed, after the second sinking, Shields contemplated returning to Delaware. Rodney cajoled him into staying, but recorded, "Shields has been a very timid companion . . . and was babyish."[16]

Upon arrival in the Mississippi Territory, Rodney made his way across the riverside village of Natchez to the seat of territorial government west of the Pearl River, Washington, Mississippi Territory. After finding lodgings and storing his trunks, Rodney began to discover what an onerous responsibility faced him as land commissioner. Two thousand and fifty-seven unprocessed land claims clogged the office over which Rodney and his fellow land commissioner Robert Williams were to preside.[17] Williams, a North Carolinian, had arrived in the territory prior to Rodney and advised him of the disarrangement in

[13]*Ibid.*, September 12, October 3, 1803.
[14]*Ibid.*, December 2, 1803.
[15]*Ibid.*, October 3, 1803.
[16]*Ibid.*, October 15, 1803.
[17]Carter (ed.), *Territorial Papers*, V, 369.

the land office. Not even the barest prerequisites of an office existed. The United States Treasury had failed to send the necessary documents for establishing an office, and the rooms in Washington, Mississippi Territory, were bereft of furniture, stationery, and firewood. Months passed while both Rodney and Williams peppered Albert Gallatin, Secretary of the Treasury, and Rodney's son for supplies and contingent expenses. All the while they had to fend off impatient settlers.

Rodney groused, "One gentleman has a map of the British grants . . . and . . . another has a map of the Spanish . . . surveys. . . ."[18] The Indian boundaries to the territory were unknown and the commission did not have the power to protect the office from unfair claims.[19] In addition, Rodney discovered that the man who served as Register of the Land Commission Board of Claims was related to a prominent family which "are interested . . . in many important and extensive claims."[20]

American frontiersmen, during both the British and Spanish administration of the territory, had settled on the fertile banks of the Mississippi River. Were their former land titles valid? What of the present and future settlers who found rich farm and timber lands immersed in legal crosscurrents which could sweep away their hard work and dreams of security? The Act Providing for the Disposal of Land South of the State of Tennessee was enacted into laws on March 3, 1803, and provided Rodney and Williams with the directives, if not the documents and office expenses they required, to adjudicate the problems presented by the myriad of land grants, commissions, warrants, and certificates issued by the Spanish, French, Indian, and United States authorities. If claims were for land cultivated and inhabited when the Spanish troops evacuated the territory, the land commission would approve them. If the lands were so occupied at the time of the passage of the law directing the disposal of the land claims south of Tennessee, then the claimants

[18] Thomas Rodney to Caesar Augustus Rodney, December 8, 1803, in Div. of MSS, Historical Society of Pennsylvania.
[19] *Ibid.*
[20] *Ibid.*

would receive preference in purchasing the land claimed.[21] Rodney and Williams began to discern the legality and precedence of the claims by using this law, but they predicted that the process would be costly and time consuming.

The court, prior to Rodney's arrival, had foundered in political discord, causing to the new judge as much confusion as did the land office. William C. C. Claiborne, Governor of the Mississippi Territory, in 1803, had sent a series of letters to Jefferson's Secretary of State, James Madison, which discussed the troubled court west of the Pearl River. The court had lost the confidence of the general populace, the governor recounted, by seldom holding sessions and when convened acted with apparent highhanded disregard of the law. Undoubtedly, much of the frustration and misunderstanding surrounding the court could have been ameliorated with the publication of the territorial laws, but the only printer in the territory, a novice, lacked the tools of his trade to accomplish the task.[22]

Peter Bryan Bruin, a merchant turned judge; David Tilton, a former law student; and Seth Lewis, the only lawyer on the bench, had been the judges. The trio magnified their collective negligence, Claiborne stated, because of their personal shortcomings. Bruin seldom attended court sessions; Tilton possessed a meager knowledge of the law, and Lewis irritated the people with his rows with the territorial legislature. Claiborne expected the impasse created by the court to dissolve with the resignation of either Bruin or Tilton. He expressed surprise when Lewis, in his opinion the best judge in the western territory, quit his post.[23] Claiborne attributed his resignation to the strong political opposition Lewis encountered in the legislature.[24]

[21]Carter (ed.), *Territorial Papers*, V, 142, 194–195.

[22]Dunbar Rowland (ed.), *The Mississippi Territorial Archives 1798–1803* (Nashville, Tennessee, 1905), I, 367, 376.

[23]Dunbar Rowland, *Courts, Judges, and Lawyers of Mississippi 1798–1935* (Jackson, Mississippi, 1935), 16–18.

[24]Rowland (ed.), *Territorial Archives 1798–1803*, I, 367, 363, 377.

Rodney, informed of this turbulent history of the court, viewed his role on the bench as that of "a serene experienced conciliating character suited to heal those animosities which party [strife] has stirred up."[25] He wrote to his son, "I am determined to hold an impartial station here, therefore I take no part in local politics."[26] Rodney could not long hold to his promise to remain above the affray of partisans or retain his judicial reserve. Events soon made him an active participant in several controversies.

The first pitted him against David Tilton's successor on the bench, David Kerr. Kerr, a former sheriff of Adams County and an itinerant schoolteacher, opposed the trial and execution of two of Samuel Mason's gang.[27] Mason, a robber and murderer, and his gang terrorized the trails leading from Nashville to New Orleans and victimized unsuspecting travelers. May and Sutton, two of his henchmen, fell into the hands of the law and were brought into the territory to stand trial before Rodney and Kerr.

Rodney pronounced sentence upon them, but Kerr refused to participate on the grounds the court did not have jurisdiction over the defendants arrested outside of the territory.[28] Bruin, absent from the court during the initial trial, joined the proceedings and to the relief of the frightened settlers who supported Rodney's opinion of the powers of the court west of the Pearl River, May and Sutton swung from the limb of the gallows tree.[29]

Kerr's hesitancy soured Rodney on the former sheriff. He de-

[25] Thomas Rodney to Caesar Augustus Rodney, December 8, 1803, in Div. of MSS, Historical Society of Pennsylvania.

[26] *Ibid.,* February 8, 1803.

[27] The exact dates for the episode concerning May and Sutton may be as much in question as the true identity of one of the desperadoes. Rodney places the events in 1803 while J. F. A. Claiborne, in *Mississippi as a Province, Territory, and State,* begins the narrative in 1802.

[28] Thomas Rodney to Caesar Augustus Rodney, January 21, 1804, in Div. of MSS, Historical Society of Pennsylvania.

[29] *Ibid.*

scribed him to Caesar Augustus as possibly the most unpopular man in the territory.[30] In contrast, Rodney discovered that the majority of the leading citizens of the territory were congenial. He found himself, he wrote, much in demand as "priest" among the landed gentry. The better sort, Rodney explained, who married far from churches and ministers, invited him to preside at their marriage rites. He traveled sixty miles to Bruin's home to officiate at his daughter's wedding. He united General George Mathews, a former governor of Georgia, and Mrs. Mary Carpenter in marriage and presided at the ceremonies of George Poindexter and Lydia Carter, the daughter of a wealthy farmer. His raftmate, William Shields, set his cap for Miss Peggy Dunbar, daughter of William Dunbar, whom Rodney described as "one of the most wealthy men in the territory . . . a man of great science and . . . once surveyor-general under the Spanish." When Peggy resisted Shields' charms, he settled for fifteen-year-old Victoria Benoit, the daughter of an equally successful planter.[31]

Rodney did not confine his friendship to the Jeffersonian Republicans in the territory. He became acquainted with the settlers of the Federalist persuasion and even supported the candidacies of Colonel Benijah Osmun and Colonel Joseph Pannill for the office of Governor of the territory.[32] Robert Williams, Rodney's fellow land commissioner, who had left the territory for Washington, D.C., in 1804, to lobby for more precise instructions and aid concerning the land commission, opposed both Osmun and Pannill's bids for the office and took the position for himself.[33] This action angered Rodney, and when

[30] Thomas Rodney to Caesar Augustus Rodney, February 15, 1805, in Div. of MSS, Library of Congress.

[31] Thomas Rodney to Caesar Augustus Rodney, March 2, 1804, May 18, 1804, in Div. of MSS, Historical Society of Pennsylvania; Thomas Rodney's Diary, undated entry, in New York Public Library; Thomas Rodney to Caesar Augustus Rodney, April 18, 1804, in Div. of MSS, Historical Society of Pennsylvania; *Ibid.*, Feb. 1807; *Ibid.*, April 18, 1804.

[32] Thomas Rodney to Caesar Augustus Rodney, March 21, 1804, in Div. of MSS, Historical Society of Pennsylvania.

[33] Carter (ed.), *Territorial Papers*, V, 368.

Williams returned to the territory, the two men began a quarrel which continued throughout their public careers. Only the events surrounding Aaron Burr's adventures in the Mississippi Territory suspended the hostilities Rodney and Williams felt for each other.[34]

Prior to Burr's appearance in the territory, the western border of the United States' possessions had been set aflame with the sparks of fear, suspicion, and distrust of the Spanish in West Florida. The Pinckney Treaty of 1795 settled for a time the boundary between the United States and Spain at the thirty-first parallel, but American settlement in the western territories provoked numerous border incidents. The Kemper affair was just one of these incidents which spread rumors of Spanish reconquest of the Mississippi Territory throughout the area. Samuel, Reuben, and Nathan Kemper of Pinckneyville, Mississippi Territory, claimed land held by the Spanish. They precipitated a series of raids across the border into Spanish held lands which resulted in the kidnapping of Samuel Kemper from his tavern in Pinckneyville by five masked men thought to be Spanish citizens. Kemper returned to his home a day later bedraggled and beaten.[35] Before the chastised Samuel and his brothers could retaliate against the alleged Spanish outrage, Rodney learned of their plans for revenge and directed that each of them be placed under a bond of a thousand dollars "for their good behavior respectively toward the country and subjects of the King of Spain."[36]

Rodney wanted to prevent further border incidents because he believed, as did many of the other territorial settlers, that Spain planned the reconquest of Louisiana and the Mississippi Territory. The Kempers might provide an excuse for invasion.

---

[34] Claiborne, *Mississippi as Province*, 258.

[35] *Mississippi Messenger* (Natchez), November 12, 1805.

[36] Thomas Rodney to unnamed person, October 7, 1805, in Div. of MSS, Historical Society of Pennsylvania; Thomas Rodney to Caesar Augustus Rodney, January 16, 1805, in Div. of MSS Library of Congress; *Ibid.*, September 7, 1805; Deposition by Arthur Cobb Turner relating to the Kemper affair, September 14, 1805, in Mississippi Department of Archives and History, Jackson.

Using the nom de plume of Hermes, Rodney essayed a series of letters to the newspapers of the territory, warning the Spanish off American lands and reminding the territorial settlers of the nation's glorious origins.[37] He wrote that many of the victorious soldiers of the American Revolution were just waiting in ready retirement to jump to the call of battle.[38] To his son, Rodney expressed the fear "that the Spanish design attempting to recover Louisiana."[39] His letters written under the disguise of Hermes served, in his opinion, to warn of the dangers of possible Spanish reinvasion, but also they reflect the growing atmosphere of uncertainty most settlers in the Mississippi Territory felt in 1805.

Into this rumor-laden environment, Aaron Burr entered, sparking anew the gossip of Spanish inspired skulduggery. Rodney noted Burr's arrival in the territories in July of 1805, recording, "Mr. Burr the late vice-president past by Natchez two weeks ago to Orleans. I did not see him," Rodney continued, "he is to return to spend the summer."[40] Burr's visit in 1805 came on the heels of his duel with Alexander Hamilton and was the first of two trips he made to the western territories. By the time the former vice-president returned to the Mississippi Territory in 1807, Rodney had written numerous Hermes letters and several notes to his son warning of impending trouble with the Spanish and possibly with the British whom Rodney loved less than he did the Spanish.[41] The settlers, he said, were expecting Spanish invasion any day, and Rodney suggested a force of both regular and militia troops be stationed in the terri-

[37] The fourteen items, mostly letters signed "Hermes," represent the Mississippi Department of Archives and History's Thomas Rodney Collection.

[38] Thomas Rodney, as Hermes, letter concerning Spanish aggression (Mississippi Department of Archives, n.d.).

[39] Thomas Rodney to Caesar Augustus Rodney, September 30, 1806, in Div. of MSS, Library of Congress.

[40] *Ibid.*, July 10, 1805.

[41] The emergence of the Hermes letters adds a new dimension to Thomas Rodney's life in the Mississippi Territory. They give the reader an insight into his secretive personality and expose his deepest thoughts about subjects which he refused to discuss directly in any other guise except that of Hermes.

tory as a deterrent to invasion and conspiracy.[42] He concluded his reports to his son, "A general rumor and almost belief pervades this territory that there is a deabolical [sic] conspiracy formed of Persons in this and the territory of Orleans and others against the U.S."[43] Rodney himself doubted such a plot existed, but recorded, "So much are the minds of the people alarmed and agitated with the sound of this project that legal investigations are in progress."[44] As judge and patriotic citizen, Rodney assumed the conspiracy possible, but highly improbable. As Hermes, he warned of invasion, not boring from within. If the conspiracy allegations became an eventuality, he thought the "vigilence" and "strong arm" of the government could suppress it.[45]

By early December, 1806, Rodney learned more details of the alleged plot. A group of adventurers, he reported, led by an important former government official, possibly Burr, and aided by General James Wilkinson of the Orleans Territory, in conjunction with either Spanish or British military support would gain control of Kentucky, Tennessee, Louisiana, the Floridas, and part of eastern Mexico. Burr, the gossip continued, stood ready at the confluence of the Ohio and Mississippi Rivers with a large army of men while General Wilkinson in New Orleans prepared the Orleans Territory for conquest.[46] Rodney remained incredulous as the rumors gained support in the minds of even his most responsible friends and associates.

Mixing fear and circumstances, many settlers saw in every event the hint of treason and the hand of betrayal. General Wilkinson's behavior became the focal point of many suspicions. An arrogant and headstrong individual, Wilkinson fanned the embers of conspiracy for his own purposes. Several

---

[42] Thomas Rodney to Caesar Augustus Rodney, January 27, 1806, in Div. of MSS, Library of Congress; *Ibid.*, March 31, 1806; *Ibid.*, August 18, 1806.

[43] *Ibid.*, November 11, 1806.

[44] *Ibid.*

[45] *Ibid.*

[46] Thomas Rodney to Caesar Augustus Rodney, November 21, 1806, in Div. of MSS, Historical Society of Pennsylvania.

of his regular army officers resigned because of his irrascible nature and arbitrary decision to order "all the troops to Orleans and requiring five hundred militia from this territory . . . and sending all the arms and ammunition . . . without any necessity . . . [is] strong evidence of some nefarious design. . . ."[47] Rodney questioned both Wilkinson's supporters and his critics and concluded, ". . . it is hard for me to believe that an old revolutionary soldier [like Wilkinson] now enjoying the highest favor of government could connive in such a plot against the government that employed him."[48]

Christmas and extra duties of the territorial Supreme Court as well as the signing of Pre-emption Certificates for the land commission kept Rodney busy until January 12, 1807, when he resumed his narrative of the alleged conspiracy. President Jefferson's message concerning Burr, Rodney informed his son, "arrived here by last mail and the letter seems to give new agitation to the idea of the Burr Conspiracy."[49] The territory had been primed for years for either invasion or a treasonous revolution from within and Jefferson's letter verified their fears. His message, issued November 27, 1806, warned the citizens of the territories from participating in any attempts to gain control of Spanish lands. Beverly Chew, a recent arrival in the Mississippi Territory from Nashville, added to the agitation created by the President's message. He told, with lurid descriptions, of Burr's marshalling of men and boats in the Tennessee capital and then slipping out of the city bound for conquest of the lower Mississippi.[50] Cowles Mead, secretary of the western territory, on the strength of Chew's alarming report, convened the legislature so that he and its members could prepare the militia for Burr's predicted invasion. Mead, at the legislature's direction,

---

[47] Ibid.

[48] Rodney specifically talked to a Captain Carter who was taking dispatches to Washington, D. C. The others were a Captain Smith and a Lieutenant Meade; Thomas Rodney to Caesar Augustus Rodney, November 21, 1806, in Div. of MSS, Historical Society of Pennsylvania.

[49] Thomas Rodney to Caesar Augustus Rodney, January 12, 1807, in Div. of MSS, Library of Congress.

[50] Ibid.

organized 285 men for the general defense and welfare of the territory.[51] The state of excitement appeared unbearable, and few listened to a Mr. Pinter from [New] Jersey who traveled down the river within days of Chew yet witnessed no preparation for treason or revolution.[52]

Rodney, at first bemused by the reaction of the general populace and particularly by that of his friends, grew alarmed at the continuing frenzy swirling about him. He remembered the scars he and his brother suffered during the American Revolution. Rodney's concern increased when he learned of Wilkinson's wholesale arrest of alleged conspirators in New Orleans. Wilkinson based his actions upon a letter he claimed Burr had written to him.[53]

The practice of military arrest repulsed Rodney and, however ready he stood to defend the union, he would not, he stated, allow citizens' rights to be trampled because all Americans must be protected by "the Consitiution and laws of our contry."[54] The old judge had long expressed his belief and complete support of the innocence of the individual until proven otherwise in a court of law. And he, as so many other men who fought in the American Revolution, believed the military must be subordinate to the civil authorities. When advising his son Caesar in a court case two years earlier, Rodney had written, "When high officers are accused of high crimes and misdemeanors the popular alarm against them is apt to be great."[55] Thus, Rodney would tolerate only orderly conduct from both the alleged conspirators and the military if he had the chance to put his opinions and beliefs into practice.

His opportunity came when an anxious militia arrested Burr. "The great Bubble about Col. Burr has busted," Rodney

[51] Cowles Mead to the Honorable Legislative Council and House of Representatives, n. d., in *Governors' Records*, Ser. A, VII, Mississippi Department of Archives and History, Jackson.

[52] Thomas Rodney to Caesar Augustus Rodney, January 12, 1807, in Div. of MSS, Library of Congress.

[53] *Ibid.*, February 10, 1805.

[54] *Ibid.*, January 12, 1807.

[55] *Ibid.*, February 10, 1805.

wrote, "—Upon hearing he had moved . . . down the river the militia . . . was prepared to oppose any hostile or other attempt contrary to the laws of the United States."[56] Being confronted by Cowles Mead and the militia at the mouth of Bayou Pierre near the present-day city of Port Gibson, Mississippi, Burr moved his boats from their moorings to a position across the river out of the reach of Mead and his men. He informed the Secretary there was no cause for alarm. He was, Rodney reported, only in the territory to settle a tract of land on the Ouachita River. Burr, the old judge wrote, advised Mead, "not to arm citizens against citizens and thereby cause civil war." Mead misconstrued the statement, thinking Burr intended armed attack upon the citizens of the territory. He "turned out" the militia with "great readiness" and "spirit" to face Burr's men.[57] Alarmed at this misunderstanding of his conversation with Mead, Burr informed the secretary that he would surrender, "if he could be assured of protection." Mead agreed, and Burr surrendered to Attorney General Richard Poindexter; Major Shields, an aid to the governor; and Colonel Richard Claiborne, who had come up to Coles Creek near Burr's flotilla with three hundred men of the militia to face Burr's alleged invasion.[58]

Rodney examined Burr preparatory to Burr's appearance before the Supreme Court of the territory. He described himself as a settler with a large tract of land to occupy and claimed that he was in no way connected with the Spanish government. He disavowed Wilkinson's accusation of a treasonous letter, saying that the letter and the charge of treason were fictions of the general. Burr further explained the confusion about himself and his expedition. He told Rodney that he had declared "if there was a Spanish war he would offer his services to government and

[56] *Ibid.*, January, 1807.
[57] *Ibid.*
[58] An excellent account of the flurry and fluster which surrounded the delicate and yet absurd negotiations between Burr and the territorial officials can be found in the *Governors' Records*, VI-VIII, Mississippi Department of Archives and History.

raise all the force he could to go with him against that country."[59] From that statement, he continued, stemmed the misconstruing of his motives in coming to the territory. Burr, Rodney recorded, had revealed his plans to John Breckinridge, the United States Attorney General, and Breckinridge had replied, Burr said, that ten thousand settlers, well armed, "would be agreeable to the United States . . . that a strong frontier was necessary and desired in that quarter of the country."[60] As Rodney had read earlier in a Kentucky paper, Breckinridge had died, and Burr's explanation was the only one which could be relied upon.[61]

Rodney's examination of Burr's ten boats left little doubt in the judge's mind that the one hundred men who traveled with Burr were too poorly armed to "exert any degree of military force."[62] Despite his conclusion about the so-called invasion Rodney advocated that Burr's project should be legally investigated. If he were innocent, Rodney confided to his letters, the nation should know of it, and for that reason, Rodney stated, Burr was brought before the territorial Supreme Court of Mississippi West of the Pearl River.

The court met on Monday, February 2, 1807, Burr had posted bail for his appearance at court, and on Tuesday a grand jury was impaneled. Attorney General Poindexter refused to find a bill on the depositions before him and questioned the court's right to try Burr since the court did not possess federal jurisdiction. This question had previously arisen in the trial of two of Mason's gang, and Rodney's opinion then and in Burr's case was that the court did have jurisdiction. "Mr. Burr himself rose and acknowledged the Jurisdiction," Rodney recorded, "and the Court had no doubt on this question."[63] Poindexter remained

[59] Thomas Rodney to Caesar Augustus Rodney, January, 1807, in Div. of MSS, Library of Congress.

[60] *Ibid.*

[61] *Ibid.*, January 12, 1807.

[62] *Ibid.*, January, 1807.

[63] Thomas Rodney to Caesar Augustus Rodney, February, 1807, in Div. of MSS, Historical Society of Pennsylvania.

adamant and would not send a bill to the grand jury. The court ignored his refusal, and the hearing into the case continued on into the afternoon, at which time the jury acquitted Burr. His counsel asked the court if the recognizance which had been placed upon Burr could be discharged and Judge Bruin supported the appeal, but Rodney opposed it, splitting the court and thus denying the request.[64] Rodney's action in keeping Burr tied to the court is unexplained in his letters and notes, but events quickly provided some possible answers.

Rodney, on the fifth, traveled to the Benoit plantation to marry his friend William Shields to Victoria Benoit. "On the seventh still cold," Rodney returned to Washington to call Burr out on his recognizance and then adjourned the court until the next term. Burr had fled the jurisdiction of the court. The governor issued a proclamation offering $2,000.00 for the capture of Burr, and all of his men who could be found were placed under guard. The search for Burr and the detention of his men must have been bone-chilling business, as Rodney noted the temperature was down to eleven degrees.[65]

The old judge ruminated on the Burr affair, comparing it to the Kemper debacle. He had fined the Kempers for their sortie into Spanish territory, and he had kept Burr tethered to the court, no doubt to control his future actions. Burr, in Rodney's opinion, in contrasting him to the Kempers, "only appeared the greatest Don Quixote. . . ."[66]

Rodney's greater concern centered upon the men who were conducting the hunt for and the arrest of Burr. He stated they would give a greater shock to the Constitution than Burr and ten thousand armed men in open rebellion. He pitied Burr, as his letters reveal. "He does not," Rodney wrote, "appear to me to possess a mind in condition and competence to plan or execute such an enterprise [as a rebellion] . . . his aspect appeared

[64] *Ibid.*
[65] *Ibid.*
[66] Thomas Rodney to Caesar Augustus Rodney, February, 1807, in Div. of MSS, Historical Society of Pennsylvania.

that of distress—not one promoted of the strong genius of certain success."[67] When Wilkinson's troops arrived at Natchez to take Burr back to New Orleans, Rodney was relieved that Burr had fled. "I am determined," he vowed, "to be firm in maintaining the Constitution and laws . . . I will not deviate even to please the president. . . ." The military may arrest, Rodney added, but the court must try citizens, and eventual accounting by the military must be given to the civilian authority. ". . . If arms are to rule I know my station," Rodney continued, "—I believe . . . Burr if guilty had better escape than that the Constitution and laws should be violated by those acting under them."[68] Governor Williams concurred with Rodney, pledging to support the "civil authority" as stated in the Constitution. Neither man wished to see civil discord created by either alleged traitors or military officers bent upon burnishing their reputations.

The structure of territorial government had been given a mighty blow, with Burr's alleged conspiracy hammering on one side and General Wilkinson threatening justice and civil authority on the other; but to Rodney's relief the tenuous bond fostered by the Constitution and the desire for lawful conduct held fast against all aspects of the Burr debacle. When Lieutenant Edmund Pendleton Gaines recaptured Burr in Alabama, Rodney expressed gratification. He wrote, "I am very glad . . . that he [Burr] has [been] taken and that he will have to answer for his misdeeds where and at a time when perhaps they will be better known than when he was before the grand jury here."[69]

When he fled the Mississippi Territory, Burr left behind a trail strewn with unanswered questions, blighted reputations, political animosities, and unexplained behavior. Colonel John Ellis, a plantation owner and associate of Rodney's, admitted to the old judge that his former advocacy of arbitrary measures against Burr prior to the former vice-president's arrival in the

[67] *Ibid.*
[68] *Ibid.*
[69] *Ibid.*, March 1, 1807.

19

territory had, upon examination of Burr's boats and men, been completely misplaced. Wilkinson gained no advantage from his military arrest, and slowly the day-to-day existence of territorial life resumed its pace.

Rodney received a summons which he quoted in his notes, "to attend the circuit court . . . in the case of Mr. Burr on the 22nd of this month [April, 1807] which day," Rodney commented, "was past before the summons arrived."[70] The old judge, Poindexter, Mead, and Colonel Fitzpatrick were called to attend the trial which was held in Richmond, Virginia, but Rodney fell ill with a fever which haunted him the remainder of his life in the territory. Unable to attend the second trial of Burr, Rodney turned his attention to Governor Williams, who had disposed the court of its meeting rooms. In this episode, Rodney drew the lines of partisian politics and despite his disavowal became an active participant in the rough and tumble of territorial power struggles.

The controversy began shortly after Williams returned from a visit to his family in North Carolina. His stay, from April, 1806, to January, 1807, had been prolonged, and Secretary of the Territory Cowles Mead served as acting governor in Williams' place. Upon his return, Williams dismissed Mead from office. "The patriotic ardor of Mead's conduct, Rodney commented in his letters, "in the case of Burr was much approved of here by the Republicans."[71] Upon hearing of Mead's dismissal, his friends immediately elected him to the territorial legislature, a stratagem which infuriated Williams.[72]

Despite the hostility generated by Mead's dismissal, Rodney attempted to maintain cordial and correct relations with the governor. "Our public duties," wrote the old judge, "require that the governor and myself should act in a polite and social manner—this perhaps may not be altogether pleasing to some—

[70] *Ibid.*, May 25, 1807.
[71] *Ibid.*, September 1, 1807. Mead, a lawyer from Georgia was appointed Secretary of the Mississippi Territory in March, 1806, and served until dismissed by Williams.
[72] Thomas Rodney to Caesar Augustus Rodney, September 1, 1807, in Div. of MSS, Historical Society of Pennsylvania.

who are abusing him."[73] When Williams began attacking George Poindexter, a young man Rodney considered a second son, the old judge's composure was shattered. Poindexter, who on March 4, 1807, began his first term as a delegate from the Mississippi Territory to the Tenth Congress, had practiced law in Natchez and Washington, served as attorney general of the territory during Governor Claiborne's administration, and had held a seat in the territorial general assembly in 1805.[74] Williams' hatred of Poindexter apparently stemmed from the young man's rapid rise in territorial politics. "Indeed," Rodney wrote, "the governor one way or another has offended all the Republican party here, and they treat him with great asperity."[75]

Williams dismissed other of Rodney's associates, including Colonel Ferdinand Leigh Claiborne. Colonel Claiborne and Governor W. C. C. Claiborne of the Orleans district were brothers, and the colonel's dismissal angered the Orleans governor.[76] Colonel Claiborne accused Williams of collusion with Burr and of favoring the Federalist cause. The conflict between the two men reached a climax October 17, 1807, when the governor ordered the county troop of horsemen separated from Claiborne's command. Claiborne resisted, and Williams revoked his commission.[77] The struggle between the two went deeper than the fight over who would control the Adams County troop of horsemen. Williams resented the courtmartial proceedings against one of his aides-de-camp, John F. Carmichael, which occurred while he visited in North Carolina. Poindexter, smarting from Williams' criticisms, lobbied against the governor in the nation's capitol. He told the Secretary of State James Madison that Carmichael "was strongly suspected of Burrism. . . ."[78] The momentum against Williams grew both in the territory

[73] *Ibid.*, June 22, 1807.
[74] *Biographical Directory of the American Congress 1774–1961* (Washington, D. C., 1961), 1466.
[75] Thomas Rodney to Caesar Augustus Rodney, September 1, 1807, in Div. of MSS, Historical Society of Pennsylvania.
[76] Carter (ed.), *Territorial Papers*, V, 564.
[77] *Ibid.*, 563–68, 573–78.
[78] *Ibid.*, 605.

and in Washington. It continued to build in both places when Claiborne's resignation was followed by that of Joseph Sessions and of Jesse Carter, both majors in the first regiment of the Mississippi militia. The remaining officers and men sent a petition to President Jefferson supporting Claiborne. "Your Excellency might inquire," their letter stated, "why the Governor alone should be blind to the value of this officer . . . we . . . believe that Governor Williams has a total distaste to everything like Republicanism."[79] Williams' public blasts against Claiborne and his charges of Federalism against Republican supporters, Rodney noted, ". . . lost [the governor] the confidence and provoked the resentment of the Republicans without obtaining the friendship of the Feds."[80]

Critics assailed Williams on all sides, but he aggravated their assaults by his own mendacity. He revoked Theodore Starke's commission as clerk of Adams County Circuit Court on October 7, 1808, and a few days later revoked Beverly R. Grayson's commission as Clerk of the Supreme Court, Auditor of Public Accounts, and Justice of the Quorum.[81] When Rodney informed Poindexter of the continued acts of political intemperance by Williams, he compared him to "a man whose mind is deranged."[82]

Ferdinand Leigh Claiborne, the former Lieutenant Colonel of the First regiment of the Militia, agreed with Rodney, but called upon the judge to discuss a matter which he then thought unrelated to the activities of the governor. Major Richard Claiborne, having the same name as the Colonel and Governor Claiborne but related to neither, had compromised the Claiborne name, and Colonel Claiborne sought Rodney's advice concerning Richard's conduct. He had been seen riding in a carriage with a "Mrs. M.," a lady of ill repute. The brothers Claiborne requested Rodney's assistance in dealing with the young man so

---

[79] Ibid., 571.
[80] Ibid., 564.
[81] Ibid., 654–57.
[82] Ibid., 656.

that the Claiborne's name would not be compromised in the future.[83] When confronted, in Rodney's chambers, with the accusation, Richard blamed the governor, who had requested he escort "Mrs. M." about the village. He revealed the fact that Williams' visit to his family in North Carolina was for the purpose of seeking a divorce from his wife and that the governor then planned to marry "Mrs. M." This information of the governor's conduct provided Rodney, the Claibornes, and their friends with the strongest and most effective weapon against Williams. "The whole [affair]," Rodney stated, "makes Gov. W. appear in a horrid point of view—Mrs. M. was well known in this town as a common strump [et]."[84] Poindexter, from congress, informed James Madison and other cabinet members of Williams' conduct, ". . . the flagrant act of moral turpitude commited by Governor Williams has disgraced him with all parties. . . ."[85] Rodney wrote to his son, now Jefferson's Attorney General, "Alas, America! When you have such gov[ernors] desperate are the deeds that shun the light. . . ."[86]

In an effort to counter the memorial circulated by Colonel Ferdinand Leigh Claiborne's friends, the attacks made upon his character by Mead and Poindexter, and the revelation of his private life, Williams wrote to the President. He claimed his administration was as loyally Republican as any other state or territorial official. Unfortunately for Williams, his opponents' charges weighed against him. He undoubtedly realized his position could no longer be defended and informed Jefferson, "I intend going out of office with you. . . ."[87] He offered his resignation to the President February, 1809, to take effect on March 4, of that year. In defeat Williams would not call a truce to his attacks upon the government of the Mississippi Territory. On

[83] Dunbar Rowland (ed.), *Official Letter Book of W. C. C. Claiborne 1800–1816* (Madison, Wisconsin, 1917), VI, 251.

[84] Thomas Rodney Personal Memo, December 13, 1807 in Div. of MSS, Historical Society of Pennsylvania.

[85] Carter (ed.), *Territorial Papers*, V, 700.

[86] Thomas Rodney Personal Memo, December 13, 1807, in Div. of MSS, Historical Society of Pennsylvania.

[87] Carter (ed.), *Territorial Papers*, V, 661.

March 1, 1809, he announced the territorial assembly to be dissolved.[88] Williams explained to the Secretary of State, "With such a Legislature it was impossible to get along as the public interest required. . . ."[89] He added that the citizens of the territory would vote in July for a new assembly and that no inconvenience would occur. He could not, Williams concluded, turn the government over to his successor while "a set of men . . . retain their political existence who so little regard the public interest as this majority. . . ."[90] He then attempted to renege on his resignation, but Jefferson refused to allow the wild man of territorial politics to remain in office.

Rodney enjoyed the governor's imbroglio. He advised those who questioned Williams' right to administer in the territory. He allowed the Claibornes to meet in his room to discuss the odious "Mrs. M.," and he served as Poindexter's ears while Williams dismissed officials in every phase of territorial government. "His Nefarious changes of Military officers," Rodney wrote, "has disorganized the Militia. His frequent Changes of Magistrates, and Civil officers to git in Such as will servilely support him . . . contrary to the free spirit of Americans degraded the Civil Department."[91] Poindexter, upon receiving such information, did the spade work against Williams in the nation's capitol. In all, Rodney observed, contributed, and commended Williams' downfall. It proved to be the old judge's last involvement in the political life of the territory. The fever he contracted while making preparations to attend the Burr trial in Richmond, Virginia, flared up and removed him from public life. He died in 1811.

Rodney relished his life in the Mississippi Territory. The politics and the people fascinated him to such a degree that he spent his last years participating in and recording the important events of Mississippi's early territorial history. His friends

[88] *Ibid.*, 616.
[89] *Ibid.*, 618.
[90] *Ibid.*, 713.
[91] *Ibid.*, 656.

wished to erect a monument to his memory, but the plans for his memorial became a political issue and his allies "grew fearful to apropriate money for the monument . . . should [it] be made a handle against them at some future election."[92] Rodney remains little known, a footnote to the greater narrative of territorial development and a victim, after death, of the political life he said he avoided, but so greatly enjoyed.

BIBLIOGRAPHY

Manuscript Collections

Historical Society of Delaware. Thomas Rodney MSS.
Historical Society of Pennsylvania. Thomas Rodney MSS.
Library of Congress. Thomas Rodney MSS.
Mississippi Department of Archives and History. Thomas Rodney MSS; *Governors' Records*, Ser. A, VI-VIII.
New York Public Library. Thomas Rodney MSS.

Articles and Newspapers

Carter, Clarence E. "The Transit of Law to the Frontier," *Journal of Mississippi History*, XVI (July, 1954), 183–192.
Gratz, Simon. "Thomas Rodney," *Pennsylvania Magazine of History and Biography*, XLV (1921), 34–65.
Johnson, Allen, and Dumas Malone (eds.). "Thomas Rodney," *Dictionary of American Biography*, XVI, New York: Charles Scribner's Sons, 1928–1937, 83–84.
————. "Philip Nolan," *DAB*, XIII, 1934, 543–544.
Reed, H. Clay. "Delaware Constitution of 1776," *Delaware Notes*. Newark, Delaware: University of Delaware, 1930, 7–42.
Mississippi Messenger. Natchez, Mississippi. November 12, 1805, 1.

Books

Abernethy, Thomas Perkins. *The Burr Conspiracy*. New York: Oxford University Press, 1954.
Binkley, Wilfred E. *American Political Parties: Their Natural History*. New York: Alfred A. Knopf, 1964.
Biographical Directory of the American Congress 1774–1927. Washington, D.C.: U.S. Government Printing Office, 1928.

---

[92] Nehemiah Tilton to Caesar Augustus Rodney, May 7, 1811, in Div. of MSS, Historical Society of Delaware.

Biographical Directory of the American Congress 1774–1961. Washington, D.C.: U.S. Government Printing Office, 1961.

Carter, Clarence E. (ed.). *The Territorial Papers of the United States,* V. Washington, D.C.: U.S. Government Printing Office, 1938.

Claiborne, J. F. H. *Mississippi as a Province, Territory, and State.* Jackson, Mississippi: Power and Barksdale, 1880.

Correspondence of the Late President Adams. Boston: Everett and Munroe, 1809.

Foley, John P. (ed.). *The Jefferson Cyclopedia.* New York: Funk and Wagnalls Company, 1900.

Hamilton, William Baskerville. *Thomas Rodney: Revolutionary and Builder of the West.* Durham: Duke University Press, 1953.

Mott, Frank L. *Jefferson and the Press.* Baton Rouge: Louisiana State University Press, 1943.

Public Archives Commission of Delaware. *Revolutionary War,* II. Wilmington, Delaware, 1919.

Rowland, Dunbar. *Courts, Judges, and Lawyers of Mississippi 1798–1935.* Jackson, Mississippi: Press of Hederman Bros., 1935.

—— (ed.). *The Mississippi Territorial Archives 1798–1803,* I. Nashville, Tennessee: Brandon Printing Company, 1905.

——. *Encyclopedia of Mississippi,* III, Atlanta: Southern Historical Publishing Association, 1907.

—— (ed.). *Official Letter Books of W. C. C. Claiborne 1800–1816,* VI, Madison, Wisconsin: Democrat Printing Company, 1917.

Samuel, Ray, Leonard V. Huber, and Warren C. Ogden. *Tales of the Mississippi.* New York: Hastings House, 1955.

Ryden, George Herbert (ed.). *Letters to and from Caesar Rodney, 1756–1784.* Philadelphia: University of Pennsylvania Press, 1928–1937.

Samuel Dale
1772–1841

Frontiersman
of the Old Southwest

BY NANNIE PITTS MCLEMORE*

Toward the end of General Samuel Dale's eventful life, when he had settled in Mississippi, his final home, he could reflect upon his part in the developing of the Old Southwest. J.F.H. Claiborne wrote down the facts of Dale's remarkable and heroic career, and these show the role Dale played in settling the frontier.[1] Today these events are seen as the currents of Jeffersonian democracy moving westward and as America's deeds in a policy of manifest destiny. In the Old Southwest, which comprised Mississippi Territory, Dale, as Claiborne's narrative shows, left an indelible mark. Though Dale was always a hardy pioneer, he was at various times likewise a government scout, an Indian fighter, a soldier in the War of 1812, a wagon master, a trailblazer, a participant in the convention which met to divide Mississippi Territory, and a representative in the legislatures of Alabama and Mississippi.

Dale was of Scotch-Irish extraction. The Scotch-Irish in America, for the most part, were descendants of inhabitants of the lowlands of Scotland who had been settled in rebellious northern Ireland in the early 1600s as loyalists to the British

---

*Before her death on January 24, 1980, the author had written the first draft of this essay and had planned to spend another month completing it. Her son, Harry K. McLemore, with Pam Sullivan, Mrs. McLemore's assistant, prepared the essay for publication.

[1] Most of the information in this essay is drawn from J.F.H. Claiborne's *Life and Times of Gen. Sam Dale, the Mississippi Partisan* (New York: Harper and Brothers, 1860). Claiborne's narrative, which is composed in a form which presents itself as Dale's autobiography, is the principal resource from which most authors who have written about Dale have drawn facts about his life and career. "As originally written," Claiborne states in the preface, "the narrative was almost literally in his [Dale's] own words."

crown. Like many others of Scotch-Irish descent, both Dale's father and mother were natives of Pennsylvania. After their marriage they moved to Rockbridge County, Virginia, and Dale, the eldest of nine children, was born there in 1771. They moved again, to the forks of the Clinch River, Washington County, and for a time settled on land they acquired there.

Since this plot was unprotected, the Dales and their neighbors built a stockade called the Glade Hollow Fort, in which each family occupied a small log cabin. Women and children remained within the stockade while the men went out to till the soil, with their guns handy in case of an Indian attack. A few sentries, Dale reported, were constantly on the lookout, and when there was evidence of Indians, all the families fled to the stockade for protection. Dale described living on the frontier as "a wild precarious life, often interrupted by ambushes and massacres, but no one of that hard frontier race was ever known to return to the [safe] settlements."[2]

Dale exemplified this uncertainty of the "precarious" existence by describing what traditionally could happen even when a pleasure like a wedding occurred as a relief from the custom of hardship and vigilance. Once when there was to be a wedding in another settlement, the Dales planned to attend. They began their trip with some anxiety, since they left their house unguarded and since Indians were known to inhabit the lands all around them. "Folks," Dale said, "did not calculate consequences closely, and the temptation to a frolic—a wedding, a feast, and a dance till daylight and often for several days together—was not to be resisted, and off we went."[3] When they reached the settlement, they found a pile of ashes and six or seven corpses, tomahawked and scalped. However, the bride and bridegroom had escaped in different directions, but they were reunited and later married.

By 1783 the Dale family, like the multitudes of migrating pi-

[2] *Ibid.*, p. 16.
[3] *Ibid.*, p. 19.

30

oneers of the time, had moved again. In the vicinity of Greensborough, Georgia, the family expected better living conditions, but they knew soon enough that they were in the midst of hostile Creeks and Cherokees. The Dales found it necessary to seek shelter in Carmichael's Station, a stockade of thirty families which provided practically the same kind of life that they had experienced in Virginia. The Georgia frontier, like Virginia, offered only uncertainty and, very often, trouble. One fall, for instance, several hundred bushels of corn had been harvested and hauled into the stockade. In the dead of night the Dales were startled by awful yells and a blazing light. Indians at first had silently approached, bringing fire in a cow's horn to prevent their being detected, and had ignited the shucks. As the fire roared, Dale's father and mother each seized a rifle and stood in the door while he and his brother ran to the corn pen and pulled down the rails on the blazing shucks and soon put out the flames. Throughout Dale's youth his experience was marked by such narrow escapes from death and by the loss of many friends.

> So passed the days of my youth. Inured to every hardship, living on the coarsest food, earning our bread with our rifles cocked and primed, often witnessing the ruin of homesteads and the murders of families, my own life constantly in jeopardy, yet ever hopeful, ever relying on Providence, ever conscious of my duty to my fellow-men, never counting a personal risk for others as a merit, but only as a duty, and, in spite of privation and dangers, loving the wilderness to the last.[4]

When Indians ceased to be a threat, his father, in 1791, contracted for and moved the family to a tract three miles from Carmichael's Station. As payment he promised seven thousand pounds of tobacco. Feeling the promise of prosperity and safety, they built a cabin and made a clearing. However, their hopes were dashed. "The blind staggers got among the horses and

---

[4] *Ibid.*, p. 31.

killed all but one," and then the following Christmas Dale's mother died. A week later his father, broken-hearted, followed her to the grave.

> Never have I felt so crushed and overpowered by the feeling of help-lessness and isolation. I was under twenty years of age; no foot of earth could be called our own. We were burdened with debt. No kindred blood or oppulent friends to offer us sympathy or aid; eight brothers and sisters, all younger than myself, and one infant, look-ing to me for bread, and the wilderness around our lonely cabin swarming with enemies.[5]

After all the children had cried themselves to sleep, Dale went to the graves of his parents and prayed. He was a despair-ing boy, but when he arose he was a hopeful and resolute man. He said he had faith in Providence and in himself so that when the children awoke he was able to meet them with a smile and a cheerful spirit.

In 1793 the Indians became restless as white settlers con-tinued to come into the territory. The governor of Georgia au-thorized Captain Foote to organize a troop for the protection of the frontier. When Dale was able to find a reliable old man to tend to the farm and to the Dale children, he enlisted as a gov-ernment scout. He was equipped with a coonskin cap, a bear-skin vest, a short hunting shirt and trousers of homespun, buckskin leggings, and a blanket, and behind his saddle he had a wallet for parched corn, flour, or any kind of personal posses-sion, a long rifle, and a hunting knife. His pay for scouting, along with the proceeds from a first-rate crop of tobacco made on the farm by the children, enabled him to pay off more than half the money owing on the Dale land. They also had an abun-dant supply of provisions for the winter. In the next year he was able to pay off the entire debt. He said that the "household grew up with thankful hearts to an overruling Providence."[6]

Until 1796 Dale continued as a frontier scout. Then he

[5] *Ibid.*, p. 35.
[6] *Ibid.*, pp. 36–37.

started a business of trading and bartering goods. He purchased a four-horse wagon and went to Savannah and engaged in wagon trade during the winter. When spring came, he put his horses to the plow and aided his brothers in making a crop. For a few years he engaged in trading with the Creek Indians, bartering for cattle, hogs, peltry, hides, and tallow, which he carried to the seaboard and sold.

During the first year of the nineteenth century there was a brisk emigration from Georgia and the Carolinas to the Creek and Choctaw lands in Mississippi Territory. Dale contracted to move many of these pioneers through the Creek nation. He put three wagons and teams into the business of transporting these families. On the return trips he would bring back loads of Indian produce, which he sold on the seacoast. In 1803 he and Ellick Saunders, a half-blood, served as guides to mark out a highway through the Cherokee nation. Then they set up a trading post on Hightower River. The products their wagons picked up on these trips were sold in Charleston.

Dale returned to scouting at about the time of the massacre at Fort Mims, August 30, 1813. In Indian fighting he had received a severe wound which continued to give him great pain. A ball had struck him in the left side, and it had moved from under his ribs to his backbone. Though he continued to suffer much pain, he went to Fort Madison, situated at the fork of the Alabama and Tombigbee Rivers, near Choctaw and Creek Territory.

The general alarm which spread with the news of the massacre at Fort Mims brought Dale new duties. He took charge of Fort Glass, a small stockade about a quarter of a mile from Fort Madison, where there were fifteen families. Determined to prevent another massacre, Dale arranged a means to light up the approach to the fort for a circuit of a hundred yards. At his suggestion the women wore men's hats so that Indians would believe there were more men inside the fort.

On November 13, 1813, while scouting near Random's Landing in Monroe County, Dale and three of his men surprised a band of warriors in two canoes. Dale leaped into one canoe and killed seven of the Indians singlehandedly. This combat lasted only ten minutes. Altogether Dale and his men were able to kill twelve Indians. Although the white men escaped death, Dale's shoulder was dislocated.

It was decided that for further protection a new fort was to be built on Weatherford's Bluff. This stockade, called Fort Claiborne, was two hundred feet square and was protected by three block houses and a halfmoon battery which commanded the river. Dale said that the fort was built chiefly for the security of magazines intended for General Jackson. Without these supplies, General Jackson could not have been able to keep the field. Dale believed the most serious fear for the American forces was the fact that the Indians could go to Pensacola, which was held by the Spanish, and obtain firearms. Dale said that "he wished to God he was authorized by General Flournoy to take that sink of iniquity, the depot of Tories and instigators of disturbances on the southern frontier."

Dale was aware that much of the strength of Indians lay in their superstitions. He recounted how, to discredit these, an expedition by whites onto sacred Indian lands undermined the Indians' reverence for their tribal spokesmen. Colonel Russell, with the third regiment, and the general resolved to make this expedition to "holy ground" east of Alabama into the heart of enemy territory, 120 miles from the stockade. It was a stronghold of Indians who had been taught that if a white man dared to tread upon these lands the earth would open up and swallow him. If enemy Indians were taken on these lands, they were burned at the stake.

Though it was the dead of winter and though the troops were poorly clothed and without supplies, they traveled into this forbidden territory. On Christmas Day General Claiborne, his officers, and men ate a meagre dinner of boiled acorns and parched corn. However, despite such privations as cold weather and inadequate food they realized the importance of this bold movement into the heart of the Indian nation. The expedition proved a success, Dale reported, for it destroyed the Indians' confidence in their prophets, and it proved what volunteers, even without shoes, clothing, blankets, or provisions, would do for their country. To Fort Claiborne the volunteers returned barefoot, with eight months' pay due them.

Dale reported other privations he had witnessed. Another group of soldiers lived on acorns, hickory nuts, rats, and mice. He saw one soldier offer two dollars for a rat, but the owner would accept not less than ten dollars. By purchasing two horses, the troops subsisted on horseflesh until they arrived at Fort Claiborne. Exposure and privations affected Dale's old wound and brought on inflammation. He said that Dr. Neal Smith, a surgeon at the stockade, skillfully extracted the ball which had been in Dale's body since the Battle of Burnt Court.

Toward the close of December, 1814, while Dale was engaged in a business transaction at the Creek agency in Georgia, an express message arrived for General Jackson from the secretary of war. It was supposed that the general was near New Orleans preparing for the defense against the rumored British invasion. General McIntosh, in command of the Georgia troops then in that vicinity, urged Dale to take charge of delivering the dispatches. Dale knew that, to deliver them, he had to pass through a territory of vengeful Indians, but he accepted the trust. That same night, taking only a blanket, a flint and steel, his pistols, and a wallet of Indian flour for himself and his horse, he left. On Paddy, his reliable horse noted for his wind and muscle, Dale made the trip of eight-hundred miles in seven and one-half days. On January 8, 1815, he learned that the general was with the army on the plains of Chalmette. Galloping astride Paddy to the battlefield, Dale thus became an eyewitness of the Battle of New Orleans. As he arrived, the roar of artillery told him that the battle was in full blast. The British advanced in columns and cheered loudly as they marched toward the American forces. When they were near enough, there was a blaze of gunfire, a crack of small arms, and a deafening roar of artillery. When the smoke cleared away, the field was covered with dead and wounded. The British columns were in retreat, "not," Dale said, "flying ingloriously, but staggering back, like men reeling under unexpected and overpowering blows."[7] This was the first time that Dale, a backwoodsman, had ever seen a military battle. He was accustomed to ambuscades in the wilderness and to the kind of hand-to-hand combat typical of the frontier. This was a sight that he never forgot. The British very much impressed him with "the heroism of their officers, who rushed to the front, waving their swords, and rallied their men into the very jaws of death, and cheering died."[8]

It was after midnight before Dale could see General Jackson to deliver the dispatches. Jackson tore them open, read them, and exclaimed, "Too late; too late; they are always too late at Washington." Though Dale had reached New Orleans in record time, the dispatch papers arrived outdated and useless. Thus, as Jackson learned from them, the battle at New Orleans had been fought after the treaty of peace had been signed.[9]

Jackson congratulated Dale on the quickness of his journey, and for Dale's long ride back to Milledgeville Jackson offered him another horse, but Dale preferred to keep his faithful Paddy. Jackson doubted that the same horse could survive the return trip, but Dale told Jackson, "He is like myself, general, very tough." Dale said he was able to ride so fast because he rode with "an empty belly and no saddlebags." He set out the next day, and when he reached Georgia, everyone wanted to hear in detail his eyewitness report of the Battle of New Orleans. "I shall never fear for my country," he said, "while such a spirit prevails."[10]

With the end of war Dale resumed his business as a merchant at Dale's Ferry. It was difficult, however, for him to concentrate solely upon business and not engage in the active affairs of the frontier. Holmes, governor of Mississippi Territory, appointed him colonel of the militia, assessor and collector for Monroe

[7] *Ibid.*, p. 150.
[8] *Ibid.*
[9] *Ibid.*, p. 151.
[10] *Ibid.*, p. 164.

36

County, and commissioner to take the census, organize beats or precincts, with blank commissions for justices of the peace, sheriff, constables, and other civil officers. At first Dale protested, but at the governor's insistence he accepted.

In 1816 Dale was elected to be a delegate to the convention called to divide Mississippi Territory, the western portion to form a new state of Mississippi. The convention was assembled on the Pearl River at the house of John Ford. General Cowles Mead, whom Thomas Jefferson had appointed secretary of Mississippi Territory, presided. When it came to the final vote, Dale, representing Monroe County, voted for the division of the Territory and for the western part of the Territory to be admitted to the Union.[11]

Dale's participation in the convention prevented his being in Dale's Ferry to attend to his business. He reported that he felt a duty, moreover, to the settlers as they continued the migration into newly opened lands. By 1817 he found that his duties to his nation and to his community had caused him to neglect his mercantile interests. In that year business, he said, was "disastrous."

"The influx of immigrants was incessant, and, of course, they came destitute of provisions and without means." Dale reported that the settlers' first demand was for bread. He said that their demands were made with "tears, with persuasions, and even with threats." He could not refuse. With his personal cash savings of four thousand dollars, he traveled to Mobile to invest it for the settlers' needs and to buy provisions for them. He sold goods to them on credit, and many never repaid him. It caused Dale financial ruin.

He was elected to be a delegate to the first general assembly in the Alabama Territory which met at St. Stephen. At this time Governor Bibb conferred on him the commission of colonel because there was still unrest among Indians in the territory. When several families were murdered in what later became Butler County, Alabama, Dale hastily recruited thirty

---

[11] Clarence Edwin Carter, ed., *The Territorial Papers of the United States*, vol. 5 (Washington, 1937), p. 708.

volunteers and they marched in the direction of the hostile outbursts to inter the bodies of the dead. Among those slain and mutilated by the Indians was Captain William Butler, whose heart had been cut out and suspended on a stake. For several months Dale was engaged in warring with Indians. He and his men strengthened Fort Bibb and erected Fort Dale to provide some degree of security from murderous raiding parties. Acts of cruelty persisted as Indians crept out at night to attack, though by day they hid in the swamps and cane brakes of Chulatchee, Bogue Chitto, Warren, and Sipsey rivers. Finally, as Dale reported, these Indians were so closely pursued that they secretly left the vicinity.

Alabama became a state in 1818, and again Dale returned to politics to serve in 1819–20 in the Alabama legislature, which met at St. Stephens and Cahawba. In 1821 Dale and three others were appointed to locate public roads from Tuscaloosa to Pensacola and then to Fort Alabama. He said that they were engaged in hard labor for seventy-eight days.

In the same year the legislature of Alabama adopted resolutions referring to Dale's military service in gratifying terms and conferred on him both a pension and the rank of brigadier general by brevet in the state militia. In their proclamation the legislators expressed both their gratitude and their description of Dale's financial and physical condition.

> Whereas the territory now comprising the State of Alabama was, during our late war with Great Britain, subjected likewise to the barbarities of savage warfare; and whereas our venerable citizen, Col. Samuel Dale, was the first to interpose his aid for the defense of our people, and endure privations and hardships that have impaired his constitution and reduced him to indigence; and whereas the said Dale, not having had it in his power, owing to the situation of the country, to preserve his papers and vouchers to establish his claim on the United States government, and has failed to receive even justice from that quarter; and whereas we, the representatives of the people of Alabama, feel it a duty to them and ourselves to manifest our gratitude for his distinguished services; therefore
>
> Be it enacted by the Senate and House of Representatives, that

the treasurer be and is hereby required to pay to the said Col. Samuel Dale half the pay now allowed by the United States to colonels in the army. And that he is hereby declared a brigadier general in brevet in the militia of this state, and shall rank as such whenever called into service. And the treasurer is authorized and required to the said brevet Brigadier General Samuel Dale, the half pay as aforesaid, for aid during his life, out of any money in the treasury not otherwise appropriated.[12]

When Jackson became president, Dale traveled to Washington, hoping to be paid money he felt was due him for furnishing corn and other supplies to troops during the war. He was entertained at the White House, and in returning home he passed through Virginia, and while visiting again the graves of his parents in Georgia, he was deeply moved to tears.

He came to Mississippi, where he had settled, and served in the legislature in 1822 to represent Lauderdale County. From Iacha-hopa he purchased a reserve of two sections of land, near Daleville, in Lauderdale County.

From 1825 to 1828 he served again in the state legislature. Then in 1831 he entered the emigration service. Dale and Colonel George Gaines were commissioned by the secretary of war, according to the Treaty of Dancing Rabbit Creek, to remove the Choctaws to their new homelands on the Arkansas and Red Rivers. Though Dale did not fully agree with the purposes of his mission, it fell his duty to "collect and transport the Indians that remained on ceded land." By the treaty all their lands east of the Mississippi River except special reservations had been ceded to the United States.

In Dale's view the treaty "was brought about by pressure. The Indian is ever averse to the surrender of land. Though only tenants in common, they have a superstitious reverence for the soil of their birth and the ashes of their ancestors."[13] He felt that they had been brave fighters in defending their homes, and he believed that the achievements of the Creeks could "rival

[12] Claiborne, p. vi.
[13] Ibid., pp. 173–174.

the prodigies of antiquity." Dale seemed to lament the dominion that the Mississippi legislature extended over the Choctaws, for the treaty "extinguished the powers and authority of the chiefs, abolished the tribal immunities and penalties, and . . . subjected the untutored Indian to the cupidity and cunning of a dominant and instructed race."[14]

As the agent who transported them from Mississippi, Dale, the old Indian fighter and man of the frontier, was very much moved by the plight of the Choctaws:

> I have found the great body of Choctaws very sad; making no arrangements, until the last moment, to remove; clinging around their humble cabins, and returning again and again to the resting places of their dead. Even the sternest warriors, trained to suppress every emotion, appeared unmanned, and, when we camped at night, many of them stole back, in the darkness, twenty, thirty, even forty miles to take "a last fond look" at the graves of their household, soon to be trampled upon by a more enterprising and less sentimental race.[15]

Weakened by his old injuries, many of them inflicted by Indians like those whom he was transporting from their tribal lands, Dale was not physically well enough to travel the full way with them. While Dale was on the trail with with the migrating Choctaws, his horse fell in the woods and rolled over him. His shoulder was again badly dislocated and he received other injuries. These forced his retirement from emigration service.

To his final days Dale grieved for the Indians, for he well understood them. He "extolled their courage, their love of country, their tenderness to their children, and their reverence for the dead."[16]

Claiborne recalls the heroic Dale as quiet, self-effacing, "taciturn and grave of face and manner." He reports that Dale

[14] Ibid., p. 175.
[15] Ibid.
[16] Ibid., p. 232.

seldom laughed and that he spoke in low tones. Claiborne notes further that Dale was "six feet two inches, erect, square-shouldered, raw-boned, and muscular, noted particularly for the great length and strength of arm."[17]

> He was a man of singular modesty, silent and reserved, and rarely alluded to his own adventures. He was a man of truth, and possessed the confidence and esteem of many eminent persons.[18]

On May 24, 1841, on the lands which he had acquired from Ia-cha-hopa and on which he had resided for ten years, Sam Dale died in his seventieth year. He was buried near this last home at Daleville. Today near this site is a state park established as a tribute to Dale and his fearless leadership in the affairs of the Old Southwest.

SELECTED BIBLIOGRAPHY

Carter, Clarence Edwin, ed. *The Territorial Papers of the United States*. Vols. 5, 6. Washington, D.C.: United States Government Printing Office, 1937.

Claiborne, J.F.H. *Life and Times of Gen. Sam Dale, the Mississippi Partisan*. New York: Harper and Brothers, 1860.

Flynn, Robert, and Edna Wood Fraser. "The Indians Called Him 'Big Sam.'" *The Birmingham News Magazine*, November 5, 1967, p. 15.

Foster, John. *Southern Frontiersman: The Story of General Sam Dale*. New York: William Morrow and Company, 1967.

"Sam Dale." *Dictionary of Alabama Biography*. Chicago: S. J. Clark Publishing Company, 1921, III, 451.

"Sam Dale Park Is Dedicated." *Commercial Appeal*, October 14, 1968, p. 21.

Pickett, Albert James. *History of Alabama, and Incidentally of Georgia and Mississippi, from the Earliest Period*. 2 vols. Charleston: Walker and James, 1851.

[17] Ibid., pp. 231–232.
[18] Ibid., p. vii.

Greenwood LeFlore
1800–1865

Greenwood LeFlore

Greenwood LeFlore:
Farsighted Realist

BY EMMIE ELLEN WADE

The name Greenwood LeFlore is a familiar one in Mississippi because of the city of Greenwood and the county of Leflore. Once remembered as a wealthy planter and the builder of Malmaison, one of the most beautiful antebellum landmarks in the state, LeFlore has been almost forgotten since the destruction of this home by fire in 1942. His greatest significance, however, is in the role he played as chief of the Choctaws who signed the Treaty of Dancing Rabbit Creek, ending the Choctaw nation in Mississippi. Since this treaty opened up for settlement millions of acres of the richest land in the state, Mississippians were doubtless grateful to LeFlore. But did his actions entitle him to be regarded as a hero or was he an unscrupulous opportunist who exploited his people for his own gain?

So many discrepancies and contradictions are found in the LeFlore biographies that it is impossible to give a completely authentic account of his life. However, fitting the accepted details into the general history of his times can provide a proper perspective. One fact is indisputable. The Choctaw nation in Mississippi was doomed because the policy of removing all Indians east of the Mississippi River into the western area designated as Indian Territory had become generally accepted. Even John Quincy Adams, who as president was concerned that the Indians should be fairly treated, did not oppose the Indian policy. Once Andrew Jackson became president, the removal of the Indians became a certainty. The real question was not would they be removed but how soon and under what circumstances.

A brief examination of federal policy in regard to the Choc-

43

taws shows continuous inroads on their lands. In 1801 the federal government persuaded both the Choctaws and Chickasaws to cede lands needed for constructing the Natchez Trace; in 1803 a cession of over two and a half million acres was acquired by the Treaty of Fort Adams; in 1805 by the Treaty of Mount Dexter over four million acres of Choctaw land was made available for settlements; in 1816 another treaty concerned land on the middle Alabama-Mississippi lines; and in 1820 the renowned Pushmataha signed the Treaty of Doak's Stand giving up over five million acres in return for land in the Indian Territory to which the Choctaws were encouraged to move.[1] However, it was the Treaty of Dancing Rabbit Creek signed by Greenwood LeFlore and other Choctaw leaders that brought an end to the existence of the Choctaw nation in Mississippi as those who did remain were no longer under tribal organization and rules but were subject to Mississippi government and laws.

To understand the young chief who was only thirty years old at the time he played such an important part in the Treaty of Dancing Rabbit Creek, some knowledge of his background is necessary. The LeFlore story began with the appearance of Louis LeFleur, a young French-Canadian, who came first to Mobile with several brothers and a sister. (The name LeFleur was later changed to LeFlore, supposedly to simplify the spelling.) LeFleur later accepted an appointment by the United States government to establish a trading post in Choctaw Territory. One of the first persons the young man encountered in Indian Territory was a beautiful Choctaw girl named Rebecca Cravat. If he spoke to her in French, she probably understood him, as her father was John Cravat, a full-blooded Frenchman, who married a Choctaw woman and had been adopted into the tribe. Later LeFleur and Rebecca were married and settled at LeFleur Bluffs, also called LeFleur Landing, in the area of present-day Jackson.

[1] Richard A. McLemore, ed., *A History of Mississippi* (Jackson, 1973), I, 88.

Their fourth child[2] was born June 3, 1800, at LeFleur Bluffs and named Greenwood in honor of an English sea captain and former partner of LeFleur. When Greenwood was twelve years old, the family moved, establishing a tavern on the Natchez Trace in an area which was soon called French Camp, as it is still known today. Among the travelers who stayed at the LeFlore establishment was Major John Donley who had the United States government contract to carry the mails from Natchez to Nashville. Major Donley was attracted to the young Greenwood as he played with his brothers and sisters outside the tavern. Apparently the young boy felt a mutual attraction to Major Donley, for, according to LeFlore family tradition, the boy Greenwood followed his father and Major Donley about attempting to listen to their conversations. Since he spoke only Choctaw and Major Donley did not, he could understand very little of what was said. Yet he is supposed to have remarked to his brother that he would like to go to Nashville with Major Donley. When the Major came again to the LeFlore tavern on his return trip, he suggested to Louis LeFlore that he would like to take Greenwood home with him so that the boy would have the opportunity for an education. When Rebecca LeFlore was consulted about this proposal, she gave her consent, reportedly saying that it would be a wonderful advantage for him since the boy was so different from the other children.

Early in the fall of 1812, Greenwood LeFlore, only twelve years old and speaking little or no English, accompanied Major Donley to his home in Nashville where he would remain until the end of the year 1817. Rosa Donley, only two years younger, gave him the special assistance he needed in learning the English language. The close association of Greenwood and Rosa developed into romance, but when permission to marry was requested of Major Donley, it was denied because they were too young. (Greenwood was seventeen and Rosa fifteen.) The young

[2] There were thirteen LeFlore children, eleven born to Rebecca and two to her sister Nancy, whom LeFlore married after Rebecca's death.

lover apparently accepted the decision, allowing Major Donley to forget the request. Later, Greenwood asked his friend what he would dc if he loved a girl but was not allowed to marry her. Major Donley, not thinking about his own daughter, replied that he would take her away and marry her. The young couple immediately followed this advice and were married at a friend's house on December 4, 1817. The Major was at first very angry but soon relented and invited the young couple to return home. They remained with the Donleys for a short time but were soon on their way to Mississippi, which had just been admitted to statehood, to make their home there.

Little is known of their first years in Mississippi except that their first home was a "humble log cabin,"[3] but LeFlore's father was probably in a position to aid his ambitious young son. Louis LeFlore had fought with Pushmataha and Andrew Jackson against the Creek Indians in the War of 1812 and was respected by Indians and whites alike. LeFlore had also achieved some financial success with his tavern at French Camp and possibly had acquired other landholdings as well. When the Treaty of Doak's Stand was negotiated in 1820, Greenwood LeFlore petitioned the United States Government to become an American citizen entitled to possess land grants in his own right instead of under tribal custom. General Andrew Jackson, who had helped negotiate the treaty, endorsed the petition, hoping that LeFlore's action would be an example to others. LeFlore's petition was granted in the Treaty of Washington in 1825, so he became an American citizen possessing his own land.

LeFlore himself hoped that the Choctaws would remain in Mississippi gradually absorbing and accepting the culture of the whites.[4] He therefore opposed removal to the Indian Terri-

[3] Florence Rebecca Ray, *Chieftain Greenwood LeFlore and the Choctaw Indians of the Mississippi Valley* (Memphis, 1936), pp. 58–59.

[4] LeFlore was not alone in believing that the Indians could be assimilated into American culture. General Edmund Pendleton Gaines, believing that Indians should be educated and allowed to live on their own lands, strongly opposed Jackson's Indian policy.

tory, proposed in the Treaty of Doak's Stand. Since the Choctaws had never taken up arms against their white neighbors
but instead had fought as their allies in the War of 1812, no
deep-seated bitterness or resentment existed between them. In
addition, the Choctaws were among the most civilized of the
Indians, no longer depending on hunting wild animals but raising their own cattle and grain.

Since the old chiefs, Pushmataha, Nittahachi, and Mashulatubbee, had signed the treaty, the Choctaw's reaction against
them probably caused LeFlore's election as chief of the Northwest District at the age of twenty-two.[5] To honor him as the
new chief, he was presented a sword bestowed upon a former
chief by President Thomas Jefferson. The sword, a magnificent
blue-steel blade with a gold-mounted handle, and the silver
medal, bearing the inscription "Peace and Prosperity" and the
date 1802, were among LeFlore's most treasured possessions
and were prominently displayed at Malmaison until it was destroyed by fire.

The new chief took his responsibilities seriously, supporting
several significant reforms. Traffic in intoxicating beverages
was forbidden,[6] and any infringement was punishable by a severe whipping. One of the first offenders was his own brother-
in-law, but the law was strictly enforced despite the relationship. Educating his people was one of his goals, so efforts were
made to establish schools. Several mission schools had been established by Presbyterian and Methodist missionaries, and he
strongly supported their efforts to convert the Indians to Chris-
tianity. He himself became a Methodist and was closely associ-
ated with the missionary, the Reverand Dr. Alexander Talley.

James W. Silver, "A Counter-Proposal to the Indian Policy of Andrew Jackson," *Journal
of Mississippi History*, IV, 207–215.

[5]Not only was he young to be elected a chief but also he was only a quarter Choctaw
and educated in the white culture.

[6]Federal laws had earlier forbidden whiskey brought into Indian Territory, but the
laws were never enforced. Angie Debo, *The Rise and Fall of the Choctaw Republic*
(Norman, 1934), p. 48.

He also sought to eliminate the Choctaw beliefs in witchcraft and the supernatural. To do this, he proposed to execute the first self-proclaimed witch himself to disprove the belief that a witch could not be killed.

Another reform supported by LeFlore was the right to a fair trial by jury. An incident described by his great-granddaughter, Florence Rebecca Ray, illustrated his efforts to achieve this. At an Indian council meeting, a warrior on horseback accidentally caused the death of another Indian when the horse, frightened by a wild war whoop, stampeded into the midst of the council. Immediately the Choctaws would have killed the young warrior according to their custom of a life for a life. LeFlore attempted to dissuade them, but, failing to do so, he stepped in front of the offender, saying that they would have to kill him first. The action proved successful, and instead of killing the young warrior, the Indians were persuaded to contribute a sum of $500 which was presented to the family of the slain man.

Despite LeFlore's efforts, only a small, loyal following supported him and his associates, who like LeFlore were not full-blooded Choctaws. The old chiefs, Mushulatubbee and Nittahachi[7], were regaining their former influence, and a power struggle was rapidly developing between the two factions, LeFlore and the "half-bloods" against the old chiefs and the "full-bloods." A conflict between the two factions was probably inevitable, as many of the Indians opposed LeFlore's progressive ideas, preferring the traditional customs.[8] LeFlore, an imperious young man, impatient with those who opposed his policies, doubtless antagonized many, particularly the old chiefs. When several of the newly-established schools were burned, LeFlore accused Mashulatubbee as the instigator of the arson.

[7]Pushmataha had died in Washington in 1824 and was buried there with military honors in Arlington National Cemetery.

[8]A similar power struggle existing between the Choctaws in the Indian Territory during the early years of the twentieth century is described by John W. Wade in "Removal of the Mississippi Choctaws," Publications of the *Mississippi Historical Society*, VIII, 397–426. Wade lived in the Indian Territory briefly and was familiar with the difference between the two factions.

In addition, LeFlore was gradually reversing his stand on the removal of the Choctaws and was considering the advisability of negotiating with the United States government, while the old chiefs were now committed to opposing all negotiations.

The end result of these differences was armed confrontation of the two factions with the threat of a tragic civil war. Conflicting stories are told about what happened next. The LeFlore account was that when Nittahachi suddenly appeared in the center between the two armed camps, LeFlore went to meet him and the two men made their peace.[9] Another account attributed the peaceful solution to the efforts of George S. Gaines, an Indian agent whom the Choctaws trusted.[10] However it was accomplished, peace was achieved and war averted.

Pressure on the Choctaws to move westward to the Indian Territory intensified after Andrew Jackson's election as president in 1828. The following year the Mississippi Legislature, certain of Jackson's support, provided extension of state laws over both the Choctaws and Chickasaws. In 1829 the legislature took further action, granting citizenship to the Indians and abolishing tribal government under penalty of fine and imprisonment. Actually the law was not enforced but apparently was intended to induce the Choctaws to leave Mississippi so that they might retain their tribal government and customs. One result of the Mississippi laws was that the Choctaw chiefs could no longer enforce prohibition regulations, and this was disastrous for the Indians. The Presbyterian and Methodist missionaries, fearing that close contact with the whites would lead to further dissipation among the Indians, also began to favor removal to the Indian Territory.

Early in 1830 the Choctaws held elections for chiefs for the three districts according to a law passed in 1826, which limited the term of a chief to four years. The chiefs elected were Green-

[9]Ray, pp. 53–57; Mrs. W.D. Deupree, "Greenwood LeFlore," *Publications of the Mississippi Historical Society*, VII, 145. According to Mrs. Deupree, David Folson rather than LeFlore met Nittahachi.

[10]George H. Ethridge, "The Mississippi Indians: Greenwood LeFlore," *Clarion Ledger*, June 11, 1939.

wood LeFlore of the Northwest District, David Folsom of Lower Laws, and John Garland of Six Towns. Folsom and Garland, both "half-bloods," resigned in favor of LeFlore, who was then chief of all the Choctaws. Why this action was taken is not clear. One source suggests that Folsom and Garland were fearful that the state law would be enforced and they would be penalized. LeFlore, however, was unconcerned because he planned to move to the Indian Territory.[11] Needless to say, the old chiefs protested this action, claiming irregularities in the election, and continued to oppose LeFlore.

Feeling that removal was inevitable, LeFlore and some of his associates wrote a treaty and sent it by a trusted friend, D. W. Haley, to be presented to the Senate. Other Choctaws, hearing about the proposed treaty, drew up a petition to the Senate expressing their opposition. The Senate rejected the treaty, not because of the expressed opposition, but apparently on the grounds that the treaty was considered to be "too favorable to the Choctaws."[12]

Meanwhile President Jackson invited the Choctaw chiefs to meet with federal agents in Franklin, Tennessee, suggesting that he himself might attend. The meeting did not take place, however, because the Choctaws expressed so much opposition that none of their leaders dared to go.[13] Perhaps the Choctaws feared that their leaders, separated from the people, might be more easily persuaded to accept a treaty giving up their Mississippi lands. This seemed to be Jackson's interpretation because his next proposal was to send agents to meet with the Choctaws on their own territory, and this meeting did take place.

On September 17, 1830, the two American commissioners, John Coffee and John Eaton, began their negotiations with the Choctaws in the area of Dancing Rabbit Creek, centrally lo-

---

[11] Debo, p. 52.
[12] Debo, p. 52.
[13] Debo, p. 52. Another source, Ethridge, states that LeFlore went to Franklin and signed a treaty which was rejected by the Senate since the Choctaws opposed it.

cated in Choctaw lands and with sufficient space to provide for all those who wished to attend. Approximately six thousand Choctaws came, some of them already encamped before the commissioners arrived. Obviously they understood the importance of this meeting and intended to see that their interests were protected. The land on which they camped was a constant reminder to them of what they were being asked to give up and perhaps strengthened them in their resolve to retain their Mississippi lands.

The federal government had contracted with General George S. Gaines to provide food for possibly three thousand people for a week. Gaines brought vast quantities of flour and corn meal as well as a sizeable number of cattle, many of which were slaughtered each day. The Indians came prepared, too, with supplies of bread, jerked venison, and hominy, so no one went hungry despite the unexpectedly large number of Indians attending.

There was also an abundance of whiskey, for the law was very much relaxed, and "all the demoralizing concomitants of civilization were to be found . . . drinking saloons, gaming tables, and every cunning contrivance" which might lessen the Choctaw resolve to retain their lands. Ironically, the only people excluded from the area were the missionaries who had come with their Indian converts but were forced to leave the area by the two federal commissioners on the grounds that "their religious instruction would have a tendency to distract the Indians' minds."[14] Religious observances were not completely excluded, however, for David Folsom led his people in "preaching, praise, and song service" each night.[15]

The Indians were encamped according to the three sections of the Choctaw Nation. LeFlore, although he was supposedly chief of all the Choctaws, was encamped with his Northeast Section and had little influence over the other two sections

[14] H.S. Halbert, "The Story of the Treaty of Dancing Rabbit Creek," *Publications of the Mississippi Historical Society*, VI, 373–377.
[15] Ray, p. 87.

dominated by Mashulatubbee and Nittahachi. The three leaders presented an interesting contrast in appearance. LeFlore wore a suit as an ordinary citizen, which apparently caused some suspicion against him and the feeling that he had made some arrangement with the commissioners. This was not true for the commissioners completely ignored LeFlore until they had failed to gain their treaty. The most resplendent of the three was Nittahachi in full Indian costume, wearing a hunting shirt fringed with beadwork, a bright shawl held in place with a silver band, silver bands on his arms above his elbows and wrists, and seven crest-shaped gadgets around his neck. Mashulatubbee, who apparently was impressed with uniforms, wore a new blue military uniform which Jackson had sent to him.

The two commissioners, Coffee and Eaton, had received clear instructions from President Jackson, a very forceful man. They were to *bring back a treaty*. No excuses would be accepted and no limitations were set on their methods in acquiring the treaty. Eaton, who played the leading role, was from Tennessee and a close friend and associate of Jackson's. He had worked unceasingly from 1824 to 1828 to elect Jackson president of the United States and had been rewarded with the cabinet post of Secretary of War.[16] His policy of treating the Indians was to alternate flattery and appeals of friendship with threats of the most alarming nature.

Commissioner Eaton began his first address to the Choctaws asserting that it was "not your lands, but your happiness that we seek to obtain. . . . Your Great Father has sent us not as traders but as friends and brothers. . . Your Great Father will guard you against all enemies." When the chiefs opposed his proposals, he changed his tactics, threatening "Choctaws had no choice . . . but were bound to sell their lands and remove.

[16] Eaton continued to serve as Secretary of War until Jackson dismissed his entire cabinet because of the "Eaton Affair." When Eaton's wife, the former Peggy O'Neal, was snubbed by Washington society, Jackson came to her defense and ordered all cabinet members to have their wives accept Mrs. Eaton. When Peggy was still snubbed, Jackson dismissed his cabinet and later appointed Eaton U.S. ambassador to Spain.

. . . If they refused, the President in 20 days would march with an army . . . build forts in their hunting grounds. . . . Their lands would be seized."[17] As the Choctaws still determined to retain their lands and would sign no treaty, the commissioners turned to Greenwood LeFlore. They apologized for their neglect of him and asked for his support. He made several proposals to be included in the treaty, saying it would be more acceptable with these provisions. The commissioners did not agree to all his proposals but Article XIV was included in the treaty. Then Eaton made one last speech, threatening the Indians with such dire calamities as "they would become paupers and beggars . . . broken up and utterly destroyed as a nation." LeFlore was ready to accept the treaty with the inclusion of Article XIV, and the other chiefs, full of fear from Eaton's speech, signed the Treaty of Dancing Rabbit Creek on September 27, 1830.[18]

LeFlore was a realist with the foresight to see that the Indians' choices were limited. The inclusion of Article XIV provided an alternative, allowing Choctaws to remain in Mississippi, which he thought made the treaty acceptable. The provisions of this Article are:

> Each Choctaw head of a family, being desirous to remain and become a citizen of the States, shall be permitted to do so by signifying his intentions to the Agent within six months from ratification of this Treaty, and he or she shall thereupon be entitled to a reservation of section of six hundred and forty acres of land . . . he shall be entitled to onehalf that quantity for each unmarried child which is living with him over ten years of age; and a quarter section to such child as may be under ten years of age to adjoin the location of the parent. . . Persons who claim under this article shall lose the privilege of a Choctaw citizen, but if they ever remove are not to be entitled to any portion of Choctaw annuity.[19]

[17] Halbert, pp. 373–377.
[18] Halbert, pp. 373–377; Debo, pp. 54–55.
[19] Ray, pp. 93–94. The entire Treaty of Dancing Rabbit Creek is included in this book.

The basic choices of the Choctaws, treaty or no treaty, were either to remain in Mississippi and live under the white man's government and laws or to move to the Indian Territory where they would be allowed to retain their tribal government and customs. If they accepted the Treaty of Dancing Rabbit Creek, the conditions would be more favorable than if they rejected the treaty. Actually, if the treaty had been fairly and effectively enforced, the Choctaws would not have fared too badly except that they were forced to give up their ancestral lands.[20]

Unfortunately the treaty was not effectively enforced. Government officials had no concept of the organization and administration required to move thousands of Indians into an unsettled land and to provide for them until they could care for themselves. Much of the undertaking was left to army officials to carry out with indefinite orders and limited resources, and the Choctaws were the ones who suffered. The government also failed to provide honest Indian agents to supervise the selling of the Choctaws' cattle and other properties as they prepared to move, and most of them were exploited by the unscrupulous whites who flocked into the area. Eventually, however, as the Choctaws recovered from the shock of their removal and adjusted to their new life, they began to prosper in the Indian Territory.[21]

The Choctaws who fared the worst were the ones who remained in Mississippi. According to Article XIV they had only six months in which to register for the lands to which they were entitled, so registration was quickly begun. The man appointed as Indian Agent responsible for registering the Choctaws was William Ward, by all accounts a drunkard who frequently did not open his office and generally made no effort to

[20] The whites and perhaps LeFlore himself did not fully appreciate the Choctaws' regard for their lands. Generations had lived there, their ancestors were buried there, and they had an almost spiritual attachment to their lands. Americans were more nomadic than the Choctaws, and few Mississippians, including LeFlore, had lived in the same area for more than two generations.

[21] Debo, p. 56. According to Debo, the wealthiest Choctaw in the Indian Territory possessed even more than LeFlore with his five large plantations, 500 slaves, interests in trading establishments, and a number of steamboats.

assist the Indians. Some of the uneducated Indians brought sticks to show the number of children, a long stick indicating children over ten and shorter ones for the younger children. Ward was said to have taken the sticks and thrown them away without making any effort to properly register the man and his family. He was also accused of having told Indians that they were properly registered when they had not been registered at all. He showed no concern about the registration books, leaving them unattended or even loaning them on request, so that a white man, wanting land registered to an Indian, could simply scratch out the Indian's name and acquire the land.

As more Indians sought to remain in Mississippi than had been anticipated, registration was closed after three months instead of the prescribed six. Comparatively few Choctaws succeeded in acquiring titles to their land and keeping them from the unscrupulous land agents and rapacious white neighbors. Most of the Indians remaining in Mississippi were doomed to a miserable existence, living on undesirable but unclaimed land to which they had no legal title.[22]

How LeFlore reacted to the exploitation of the Choctaws is not known, but, according to Miss Ray, he made a trip to Washington, personally appealing to President Jackson. Earlier he had made a similar trip requesting Jackson to remove a dishonest Indian agent from his position. Jackson at first refused, but thinking LeFlore's friendship too important to lose, eventually conceded to LeFlore's persistence. LeFlore's second trip, however, ended in failure as Jackson now had his treaty and no longer needed LeFlore's influence. According to Miss Ray, the Choctaws' resentment of LeFlore stemmed from his inability

[22] Halbert, pp. 373–377. The federal government made two attempts to make restitution to Choctaws cheated out of their lands. A Congressional Act in 1842 provided a commission to hear Choctaw claims, but again land speculators and greedy whites made so many fraudulent claims that nothing was accomplished. Franklin L. Riley, "Choctaw Land Claims," *Publications of the Mississippi Historical Society*, VIII, 345–396. The Curtis Bill of 1892 and subsequent bills provided Mississippi Choctaws were entitled to lands in the Indian Territory partly to make restitution and partly to move Mississippi Indians from that state. Wade, "Removal of Mississippi Choctaws," *Publications of the Mississippi Historical Society*, VIII, 397–426.

to assure fair treatment for them. She asserted that this was the reason LeFlore did not move to the Indian Territory as he had earlier intended but instead remained in Mississippi.

The exploited Choctaws, feeling frustrated and helpless, looked for someone or something to blame for their misfortunes; and many whites, too, perhaps appalled at what had happened to the unoffending Choctaws, looked for a scapegoat. LeFlore was the logical candidate. In the first place he was a "half-blood" and therefore suspect to both Indians and whites.[23] In the second place he had claimed to be chief of all the Choctaws; he had helped negotiate the treaty in the final stages and had readily signed it, encouraging his people to accept it, too.[24] Finally, he had not only remained in Mississippi but was very wealthy, living the life of a successful Southern planter, which was in great contrast to the Mississippi Choctaws and to most of the whites as well. Many Mississippians believed that "bribes," received for signing the treaty, were the basis of his wealth.

It is true that Article XV of the treaty allotted four sections of land to LeFlore, but equal amounts of land were provided for Mashulatubbee and Nittahachi, and in addition David Folsom and at least eight other Choctaw leaders received land grants. According to several accounts of LeFlore, he was already a wealthy man by 1830, and he would have continuing success, acquiring 15,000 acres of land in Mississippi and interests in a company owning 60,000 acres in Texas. Whenever he was accused of having taken bribes, he answered, "Which is worse— for a great government to offer a bribe or for a poor Indian to

---

[23] *Biographical and Historical Memoirs of Mississippi* (Chicago, 1891), p. 81 states that LeFlore "earned from the tribe the many maledictions heaped upon him. Greenwood LeFleur was no better or no worse than the Pitchlyns, Colberts, McKees, Allens, and Folsoms [all half-bloods]. They were squawmen, and as such lost to all sense of morals and decency, the history of one is the history of all."

[24] In explaining the treaty LeFlore is supposed to have said, "My children, for your good I have signed the Treaty. Kill me if you wish; shoot me here," pointing to his heart. Ray, p. 100. One wonders how the mature Indians reacted to being addressed as children.

accept one?"[25] Actually, Indian chiefs traditionally received land grants and/or annuities, and similar provisions are found in previous treaties not signed by LeFlore. A refusal to accept the land grants would not have benefited the Choctaws nor would it have changed his image with them. Another accusation against him was that he encouraged the Indians to sell out to him and to proceed in small groups to the Indian Territory, thereby causing them great suffering since the government had not made provisions for them.[26] Since adequate provisions were never made, LeFlore's explanation that the independent groups could travel by water and proceed more rapidly would seem logical.

Personal reasons may have influenced LeFlore in his decision to remain in Mississippi. His wife, Rosa Donley LeFlore, died October 3, 1829, after twelve years of marriage, leaving a daughter, Elizabeth, and a son, John. Conceivably, LeFlore hesitated to move his young children, who had so recently lost their mother, from their home and familiar surroundings. A year or two after Rosa's death, he married a second wife, Elizabeth Cody. She was a niece of Cherokee Chief John Ross and a cousin of Buffalo Bill, but she died within a year after their marriage. Since accounts of LeFlore portray him as a devoted husband, father, and grandfather, concern for his unsettled family could have influenced his decision to remain in Mississippi. In 1834 LeFlore was married to Priscilla Donley, the sister of his first wife, and once again he eloped with his bride because she was so young.[27] Priscilla LeFlore lived until 1910, long after her husband's death in 1865.

A new career opened up for LeFlore in 1835 when he was

[25] Ray, p. 100. In addition to land grants, annuities of $250.00 were provided for the chiefs as long as they retained their positions. LeFlore may have received the annuity once or twice but the Choctaws soon repudiated him as their chief.

[26] Grant Foreman, *Indian Removal: The Emigration of the Five Civilized Tribes of Indians* (Norman, 1932), pp. 193–195. Foreman suggests that LeFlore profited at the expense of these Indians.

[27] Priscilla Donley was an infant at the time of her sister's marriage to LeFlore and was only sixteen when she married him.

elected state representative for Carroll County, newly established from the Choctaw lands, and several years later he was
elected as a senator. During his years in the legislature he supported many of the same policies which he had favored as a
Choctaw chief, with particular emphasis on education and prohibition.[28] He apparently made no lasting contributions and is
remembered largely for an amusing incident in which he par-
ticipated. Many of the legislators, wanting to impress others
with their learning, used Latin words and phrases in their
speeches. One erudite young man carried this practice to an extreme by delivering an entire speech in Latin. LeFlore immediately arose from his seat and began to address his colleagues
in Choctaw. Despite efforts to stop him, he continued speaking
in Choctaw for at least an hour. He later asked which was the
more interesting, the Latin or Choctaw speech.

While his legislative career was brief and uneventful, he was
quite successful as a planter.[29] He had an abundance of fertile
lands, approximately four hundred slaves, and was an astute
businessman who made the most of his resources. His cotton
was ginned on his own plantations but had to be sent for shipment on the Yazoo River to a town known as Williams' Landing. Williams had built a shed in which the cotton was stored,
protecting it from the weather, and charged the planters for this
storage. When an excess of cotton accumulated, Williams left
LeFlore's cotton in the mud outside the shed but charged him
for storage nevertheless. LeFlore was indignant and as a result
decided to build his own town.

He bought land at the junction of the Yazoo and Tallahatchie
Rivers, several miles from Williams' Landing, and established a
town named Point LeFlore. First he built a sawmill to provide
lumber for needed buildings, and soon a church, hotel, schoolhouse, post office, and stores were erected. Because a road was

[28] Robert Lowery and William McCardle, *A History of Mississippi* (Jackson, 1891), p.
452. According to Miss Ray, LeFlore was elected in 1831, but the first representative
listed for Carroll County, LeFlore, is in 1835.

[29] Whether LeFlore was not re-elected or decided to devote full time to his business
enterprises is not known.

necessary to enable planters to bring their cotton for shipment, he built a turnpike, which included fourteen bridges and cost $75,000. The turnpike was well-maintained and attracted trade from as far away as sixty miles. Planters, bringing their cotton to Point LeFlore, were allowed free use of the turnpike, and many availed themselves of this privilege. To complete this business venture, LeFlore acquired a steamboat to transport the cotton and bring needed goods for the town. The town prospered until a lack of interest from either LeFlore or his heirs caused it to decline and eventually to die out completely. Ironically, Greenwood, the town which bears his name, later developed on the site of Williams' Landing.

Shortly after he married Priscilla Donley, LeFlore built a modest frame house in which they lived for almost twenty years. By the 1850s he had accumulated great wealth and was ready to build his mansion. He selected a beautiful spot nearby on a gradually sloping plateau, had pine and cypress trees cut and sent to his sawmill, and then had the wood carefully seasoned for over a year before it was used. The architect, James Clark Harris from Georgia, became LeFlore's son-in-law shortly after the completion of the house. While supervising the construction of the house, Harris fell in love with Rebecca Cravat LeFlore, the youngest of the LeFlore children and the only child of Priscilla LeFlore. He asked permission to marry her rather than to receive pay for his services. One of the most spectacular occasions celebrated at Malmaison was the wedding of Harris and Rebecca, who received a plantation and a hundred slaves as a wedding gift from her father.[30]

In his early years LeFlore had greatly admired Napoleon until he divorced his wife Josephine. LeFlore's reaction was sympathy for Josephine who he felt had been wronged. For this reason he named his new home Malmaison in honor of Josephine, whose home was known by that name during the unhappy

---

[30] Ray, pp. 67–68. Actually, a double wedding was held, as LeFlore's granddaughter, Martha Halsey, was married at the same time, and she, too, received a plantation and a hundred slaves for her wedding gift.

years after her divorce. Actually, the name meaning unhappy home was a misnomer because the LeFlores were very happy in their new home and enjoyed extending the lavish hospitality for which they soon became famous.

Malmaison, which followed the neo-classic design much used in Southern mansions of the times, was a two-story building with columns and porticoes on each of the four sides. The fifteen rooms were spacious, many as large as 20 x 25 x 15 feet, and most of the rooms had black Italian marble mantels. Only the parlor was furnished as LeFlore wished. Its furnishings had been ordered from France, but before other orders could be made, European shipments had ceased because of the Civil War. The parlor furniture, including over thirty pieces of the Louis XIV period, was made of gold leaf over French hickory upholstered in crimson silk brocade damask, also used for the draperies. Elaborate mirrors, an exquisite table and cabinet of tortoise shell and brass Boule work, and window shades of handpainted linen depicting famous French chateaux added to the magnificence of the room. These furnishings, including an Aubusson carpet, cost over $10,000 when purchased in the 1850's but remained remarkably wellpreserved until Malmaison burned.[31] The LeFlore family delighted in telling a story about the parlor furnishings. Before they were shipped from France, the Duchess of Orleans saw and admired their beauty. She was astounded when told that the furnishings were being sent to an old Indian chief in the United States, but she ordered an identical copy of the entire suite nevertheless.

In addition to the mansion itself, other buildings on the estate were two offices, two cisterns, two carriage houses, a smokehouse, and the outside kitchen connected by a long gallery to the house. On the vast, beautiful lawn, sodded in Bermuda grass, were many oak, sugar maple, and holly trees. One

---

[31] Ray, pp. 63–65. Miss Ray, the granddaughter of James and Florence Harris, lived at Malmaison, which was still standing at the time her book was written. Malmaison was the only property of the vast LeFlore lands still owned by a LeFlore descendant.

of LeFlore's favorite haunts was the Deer Park, an area of several acres, including a spring, enclosed by a high fence where the deer could roam at will but be protected from destructive hunters. The partially tame deer, all ages and sizes, presented a remarkable sight for LeFlore and his guests whom he invariably brought to the Deer Park. Probably his love for the deer stemmed from his Indian background, which he never forgot. He continued to be called chief, particularly in his last years as even his family and friends referred to him as the "Old Chief."

Some distance north of the mansion were the slave quarters and the stable. LeFlore, who owned many slaves, was known as a humane and kind master. His slaves were comfortably housed, well-fed, and well-clothed. Children were left in a large nursery supervised by several adults while their parents worked. A physician and a minister were kept on the estate to provide for the physical and spiritual needs of the slaves. A minister performed marriage ceremonies for the slaves, and the LeFlores furnished wedding feasts afterwards. LeFlore had an ingenuous method in determining which slaves to buy on his trips to New Orleans. He would have food brought for the Negroes, watching them as they ate. He would not buy those who dallied over their food, saying that they would not be energetic workers.[32]

His humaneness was also shown in his charity to those in need. An example of his generosity is given in a story told about him. On a trip to Carrollton he heard about an unfortunate man whose house and all his possessions had been destroyed by fire. LeFlore's reaction was not to talk about the disaster, as the others were doing but to do something about it. Writing out a check for $100, he said, "I am sorry a hundred dollars' worth; how much are you sorry, my friends?"[33] Other contributions followed, of course, and the man was no longer destitute. The story is typical of the man in that he acted when others merely talked.

[32] Ray, p. 71.
[33] Deupree, p. 149.

Although his last years were saddened by declining health and the Civil War, he enjoyed his grandchildren,[34] whom he delighted in teasing, and the numerous visitors who continued to come to Malmaison. As the crises causing the Civil War occurred, with the same farsighted realism shown during the earlier Indian question, LeFlore predicted Southern devastation and defeat, followed by years of poverty and humiliation. He was completely loyal to the United States government and outspoken in his opposition to Mississippi's seceding from the Union and joining the Confederate States. Refusing to recognize the Confederacy, he would not accept Confederate currency for any produce which was sold, nor would he support the Confederacy in any way, allowing a slave to be sold in lieu of the taxes he refused to pay. His undeviating loyalty to the Union is not easily understood considering the government's treatment of the Choctaw Indians. However, he had become an American citizen years before he had acquired state citizenship, and, in signing the Treaty of Dancing Rabbit Creek, he had pledged his allegiance to the federal government. Perhaps the Choctaws' repudiation had caused him to turn his loyalty and devotion to the Union, or perhaps it was simply the nature of the man.

Realistic and farseeing as he was, he maintained his basic integrity even when an unpopular stand caused public opinion to turn against him. Perhaps he had mellowed somewhat from the impatient young chief who would brook no opposition, for, according to Miss Ray, he lost few friends despite his unpopular stand. Other people were not so understanding, and several attempts were made to kill him as an enemy of the Confederacy. On one occasion two men managed to break into Malmaison, threatening LeFlore with a pistol. When he calmly faced them, saying, "Shoot! You only kill a poor old Indian," they were so startled that they fled from the house leaving him unharmed.[35]

[34] His grandchildren seemed to have lived either at Malmaison or close enough for frequent visits.
[35] Ray, p. 81.

When an attempt was made to burn the house, the loyal slaves succeeded in putting out the fire. Probably another factor which saved his life was his virtual confinement to Malmaison because of his failing health.

An incident involving an old friend, General Featherstone, revealed much about LeFlore and his reaction to the unfortunate circumstances of opposing the cause for which his friends were fighting. The general, preparing to camp not far from Malmaison on a cold, rainy night, thought how much more comfortable he would be enjoying LeFlore's hospitality and sent an aide to inquire if LeFlore would receive him. LeFlore's response was that he would welcome his friend but not a Confederate officer. Featherstone took the hint and, changing to civilian clothes, he and his aides enjoyed the hospitality of Malmaison for the night. Many years after the Civil War, a Memphis lawyer, writing about his experiences as a young Confederate officer, recalled vividly his visit to Malmaison and told how impressed he had been with LeFlore and his predictions which proved to be remarkably accurate.[36]

In 1863 Priscilla LeFlore took her husband, suffering from paralysis, to White Sulphur Springs, West Virginia, hoping that the hot springs there would be beneficial to his health. Although they returned a second time, LeFlore's condition continued to worsen. He was also troubled by financial difficulties. In addition to problems arising from the war, he was losing the 60,000 acres of Texas lands because of the dishonesty of his lawyer who had been sent to Texas to sell the lands.[37] Although he had been loyal to the United States, Union forces had confiscated much of his cotton and cattle,[38] and with the conclusion of the war, he had lost his slaves as well. As a young man LeFlore had energetically and optimistically faced what-

[36] Ray, pp. 68–70.

[37] LeFlore's son-in-law, Abram Halsey, had handled the Texas lands until his death. LeFlore sent a lawyer, Riley, to sell the lands, but Riley pocketed the money.

[38] Three of LeFlore's grandchildren, Louis and Rosa LeFlore and Florence Harris, held the flag for their grandfather. Ray, p. 82.

ever difficulties confronted him. Now an old man, with failing health and insurmountable financial problems, he lacked the will to struggle, but his loyal devotion to the United States continued to the end of his life. As he lay dying, he asked his grandchildren to hold the American flag over his bed so that he could look at it as long as he could see.[39] He had earlier asked his wife to wrap his body with the American flag, and she honored his request. He was buried on the grounds of his beloved home, Malmaison. The plain marble monument over his grave bears the simple inscription:

> GREENWOOD LEFLORE
> Born June 3, 1800
> Died August 31, 1865
> The last chief of the Choctaws
> east of the Mississippi.

BIBLIOGRAPHY

Biographical and Historical Memoirs of Mississippi. Chicago: The Goodspeed Publishing Company, 1891.

Debo, Angie. *The Rise and Fall of the Choctaw Republic.* Norman: University of Oklahoma Press, 1934.

DeRosier, Arthur H., Jr. *The Removal of the Choctaw Indians.* Knoxville: University of Tennessee Press, 1970.

Deupree, Mrs. W. D. "Greenwood LeFlore." *Publications of the Mississippi Historical Society,* VII, 141–152.

Ethridge, George H. "The Mississippi Indians: Greenwood LeFlore." Jackson *Clarion Ledger,* June 11, 1939.

Foreman, Grant. *Indian Removal: The Emigration of the Five Civilized Tribes of Indians.* Norman: University of Oklahoma Press, 1932.

Halbert, H.S. "The Story of the Treaty of Dancing Rabbit Creek." *Publications of the Mississippi Historical Society,* VI, 373–377.

Love, W.A. "The Mayhew Mission to the Choctaws." *Publications of the Mississippi Historical Society,* XI, 363–402.

Lowry, Robert, and William H. McCardle. *A History of Mississippi.* Jackson: R.H. Henry and Company, 1891.

McLemore, Richard Aubrey, ed. *A History of Mississippi.* 2 vols. Jackson: University and College Press of Mississippi, 1973.

Ray, Florence Rebecca. *Chieftain Greenwood LeFlore and the Choctaw Indians of the Mississippi Valley.* Memphis: C.A. Davis Printing Company, 1936.

Riley, Franklin L. "Choctaw Land Claims." *Publications of the Mississippi Historical Society,* VIII, 345–396.

Rowland, Dunbar, ed. *Mississippi.* 4 vols. Atlanta: Southern Historical Publishing Company, 1907.

Shackelford, Nora Jeanne. *The LeFlore Family and the Choctaw Indian Removal.* Thesis, Oklahoma State University, 1967.

Silver, James W. "A Counter-Proposal to the Indian Policy of Andrew Jackson." *Journal of Mississippi History,* IV (October 1942), 207–215.

Smith, Allene. *Greenwood LeFlore and the Choctaw Indians of the Mississippi Valley.* Memphis: C.A. Davis Printing Company, 1951.

Wade, John W. "Removal of the Mississippi Choctaws." *Publications of the Mississippi Historical Society,* VIII, 397–426.

Jefferson Davis
1808–1889

Jefferson Davis:
Prologue and Epilogue*

ᛁᛋᚩᛁᚳᛣᛁ

BY SHELBY FOOTE

It was a Monday in Washington, January 21; Jefferson Davis rose from his seat in the Senate. South Carolina had left the Union a month before, followed by Mississippi, Florida, and Alabama, which seceded at the rate of one a day during the second week of the new year. Georgia went out eight days later; Louisiana and Texas were poised to go; few doubted that they would, along with others. For more than a decade there had been intensive discussion as to the legality of secession, but now the argument was no longer academic. A convention had been called for the first week in February, at Montgomery, Alabama, for the purpose of forming a confederacy of the departed states, however many there should be in addition to the five already gone. As a protest against the election of Abraham Lincoln, who had received not a single southern electoral vote, secession was a fact—to be reinforced, if necessary, by the sword. The senator from Mississippi rose. It was high noon. The occasion was momentous and expected; the galleries were crowded, hoop-skirted ladies and men in broadcloth come to hear him say farewell. He was going home.

By now he was one of the acknowledged spokesmen of secession, though it had not always been so. By nature he was a moderate, with a deep devotion to the Union. He had been for compromise so long as he believed compromise was possible; he reserved secession as a last resort. Yet now they were at that

---

*This essay discussing Jefferson Davis's early life and his life after the war is taken from the first and third volumes of Mr. Foote's classic *The Civil War: A Narrative*. Volume I opens with the first portion of this excerpt, and Volume III concludes with the latter part.

67

stage. In a paper which he had helped to draft and which he had signed and sent as advice to his state in early December, his position had been explicit. "The argument is exhausted," it declared. "All hope of relief in the Union . . . is extinguished." At last he was for disunion, with a southern confederacy to follow.

During the twelve days since the secession of Mississippi he had remained in Washington, sick in mind and body, waiting for the news to reach him officially. He hoped he might be arrested as a traitor, thereby gaining a chance to test the right of secession in the federal courts. Now the news had been given him officially the day before, a Sunday, and he stayed to say goodbye. He had never doubted the right of secession. What he doubted was its wisdom. Yet now it was no longer a question even of wisdom; it was a question of necessity—meaning Honor. On the day before Lincoln's election, Davis had struck an organ tone that brought a storm of applause in his home state. "I glory in Mississippi's star!" he cried. "But before I would see it dishonored I would tear it from its place, to be set on the perilous ridge of battle as a sign around which her bravest and best shall meet the harvest home of death."

Thus he had spoken in November, but now in January, rising to say farewell, his manner held more of sadness than defiance. For a long moment after he rose he struck the accustomed preliminary stance of the orators of his day: high-stomached, almost sway-backed, the knuckles of one hand braced against the desk top, the other hand raised behind him with the wrist at the small of his back. He was dressed in neat black broadcloth, cuffless trouser-legs crumpling over his boots, the coat full-skirted with wide lapels, a satin waistcoat framing the stiff white bosom of his shirt, a black silk handkerchief wound stockwise twice around the upturned collar and knotted loosely at the throat. Close-shaven except for the tuft of beard at the jut of the chin, the face was built economically close to the skull, and more than anything it expressed an iron control by the brain within that skull. He had been sick for the past month and he looked it. He looked in fact like a man who had emerged from a long bout with a fever; which was what he was, except that the fever had been a generation back, when he was twenty-seven, and now he was fifty-two. Beneath the high square forehead, etched with the fine crisscross lines of pain and overwork, the eyes were deep-set, gray and stern, large and lustrous, though one was partly covered by a film, a result of the neuralgia which had racked him all those years. The nose was aquiline, finely shaped, the nostrils broad and delicately chiseled. The cheeks were deeply hollowed beneath the too-high cheekbones and above the wide, determined jaw. His voice was low, with the warmth of the Deep South in it.

"I rise, Mr. President, for the purpose of announcing to the Senate that I have satisfactory evidence that the State of Mississippi, by a solemn ordinance of her people in convention assembled, has declared her separation from the United States. Under these circumstances, of course, my functions terminate here. It has seemed to me proper, however, that I should appear in the Senate to announce that fact to my associates, and I will say but very little more."

His voice faltered at the outset, but soon it gathered volume and rang clear—"like a silver trumpet," according to his wife, who sat in the gallery. "Unshed tears were in it," she added, "and a plea for peace permeated every tone." Davis continued:

"It is known to senators who have served with me here, that I have for many years advocated, as an essential attribute of State sovereignty, the right of a State to secede from the Union. . . . If I had thought that Mississippi was acting without sufficient provocation . . . I should still, under my theory of government, because of my allegiance to the State of which I am a citizen, have been bound by her action."

He foresaw the founding of a nation, inheritor of the traditions of the American Revolution. "We but tread in the paths of our fathers when we proclaim our independence and take the hazard . . . not in hostility to others, not to injure any section of the country, not even for our own pecuniary benefit, but from the high and solemn motive of defending and protecting the rights we inherited, and which it is our duty to transmit unshorn to our children." England had been a lion; the Union might turn out to be a bear; in which case, "we will invoke the God of our fathers, who delivered them from the power of the lion, to protect us from the ravages of the bear; and thus, putting our trust in God and in our own firm hearts and strong arms, we will vindicate the right as best we may."

Davis glanced around the chamber, then continued. "I see now around me some with whom I have served long. There have been points of collision; but whatever of offense there has been to me, I leave here. I carry with me no hostile remembrance. . . . I go hence unencumbered by the remembrance of any injury received, and having discharged the duty of making the only reparation in my power for any injury received." He then spoke the final sentence to which all the rest had served as prologue. "Mr. President and Senators, having made the announcement which the occasion seemed to me to require, it remains only for me to bid you a final adieu."

For a moment there was silence. Then came the ovation, the sustained thunder of applause, the flutter of handkerchiefs and hum of comment. Davis shrank from this, however, or at any rate ignored it. As he resumed his seat he lowered his head and covered his face with his hands. Some in the gallery claimed his shoulders shook; he was weeping, they said. It may have been so, though he was not given to public tears. If so, it could have been from more than present tension. His life was crowded with glory, as a soldier, as a suitor, as a statesman; yet the glory was more than balanced by personal sorrow as a man. He had known tears in his time.

He was born in Christian County, Kentucky, within a year and a hundred miles of the man whose election had brought on the present furor. Like that man, he was a log-cabin boy, the youngest of ten children whose grandfather had been born in Philadelphia in 1702, the son of an immigrant Welshman who signed his name with an X. This grandfather moved to Georgia, where he married a widow who bore him one son, Samuel. Samuel raised and led an irregular militia company in the Revolution. After the war he married and moved northwest to south-central Kentucky, where he put up his own log house, farmed six hundred acres of land by the hard agronomy of the time, and supplied himself with children, naming the sons out of the Bible—Joseph, Samuel, Benjamin, and Isaac—until the tenth child, born in early June of 1808, whom he named for the red-headed President then in office, and gave him the middle name Finis in the belief, or perhaps the hope, that he was the last; which he was.

By the time the baby Jefferson was weaned the family was on the move again, south one thousand miles to Bayou Teche, Louisiana, only to find the climate unhealthy and to move again, three hundred miles northeast to Wilkinson County, Mississippi Territory, southeast of Natchez and forty miles from the Mississippi River. Here the patriarch stopped, for he prospered; he did not move again, and here Jefferson spent his early childhood.

The crop now was cotton, and though Samuel Davis had slaves, he was his own overseer, working alongside them in the field. It was a farm, not a plantation; he was a farmer, not a planter. In a region where the leading men were Episcopalians and Federalists, he was a Baptist and a Democrat. Now his older children were coming of age, and at their marriages he gave them what he could, one Negro slave, and that was all. The youngest, called Little Jeff, began his education when he was six. For the next fifteen years he attended one school after another, first a log schoolhouse within walking distance of home, then a Dominican institution in Kentucky, Saint Thomas Aquinas, where he was still called Little Jeff because he was the smallest pupil there. He asked to become a Roman Catholic but the priest told him to wait and learn, which he did, and either forgot or changed his mind. Then, his mother having grown lonesome for her last-born, he came home to the Mississippi schoolhouse where he had started.

He did not like it. One hot fall day he rebelled; he would not go. Very well, his father said, but he could not be idle, and sent him to the field with the work gang. Two days later Jeff was back at his desk. "The heat of the sun and the physical labor, in conjunction with the implied equality with the other cotton pickers, convinced me that school was the lesser evil." Thus he later explained his early decision to work with his head, not his hands. In continuation of this decision, just before his fourteenth birthday he left once more for Kentucky, entering Transylvania University, an excellent school, one of the few in the country to live up to a high-sounding name. Under competent professors he continued his studies in Latin and Greek and mathematics, including trigonometry, and explored the mysteries of sacred and profane history and natural philosophy—meaning chemistry and physics—with surveying and oratory thrown in for good measure. While he was there his father died and his oldest brother, Joseph, twenty-four years his senior, assumed the role of guardian.

Not long before his death, the father had secured for his youngest son an appointment to West Point, signed by the Secretary of War, and thus for the first time the names were linked: Jefferson Davis, John C. Calhoun. Joseph Davis by now had become what his father had never been—a planter, with a planter's views, a planter's way of life. Jefferson inclined toward the University of Virginia, but Joseph persuaded him to give the Academy a try. It was in the tradition for the younger sons of prominent southern families to go there; if at the end of a year he found he did not like it he could transfer. So Davis attended West Point, and found he liked it.

Up to now he had shown no special inclination to study. Alert and affectionate, he was of a mischievous disposition, enjoyed a practical joke, and sought the admiration of his fellows rather more than the esteem of his professors. Now at the Academy he continued along this course, learning something of tavern life in the process. "O Benny Haven's, O!" he sang, linking arms and clinking tankards. He found he liked the military comradeship, the thought of unrequited death on lonely, far-off battlefields:

> "To our comrades who have fallen, one cup before we go; They poured their life-blood freely out *pro bono publico*. No marble points the stranger to where they rest below; They lie neglected— far away from Benny Haven's, O!"

Brought before a court martial for out-of-bounds drinking of "spirituous liquors," he made the defense of a strict constructionist: 1) visiting Benny Haven's was not *officially* prohibited in the regulations, and 2) malt liquors were not "spirituous" in the first place. The defense was successful; he was not dismissed, and he emerged from the scrape a stricter constructionist than ever. He also got to know his fellow cadets. Leonidas Polk was his roommate; Joseph E. Johnston was said to have been his opponent in a fist fight over a girl; along with others, he admired the open manliness of Albert Sidney Johnston, the high-born rectitude of Robert E. Lee.

Davis himself was admired, even liked. Witnesses spoke of his well-shaped head, his self-esteem, his determination and personal mastery. A "florid young fellow," he had "beautiful blue eyes, a graceful figure." In his studies he did less well, receiving his lowest marks in mathematics and deportment, his highest in rhetoric and moral philosophy, including constitutional law. But the highs could not pull up the lows. He stood well below the middle of his class, still a private at the close of his senior year, and graduated in 1828, twenty-third in a class of thirty-four.

As a second lieutenant, U.S. Army, he now began a seven-year adventure, serving in Wisconsin, Iowa, Illinois, Missouri, where he learned to fight Indians, build forts, scout, and lead a simple social existence. He had liked West Point; he found he liked this even better. Soon he proved himself a superior junior officer, quick-witted and resourceful—as when once with a few men he was chased by a band of Indians after scalps; both parties being in canoes, he improvised a sail and drew away. In a winter of deep snow he came down with pneumonia, and though he won that fight as well, his susceptibility to colds and neuralgia dated from then. He was promoted to first lieutenant within four years, and when Black Hawk was captured in 1832, Davis was appointed by his colonel, Zachary Taylor, to escort the prisoner to Jefferson Barracks.

Thus Colonel Taylor, called "Old Rough and Ready," showed his approval of Davis as a soldier. But as a son-in-law, it developed, he wanted no part of him. The lieutenant had met the colonel's daughter, sixteen-year-old Knox Taylor, brown-haired and blue-eyed like himself, though later the color of his own eyes would deepen to gray. Love came quickly, and his letters to her show a man unseen before or after. "By my dreams I have been lately almost crazed, for they were of you," he wrote to her, and also thus: "Kind, dear letter; I have kissed it often and often, and it has driven away the mad notions from my brain." The girl accepted his suit, but the father did not; Taylor wanted no soldier son-in-law, apparently especially not this one. Therefore Davis, who had spent the past seven years as a man of action, proposed to challenge the colonel to a duel. Dissuaded from this, he remained a man of action still. He resigned his commission, went straight to Louisville, and married the girl. The wedding was held at the home of an aunt she was visiting. "After the service everybody cried but Davis," a witness remarked, adding that they "thought this most peculiar."

As it turned out, he was reserving his tears. The young couple did not wait to attempt a reconciliation with her father; perhaps they depended on time to accomplish this. Instead they took a steamboat south to Davis Bend, Mississippi, below Vicksburg, where Joseph Davis, the guardian elder brother, had prospered on a plantation called The Hurricane. He presented them with an adjoining 800-acre place and fourteen slaves on credit. Davis put in a cotton crop, but before the harvest time came round they were both down with fever. They were confined to separate rooms, each too sick to be told of the other's condition, though Davis managed to make it to the door of his bride's room in time to see her die. She had been a wife not quite three months, and as she died she sang snatches of "Fairy Bells," a favorite air; she had had it from her mother. Now those tears which he had not shed at the wedding came to scald his eyes. He was too sick to attend the funeral; the doctor believed he would not be long behind her.

The doctor was wrong, though Davis never lost the drawn, gaunt look of a fever convalescent. He returned to the plantation; then, finding it too crowded with recent memories, left for Cuba, thought to be a fine climate and landscape for restoring broken hearts. The sea bathing at least did his health much good, and he returned by way of New York and Washington, renewing acquaintances with old friends now on the rise and gaining some notion of how much he had missed on the frontier. Then he came home to Mississippi. He would be a planter and, at last, a student.

He found a ready tutor awaiting him. Joseph Davis had got a law degree in Kentucky, had set up practice in Natchez, and, prospering, had bought the land which in that section practically amounted to a patent of nobility. By now, in his middle fifties, he was the wealthiest planter in the state, the "leading philosopher"—whatever that meant—and the possessor of the finest library, which he gladly made available to his idolized younger brother. Davis soon had the Constitution by heart and went deeply into *Elliot's Debates*, theories of government as argued by the framers. He read John Locke and Adam Smith, *The Federalist* and the works of Thomas Jefferson. Shakespeare and Swift lent him what an orator might need of cadenced beauty and invective; Byron and Scott were there at hand, along with the best English magazines and the leading American newspapers. He read them all, and discussed them with his brother.

Also there was the plantation; Brierfield, he called it. Here too he worked and learned, making certain innovations in the labor system. The overseer was a Negro, James Pemberton. No slave was ever punished except after a formal trial by an all-Negro jury, Davis only reserving the right to temper the severity of the judgment. James was always James, never Jim; "It is disrespect to give a nickname," Davis said, and the overseer repaid him with frankness, loyalty, and efficiency. Once when something went amiss and the master asked him why, James replied: "I rather think, sir, through my neglect."

Davis gained all this from his decade of seclusion and study; but he gained something else as well. Up to now, his four years at West Point, brief and interrupted as they were, had been the longest period he had spent at any one place in his life. His school years had been various indeed, with instructors ranging from log-cabin teachers to Catholic priests and New England scholars. When a Virginian or a Carolinian spoke of his "country," he meant Virginia or Carolina. It was not so with Davis. Tennessee and Kentucky were as familiar to him as Mississippi; the whole South, as a region, formed his background; he was thirty before he knew a real home in any real sense of the word. Now at last he had this, too, though still with a feeling of being somewhat apart. Like his brother Joseph and his father before him, he was a Democrat, and while this was true of the majority of the people in his state, it was by no means true of the majority in his class, who were Federalists or Whigs.

Then history intervened for him and solved this problem too. Previously the cotton capitalists had thought their interests coincided with the interests of capitalists in general. Now antislavery and pro-tariff agitation was beginning to teach them otherwise. In 1844, the year when Davis emerged from seclusion, the upheaval was accomplished. Repudiating Jefferson and Jackson, the Democrats went over to the Whigs, who came to meet them, creating what Calhoun had been after from the start: a solid South. Davis caught the movement at its outset.

Before that, however, in the previous December, his brother produced one more item from the horn of plenty. He had a lawyer friend, W. B. Howell of Natchez, son of an eight-term governor of New Jersey. Howell had married a Kempe of Virginia and moved south to cotton country. Joseph Davis was an intimate of their house; their first son was named for him, and their seventeen-year old daughter Varina called him Uncle Joe. Now he wrote to the girl's parents, inviting her to visit The Hurricane. She arrived by steamboat during the Christmas season, having just completed an education in the classics. She did not stay at The Hurricane; she stayed at his sister's plantation, fourteen miles away. Presently a horseman arrived with a message. He dismounted to give it to her, lingered briefly, then excused himself and rode off to a political meeting in Vicksburg. That night Varina wrote to her mother, giving her first impression of the horseman.

> Today Uncle Joe sent, by his younger brother (did you know he had one?), an urgent invitation to me to go at once to The Hurricane. I do not know whether this Mr. Jefferson Davis is young or old. He looks both at times; but I believe he is old, for from what I hear he is only two years younger than you are. He impresses me as a remarkable kind of man, but of uncertain temper, and has a way of taking for granted that everybody agrees with him when he expresses an opinion, which offends me; yet he is most agreeable and has a peculiarly sweet voice and a winning manner of asserting himself. The fact is, he is the kind of person I should expect to rescue one from a mad dog at any risk, but to insist upon a stoical indifference to the fright afterward. I do not think I shall ever like him as I do his brother Joe. Would you believe it, he is refined and cultivated, and yet he is a Democrat!

This last was the principal difficulty between them. Varina was a Natchez girl, which meant not only that her background was Federalist, but also that she had led a life of gaiety quite unlike the daily round in the malarial bottoms of Davis Bend. The Christmas season was a merry one, however, and Joseph proved an excellent matchmaker, although a rather heavy-handed one. "By Jove, she is as beautiful as Venus!" he told his brother, adding: "As well as good looks, she has a mind that will fit her for any sphere that the man to whom she is married will feel proud to reach." Jefferson agreed, admiring the milk-pale skin, the raven hair, the generous mouth, the slender waist. "She is beautiful and she has a fine mind," he admitted, with some caution at the outset.

In the evenings there were readings from historians and orators, and the brothers marveled at the ease with which the girl pronounced and translated the Latin phrases and quotations that studded the texts. The conquest was nearly complete; there remained only the political difference. In the course of these discussions Varina wore a cameo brooch with a Whig device carved into the stone, a watchdog crouched by a strongbox. Then one day she appeared without it, and Davis knew he had won.

He left The Hurricane in late January, engaged. In February of the following year, 1845, they were married. Davis was thirty-six, Varina half that. They went to New Orleans on the wedding tour, enjoyed a fashionable Creole interlude, and returned after a few weeks to Brierfield.

The house they moved into was a one-story frame twin-wing structure; Davis had planned and built it himself, with the help of James Pemberton. It had charm, but he and his young wife had little time to enjoy it. By then he had emerged from his shell in more ways than one. In 1843 he had run for the state legislature against Sergeant S. Prentiss, famous as an orator, a Whig in an overwhelmingly Whig district. Davis was defeated, though with credit and a growing reputation. The following year, taking time off from courtship, he stumped the state as an elector for James K. Polk. In the year of the marriage, Whigs and Democrats having coalesced, he was elected to Congress as representative-at-large. In Washington, his first act was to introduce a resolution that federal troops be withdrawn from federal forts, their posts to be taken by state recruits. It died in committee, and his congressional career was ended by the outbreak of the Mexican War.

Davis resigned his seat and came home to lead a volunteer regiment, the Mississippi Rifles. Under the strict discipline of their West Point colonel, who saw to it that they were armed with a new model rifle, they were the crack outfit of Zachary Taylor's army, fighting bravely at Monterey and saving the day at Buena Vista, where Davis formed them in a V that broke the back of a Mexican cavalry charge and won the battle. He was wounded in the foot, came home on crutches, and at the victory banquets in New Orleans and elsewhere heard himself proclaimed a military genius and the hero of the South. Hunched upon his crutches, he responded to such toasts with dignified modesty. Basically his outlook was unchanged. When Polk sent him a commission as a brigadier general of volunteers, Davis returned it promptly, remarking that the President had no authority to make such an appointment, that power inhering in the states alone. Perhaps all these honors were somewhat anticlimactic anyhow, coming as they did after the words General Taylor was supposed to have spoken to him at Buena Vista: "My daughter, sir, was a better judge of men than I was."

Honors fell thickly upon him now. Within sixty days the governor appointed him to the U.S. Senate. At a private banquet tendered before he left, he stood and heard the toasts go round: "Colonel Jeff Davis, the Game Cock of the South!" "Jeff Davis, the President of the Southern Confederacy!" Davis stood there, allowing no change of expression, no flush of emotion on his face. He took this stiffness, this coldness up to Washington and onto the floor of the Senate.

He would not unbend; he would engage in no log-rolling. In a cloakroom exchange, when he stated his case supporting a bill for removing obstructions from the river down near Vicksburg, another senator, who had his pet project too, interrupted to ask, "Will you vote for the Lake appropriations?" Davis responded: "Sir, I make no terms. I accept no compromises. If when I ask for an appropriation, the object shall be shown to be proper and the expenditure constitutional, I defy the gentleman, for his conscience' sake, to vote against it. If it shall appear to him otherwise, then I expect his opposition, and only ask that it shall be directly, fairly, and openly exerted. The case shall be presented on its single merit; on that I wish to stand or fall. I feel, sir, that I am incapable of sectional distinction upon subjects. I abhor and reject all interested combinations." He would hammer thus at what he thought was wrong, and continue to hammer, icy cold and in measured terms, long after the opposition had been demolished, without considering the thoughts of the other man or the chance that he might be useful to him someday.

He was perhaps the best informed, probably the best educated, and certainly the most intellectual man in the Senate. Yet he too had to take his knocks. Supporting an army pay-increase bill, he remarked in passing that "a common blacksmith or tailor" could not be hired as a military engineer; whereupon Andrew Johnson of Tennessee—formerly a tailor—rose from his desk shouting that "an illegitimate, swaggering, bastard, scrub aristocracy" took much credit to itself, yet in fact had "neither talents nor information." Hot words in a Washington boarding house led to a fist fight between Davis and Henry S. Foote, his fellow senator from Mississippi. An Illinois congressman, W. H. Bissell, said in a speech that Davis' command had been a mile and a half from the blaze of battle at Buena Vista. Davis sent an immediate challenge, and Bissell, having the choice of weapons, named muskets loaded with ball and shot at fifteen paces, then went home, wrote his will, and said he would be ready in the morning. Friends intervening, Bissell explained that he had been referring to another quarter of the field and had not meant to question Davis' personal bravery anyhow; the duel was canceled. Davis made enemies in high places, as for example when he claimed that General Winfield Scott had overcharged $300 in mileage expenses. Scott later delivered himself of a judgment as to Davis: "He is not a cheap Judas. I do not think he would have sold the Saviour for thirty shillings. But for the successorship to Pontius Pilate he would have betrayed Christ and the Apostles and the whole Christian church." Sam Houston of Texas, speaking more briefly, declared that Davis was "ambitious as Lucifer and cold as a lizard."

Out of the rough-and-tumble of debate and acrimony, a more or less accepted part of political life at the time, Davis was winning a position as leader in the Senate. Successor to Calhoun, he had become the spokesman for southern nationalism, which in those days meant not independence but domination from within the Union. This movement had been given impetus by the Mexican War. Up till then the future of the country pointed north and west, but now the needle trembled and suddenly swung south. The treaty signed at Guadalupe Hidalgo brought into the Union a new southwestern domain, seemingly ripe for slavery and the southern way of life: not only Texas down to the Rio Grande, the original strip of contention, but also the vast sun-cooked area that was to become Arizona, New Mexico, Nevada, Utah, part of Colorado, and California with its new-found gold. Here was room for expansion indeed, with more to follow; for the nationalists looked forward to taking what was left of Mexico, all of Central America south to Panama, and Yucatan and Cuba by annexation. Yet the North, so recently having learned the comfort of the saddle, had no intention of yielding the reins. The South would have to fight for this; and this the South was prepared to do, using States Rights for a spear and the Constitution for a shield. Jefferson Davis, who had formed his troops in a V at Buena Vista and continued the fight with a boot full of blood, took a position, now as then, at the apex of the wedge.

He lost the fight, and lost it quickly—betrayed, as he thought, from within his ranks. The North opposed this dream of southern expansion by opposing the extension of slavery, without which the new southwestern territory would be anything but southern. Attracted by the hope of so much gain, and goaded by the fear of such a loss, Davis and his cohorts adopted more drastic actions, including threats of secession. To give substance to this threat, he called the Nashville Convention of June 1850, and in conjunction with Albert Gallatin Brown of Mississippi, William Lowndes Yancey of Alabama, and Robert Barnwell Rhett of South Carolina, informed the North quite plainly that unless slavery was extended to the territories, the South would leave the Union. It was at this point that Davis was "betrayed," meaning that he discovered that he had outrun his constituents. Henry Clay proposed his Compromise, supported by Daniel Webster, and both houses of Congress gladly accepted it. California came in as a free state and the question of slavery was left to be settled by the various other territories at the time when they should apply for admission into the Union.

What was worse from Davis' point of view, the voters seemed to approve. All over the nation, even in Mississippi, there was rejoicing that disunion and war had been avoided. Davis could scarcely believe it; he must test it at the polls. So he resigned his seat in the Senate and went home to run for governor against Henry S. Foote, the senator with whom he had exchanged first tart remarks and finally blows. Now the issue was clearly drawn, for his opponent was a Unionist Whig of Natchez and had voted consistently against Davis, from the beginning down to the Compromise itself; the voters could make a clear-cut choice before all the world. This they did—repudiating Davis.

It was bad enough to be vanquished as the champion of secession, but to receive defeat at the hands of a man he detested as much as he detested Foote was gall and wormwood. At forty-three, in the hour of his glory and at the height of his prime, he was destroyed; or so he thought. At any rate he was through. He came home to Brierfield to plant cotton.

Then history intervened again, as history always seemed to do for him. This time the muse took the form of Franklin Pierce, who in organizing a cabinet reached down from New Hampshire, all the way to Mississippi, and chose Jefferson Davis as his Secretary of War. They had been fellow officers in Mexico, friends in Congress, and shared a dislike of abolitionists. Whatever his reasons, Pierce chose well. Davis made perhaps the best War Secretary the country ever had, and though it included such capable men as William L. Marcy of New York and Caleb Cushing of Massachusetts, he dominated the cabinet in a time of strain and doubt.

Yet the man who returned to public life in 1853 was somewhat different from the man who had left in 1851 at the behest of the voters. Rather chastened—though he kept his southern nationalism and clung to the spear of States Rights, the shield of the Constitution—he left the fire-eaters Yancey and Rhett behind him. He was no longer the impetuous champion of secession; he believed now that whatever was to be gained might best be accomplished within the Union. He strengthened the army, renovated the Military Academy, and came out strong for un-Jeffersonian internal improvements, including a Pacific Railway along a southern route through Memphis or Vicksburg, to be financed by a hundred-million-dollar federal appropriation. The Gadsden Purchase was a Davis project, ten million paid for a strip of Mexican soil necessary for the railroad right-of-way. Nor was his old imperialism dead. He still had designs on what was left of Mexico and on Central America, and he shocked the diplomats of Europe with a proclamation of his government's intention to annex Cuba. Above all, he was for the unlimited extension of slavery, with a revival of the slave trade if need be.

Returned to the Senate in 1857, he continued to work along these lines, once more a southern champion, not as a secessionist, but as a believer that the destiny of the nation pointed south. It was a stormy time, and much of the bitterness between the sections came to a head on the floor of the Senate, where northern invective and southern arrogance necessarily met. Here Texas senator Louis T. Wigfall, a duelist of note, would sneer at his northern colleagues as he told them, "The difficulty between you and us, gentlemen, is that you will not send the right sort of people here. Why will you not send either Christians or gentlemen?" Here, too, the anti-slavery Massachusetts senator Charles Sumner had his head broken by Congressman Preston Brooks of South Carolina, who, taking exception to remarks Sumner had made on the floor of the Senate regarding a kinsman, caned him as he sat at his desk. Brooks explained that he attacked him sitting because, Sumner being the larger man, he would have had to shoot him if he had risen, and he did not want to kill him, only maim him. Sumner lay bleeding in the aisle among the gutta-percha fragments of the cane, and his enemies stood by and watched him bleed. Southern sympathizers sent Brooks walking sticks by the dozen, recommending their use on other abolitionists, and through the years of Sumner's convalescence Massachusetts let his desk stand empty as a reproach to southern hotheads, though these were in fact more likely to see the vacant seat as a warning to men like Sumner.

During this three-year furor, which led in the end to the disintegration of the Democratic Party and the resultant election of a Republican President, Davis remained as inflexible as ever. But his arguments now did not prgress toward secession. They ended instead against a hard brick wall. He did not even claim to know the answers beyond debate. In 1860, speaking in Boston's Faneuil Hall while he and Mrs Davis were up there vacationing for his health—he was a chronic dyspeptic by now, racked by neuralgia through sleepless nights and losing the sight of one eye—he stated his position as to slavery and southern nationalism, but announced that he remained opposed to secession; he still would not take the logical next step. He was much admired by the people of Massachusetts, many of whom despised the abolitionists as much as he did; but the people of Mississippi hardly knew what to make of him. "Davis is at sea," they said.

Then he looked back, and saw that instead of outrunning his constituents, this time he had let them outrun him. He hurried South, made his harvest-home-of-death speech on the eve of Lincoln's election, and returned to Washington, at last reconverted to secession. South Carolina left the Union, then Mississippi and the others, and opinion no longer mattered. As he said in his farewell, even if he had opposed his state's action, he still would have considered himself "bound."

Having spoken his adieu, he left the crowded chamber and, head lowered, went out into the street. That night Mrs Davis heard him pacing the floor. "May God have us in His holy keeping," she heard him say over and over as he paced, "and grant that before it is too late, peaceful councils may prevail."

Such was Davis' way of saying farewell to his colleagues, speaking out of sadness and regret. It was not the way of others: Robert Toombs of Georgia, for example, whose state had seceded two days before Davis spoke. Two days later Toombs delivered his farewell. "The Union, sir, is dissolved," he told the Senate. A large, slackmouthed man, he tossed his head in shaggy defiance as he spoke. "You see the glittering bayonet, and you hear the tramp of armed men from yon Capitol to the Rio Grande. It is a sight that gladdens the eye and cheers the hearts of other men ready to second them." In case there were those of the North who would maintain the Union by force: "Come and do it!" Toombs cried. "Georgia is on the war path! We are as ready to fight now as we ever shall be. Treason? Bah!" And with that he stalked out of the chamber, walked up to the Treasury, and demanded his salary due to date, plus mileage back to Georgia.

Thus Toombs. But Davis, having sent his wife home with their three children—Margaret aged six, Jeff three, and the year-old baby named for the guardian elder brother Joseph at Davis Bend—lingered in Washington another week, ill and confined to his bed for most of the time, still hoping he might be arrested as a traitor so as to test his claims in the federal courts, then took the train for Jackson, where Governor J. J. Pettus met him with a commission as major general of volunteers. It was the job Davis wanted. He believed there would be war, and he advised the governor to push the procurement of arms.

"The limit of our purchases should be our power to pay," he said. "We shall need all and many more than we can get."

"General," the governor protested, "you overrate the risk."

"I only wish I did," Davis said.

Awaiting the raising of his army, he went to Brierfield. In Alabama, now in early February, a convention was founding a Southern Confederacy, electing political leaders and formulating a new government. He was content, however, to leave such matters to those who were there. He considered his highest talents to be military and he had the position he wanted, commander of the Mississippi army, with advancement to come along with glory when the issue swung to war.

Then history beckoned again, assuming another of her guises. February 10; he and Mrs Davis were out in the garden, cutting a rose bush in the early blue spring weather, when a messenger approached with a telegram in his hand. Davis read it. In that moment of painful silence he seemed stricken; his face took on a look of calamity. Then he read the message to his wife. It was headed "Montgomery, Alabama," and dated the day before.

> Sir:
> We are directed to inform you that you are this day unanimously elected President of the Provisional Government of the Confederate States of America, and to request you to come to Montgomery immediately. We send also a special messenger. Do not wait for him.
> > R. Toombs,
> > R. Barnwell Rhett . . .

He spoke of it, Mrs Davis said, "as a man might speak of a sentence of death." Yet he wasted no time. He packed and left next day.

The train made many stops along the line and the people were out to meet him, in sunlight and by the glare of torches. They wanted a look at his face, the thin lips and determined jaw, the hollow cheeks with their jutting bones, the long skull behind the aquiline nose; "a wizard physiognomy," one called it. He brought forth cheers with confident words, but he had something else to say as well—something no one had told them before. He advised them to prepare for the long war that lay ahead. They did not believe him, apparently. Or if they did, they went on cheering anyhow.

He reached Montgomery Sunday night, February 17, and was driven from the station in a carriage, down the long torch-lit avenue to the old Exchange Hotel. The crowd followed through streets that had been decked as for a fair; they flowed until they were packed in a mass about the gallery of the hotel in time to see Davis dismount from the carriage and climb the steps; they cheered as he turned and looked at them. Then suddenly they fell silent. William Lowndes Yancey, short and rather seedy-looking alongside the erect and well-groomed Davis, had raised one hand. They cheered again when he brought it down, gesturing toward the tall man beside him, and said in a voice that rang above the expectant, torch-paled faces of the crowd: "The man and the hour have met."

. . . .

By then they had nearly all come round, both sides having entered into a two-way concession whereby the victors acknowledged that the Confederates had fought bravely for a cause they believed was just and the losers agreed it was probably best for all concerned that the Union had been preserved. The first step lay in admission of defeat, and one of the first to take it publicly was Joe Johnston. Aboard a Chesapeake Bay steamer, not long after his surrender, the general heard a fellow passenger insisting that the South had been "conquered but not subdued." Asked in what command he had served, the bellicose young man—one of those stalwarts later classified as "invisible in war and invincible in peace"—replied that, unfortunately, circumstances had made it impossible for him to be in the army. "Well, sir, I was," Johnston told him. "You may not be subdued, but I am.'

Similarly, R. E. Lee encouraged all who sought his advice to take the loyalty oath required by the President's amnesty proclamation as a prerequisite to recovery of their rights as citizens, and even did so himself, barely two months after Appomattox, though nothing came of it then or later; he would go to his grave disfranchised. However, news that he had "asked for pardon" spread rapidly through the South, producing consternation, which was followed for the most part, even among those who had been die-hards up till then, by prompt acceptance and emulation. "You have disgraced the family, sir!" Ex-Governor Henry Wise sputtered when he learned that one of his sons had taken the oath. "But, Father," the former captain said, "General Lee advised me to do it." Taken aback, Wise paused only a moment before he replied: "That alters the case. Whatever General Lee advises is right."

Neither of these attitudes or reactions—Johnston's admission that he had been "subdued," Lee's willingness to pledge loyalty to a government he had sought to overthrow—was acceptable to Jefferson Davis in his own right. He did not object intrinsically to their view, so long as they applied it to themselves, but as the symbolic leader of a nation, even one that had been abolished by force of arms, he had other factors to consider. For him, the very notion of subdual was something to be rejected out of hand, if acceptance, as he conceived it, meant abandoning the principles of constitutional government. The war had been lost beyond denial, but not the cause. Nothing would ever bend him from that. He clung to the views he had held in 1861, and indeed ever since he entered public life some twenty years before. As for anything resembling an apology— which he believed was what he would be offering if he took the oath required—he would say repeatedly, first and last: "I have no claim to pardon, not having in any wise repented." No wonder, then, that Andrew Johnson referred to him as Lucifer incarnate, "the head devil of them all."

To his own people he was something else, in part because of all he had suffered, first in the granite bowels of Fort Monroe—where Miles, acting on Stanton's orders, martyred him about as effectively as Booth had martyred Lincoln—and then through much of the decade following his release on bail, a time referred to by his wife as one spent "floating uprooted." From Richmond, his trial having been put off until November, he went to Canada, where the two older of his four children were in school, then came back by way of Cuba for his health's sake, his trial having been postponed again till March of 1868, then still again until the following February. Impeachment was heading up by now in Washington, and the danger loomed of Johnson's being replaced by bluff Ben Wade, who was not above Star Chamber proceedings. On the advice of his attorneys, Davis and his family planned to sail for Europe, and did so in July, though Wade by then had been kept from becoming President by one senatorial vote. In England the former State Prisoner was entertained by high-born sympathizers and had the pleasure of dining with his old companion Judah Benjamin, fast on the rise as a distinguished member of the bar. A visit to France at the end of the year also gave him the satisfaction of declining an audience with Napoleon and Eugénie, who, he said, had "played us false" at a time when the need for friends was sore.

He had by now more than enough "floating," and his pride would not allow him to accept indefinitely from admirers the financial help he was obliged to live on while his trial was pending. Then suddenly it no longer was. Early in 1869, with the indictment quashed at last, he was free to come home and accept employment as president of the Carolina Life Insurance Company, headquartered in Memphis. He returned without his family, got settled in the business, and went back to England in late summer, 1870, for his wife and children. Docking at Baltimore in mid-October he learned that Robert Lee had died that week. "Virginia has need of all her sons," the general had replied when asked by veterans what he thought of their going elsewhere to escape the strictures of poverty and Reconstruction, and he himself had set them an example by serving, at a salary of $1500 a year, as president of Washington College, a small, all but bankrupt institution out in the Shenandoah Valley. He aged greatly in the five years left him after Appomattox, suffering from the heart ailment which his doctors now could see had been what plagued him through much of the war, when the symptoms were diagnosed as rheumatism. Stricken in late September, he lingered till October 12. Back in battle toward the end, like Stonewall before him, he called in his delirium on A. P. Hill: "Tell Hill he must come up." Then he quieted, as Jackson too had done before he crossed the river. "Strike the tent," he said, and then he died.

"Of the man, how shall I speak? His moral qualities rose to the height of genius," Davis declared at a memorial service held in Richmond in early November. It was his first public address since the end of the war, and though he was encouraged by the fervor of his reception in the one-time national capital, the passing of the great Confederate captain was the signal for the onset of a series of reversals for his former chief, the heaviest of which came two years later with the death of one of his two surviving sons. Eleven-year-old Billy, conceived in Montgomery during the secession furore and born after the removal of the government of Virginia, fell victim to diphtheria in Memphis. Settled in a house of his own for the first time in six years, and released at last, as he thought, from the life his wife described as "floating uprooted," Davis suffered this sudden deprivation only to have it followed by still another during the financial panic of '73, precipitated by the failure of Jay Cooke & Company in New York, which had marketed the huge war loans of the Federal government. Carolina Life went under, too, a chip among the flotsam, taking with it his last $15,000 and the only job he had ever had. Afloat again, he sought other ventures, some involving trips to Europe in search of backers, but nothing came of them. Though he kept his home in Memphis, even managing the expense of a wedding for his daughter Maggie in 1875, the result was that he again found himself floating rootless, his life no longer a career, but rather an existence.

When at last he found the answer, a way out of this dilemma, it was neither in Memphis nor in business. Ever since his release from prison he had had it in mind to write a personal history of the war, and even as early as his stay in Canada he had begun to look through such papers as were then available for his purpose, including duplicates of messages sent commanders in the field. One of the first he examined, however—a telegram he had addressed to Lee from Danville on the day of Appomattox, unaware that the surrender was in progress—put an end to this preliminary effort. "You will realize the reluctance I feel to leave the soil of Virginia," he had wired, "and appreciate my anxiety to win success north of the Roanoke." Mrs Davis, who was there to help him sort the documents, saw a stricken look come on his face at the memories the words called up. He pushed the papers away. "Let us put them by for a while. I cannot speak of my dead so soon," he told her. That had been nearly ten years ago, and he had not returned to them since, despite the urging of such friends as Preston Johnston, who admonished him: "I do not believe any man ever lived who could dare to tell in the light more fully what was done in the dark, than you can. It seems to be a friendly duty to warn you not to forget your design." Davis did not forget, but he was fully occupied by the insurance business: until it vanished, that is, along with what little he had left in the way of funds. Failure freed him to return to his old design; failure and necessity, and something else as well. Recently, old comrades who had shared the glory and pain of battles won and lost—ex-Confederates for the most part, though the victors also had their differences in public—had begun to turn on each other, quarreling over what they considered a proper distribution of praise and blame, especially the latter. One of the hottest of these arguments had to do with Gettysburg; Fitzhugh Lee and Jubal Early crossed swords with Longstreet, who had compounded their enmity by going over to the Republicans and his old friend Grant. Davis stayed well out of it, reserving his ire for a long-time adversary, Joseph E. Johnston, who had brought out in 1874 his *Narrative of Military Operations Directed During the Late War Between the States,* much of it devoted to unburdening himself of grievances against his former superior. "The advance sheets exhibit his usual malignity and suppression of the truth when it would effect his side of the case unfavorably," Davis informed his wife by way of warming up for the counteroffensive he now had it in mind to launch. He would write his own account, quartering much of the same ground, of course, and accordingly signed a contract with Appleton's of New York, who agreed to cover such expenses as he required for secretarial assistance.

Bustling Memphis, hot in summer, cold in winter—the scene of his loss, moreover, of the third of his four sons—seemed unconducive to the peace he believed he needed for such work. Who could write anything there, let alone a full-fledged two- or three-volume history of the war? He had found the atmosphere he wanted on a trip to the Mississippi Coast the previous November, when he wrote his wife that "the moaning of the winds among the pines and the rolling waves of the Gulf on the beach gave me a sense of rest and peace which made me wish to lay me down and be at home." Midway between New Orleans and Mobile was "Beauvoir," an estate belonging to Sarah E. Dorsey, a wealthy, recently widowed childhood friend of Varina's; "a fine place," Davis called it, with a "large and beautiful house" set among spreading live oaks "and many orange trees yet full of fruit." Receiving him now as a visitor, Mrs Dorsey offered him the use of a cottage on the grounds, "a refuge without encumbrances" in which to write his book. He quickly accepted, on condition of paying board, and by February 1877 he and a body servant had moved in. Quarters were found nearby for Major W. T. Walthall, his research assistant, and work began at once, with the added help of Sarah Dorsey herself. She had written four novels under the nom de plume "Filia," and was delighted to serve as an amanuensis, having long admired her house guest as "the noblest man she had ever met on earth."

Varina, who had never enjoyed the notion of sharing Jefferson Davis with anyone—least of all another woman, childhood friend or not—was considerably less pleased with this outcome of his quest for domestic tranquillity. She had been in Germany most of the past eight months, getting twelve-year-old Winnie settled in a girls' school in Carlsruhe, and despite urgings from her husband and Mrs Dorsey that she join them on the Coast, she remained in Europe for another eight, determined not to be a party to any such *ménage à trois* arrangement. Finally in October she returned, not to Beauvoir but to Memphis, where twenty-year-old Jeff Junior, after an unsatisfactory year at V.M.I., had accepted a place in a bank with his sister Maggie's husband. Davis himself came up at once, hoping to take her back with him, but she refused. She was pleased, however, to see him looking so well, absorbed in his work and eager to get back to it. A new urgency was on him, caused in part by the recent passing of some of the principal characters in the story he was attempting to retell. Braxton Bragg, for example, had dropped dead on the street in Galveston last year, and Raphael Semmes had been buried only the month before in Mobile. Another great raider, Bedford Forrest, was dying in Memphis even now, wasted by diabetes to a scant one hundred pounds. "I am completely broke up," he confessed to friends. "I am broke in fortune, broke in health, broke in spirit." Davis sat by his bedside the day before he died, then served as a pallbearer at his funeral on the last day of October. In the carriage, en route to Elmwood Cemetery, a companion remarked on Forrest's greatness as a soldier. "I agree with you," the former President said. "The trouble was that the generals commanding in the Southwest never appreciated him until it was too late. Their judgment was that he was a bold and enterprising raider and rider. I was misled by them, and never knew how to measure him un-

93

til I read the reports of his campaign across the Tennessee River in 1864. This induced a study of his earlier reports, and after that I was prepared to adopt what you are pleased to name as the judgment of history." Someone mentioned Brice's Crossroads, and Davis replied as before: "That campaign was not understood in Richmond. The impression made upon those in authority was that Forrest had made another successful raid. . . . I saw it all after it was too late."

He returned alone to Beauvoir, Sarah Dorsey, and his work. Varina was willing to help by mail, amplifying his recollections with her own, but not in person. "Nothing on earth would pain me like living in that kind of community," she had written from Europe, and she still felt that way about it. At any rate she did for another eight months before she relented, in part because of the heat of a Memphis summer, but mainly because her husband by then had offered to give up his present living arrangement if she would join him elsewhere. Apparently it was this she had been waiting for all along, for he no sooner made the offer than she consented to join him where he was. She arrived in July, 1878, and at once took over the job of amanuensis. Indignant at the unrelenting vindictiveness of Washington in excluding Davis from the benefits of a pension bill for veterans of the Mexican War, they settled down to work amid reports of a yellow fever epidemic moving upriver from New Orleans. Memphis and other cities and towns were still under quarantine in October when a wire reached Beauvoir to inform them that Jeff Junior had come down with the disease. Then five days later another arrived to tell them he had rallied and then died. Davis had lost the fourth of his four sons; Samuel, Joseph, William, and now Jeff. "I presume not God to scorn," he wrote a kinsman, "but the many and humble prayers offered before my boy was taken from me are hushed in the despair of my bereavement."

Work was the answer, as much for Varina as for her husband, and they got on with it, sometimes into the small hours of the night. In February the domestic strain was relieved by Mrs Dorsey, who sold Beauvoir to Davis for $5500, to be paid in three installments, then went to New Orleans to consult a physician for what turned out to be cancer. By July she was dead. Childless, she left Beauvoir to Davis, absolving him from making the other two payments. Nor was that all. "I hereby give and bequeath all my property, wherever located and situated, wholly and entirely, without hindrance or qualification," her will read, "to my most honored and esteemed friend, Jefferson Davis, ex-President of the Confederate States, for his sole use and benefit, in fee simple forever. . . . I do not intend," she had said in closing, "to share in the ingratitude of my country towards the man who is in my eyes the highest and noblest in existence." He was now the master of Beauvoir, along with much else, including three plantations in Louisiana, and Varina was its mistress.

The work went on. Reconstruction was over, but Davis still fought the war, landing verbal blows where armed strokes had failed. Soon the first of what were to be two large volumes was ready for the printer. *Rise and Fall of the Confederate Government*, he would call it; not *Our Cause*, as he had originally intended. He moved into and steadily through the second volume. On an afternoon in April 1881, he took a long nap, then at 8 o'clock that evening resumed dictation. Speaking slowly and distinctly, so that Varina would not miss a word, he tugged firmly on the drawstrings of his logic for a final explication of his thesis that the North, not the South, had been the revolutionary party in the struggle, malevolent in its effort to subvert, subjugate, and destroy, respectively, the states, the people, and the Union as it had been till then. "When the cause was lost, what cause was it?" he asked, and answered: "Not that of the South only, but the cause of constitutional government, of the supremacy of law, of the natural rights of man." It was by then well past midnight, and only the rhythmic plash of waves on the beach came through the stillness of the dark hours before dawn. He kept on, launched now onto the last of nearly 1500 pages, restating his conviction "that the war was, on the part of the United States Government, one of aggression and usurpation, and, on the part of the South, was for the defense of an inherent, unalienable right." He paused, then continued.

> In asserting the right of secession, it has not been my wish to incite to its exercise: I recognize the fact that the war showed it to be impracticable, but this did not prove it to be wrong. And now that it may not be again attempted, and that the Union may promote the general welfare, it is needful that the truth, the whole truth, should be known, so that crimination and recrimination may forever cease, and then, on the basis of fraternity and faithful regard for the rights of the States, there may be written on the arch of the Union, *Esto perpetua*.

He leaned back, sighed, and closed his eyes against the glare of lamplight. It was 4 o'clock in the morning and he was within two months of being seventy-three years old. Her pen poised above the paper, Varina looked up, ready for the next sentence. "I think I am done," he said with a tired smile.

He was done, and the book—already in type, except these final pages—came out in June. In the South it was hailed and praised. No home that could afford them was without the two thick volumes, often bound in calf, on a parlor table. The trouble was, so few could afford them, and in the North the book was largely ignored, save in a few grudging magazine reviews. Financially, it was a failure; Appleton's lost money, and Davis himself made little, despite a drawn-out lawsuit with the publisher which ensued. In August he and Varina sailed for Europe to get Winnie, and returned in late November. "The Daughter of the Confederacy," born in the Richmond White House while the guns of Kennesaw were booming, was tall and fair, with clear gray eyes and a quiet manner; she spoke, to her father's surprise, with traces of a German accent which she would never lose. Settled again at Beauvoir he looked forward to a peaceful life through whatever years were left him. Then in mid-December came news that Joe Johnston had wondered aloud to a reporter what had become of all the treasury gold Davis had taken along on his flight through Georgia. It came, he heard, to $2,500,000; yet "Mr Davis has never given any satisfactory account of it." In the hue and cry that followed, the general was obliged to run for cover, and letters poured into Beauvoir from all parts of the country, expressing outrage at the slander and admiration for its victim. Davis had won his last skirmish with Johnston, who perhaps was confirmed in his distaste for the offensive.

Still, no amount of adulation North or South could temper the former President's resolution not to ask for pardon; not even pleas from his home-state Legislature that he do so in order to be returned to his old seat in the U.S. Senate. He did however agree to come to Jackson in March, 1884, for a ceremony staged to honor him as "the embodied history of the South." Standing in the high-ceilinged Capitol chamber where he had stood just over two decades ago, near the midpoint of the war, and told the assembled dignitaries, "Our people have only to be true to themselves to behold the Confederate flag among the recognized nations of the earth," he spoke now much as he had then: "It has been said that I should apply to the United States for a pardon. But repentance must precede the right of pardon, and I have not repented. Remembering, as I must, all which has been suffered, all which has been lost—disappointed hopes and crushed aspirations—yet I deliberately say, if it were all to do over again, I would again do just as I did in 1861." His hearers caught their breath at this, then applauded with all their might the fallen leader who represented, almost alone, the undefeat of which they boasted from stumps across the land, now and for years to come. Unforgiving, he was unforgiven, and he preferred it so, for their sake and his own.

Late in the spring of the following year a Boston paper called on Davis for an expression of his views on U. S. Grant, who was dying at Mount McGregor, New York, of cancer of the throat. Bankrupt by a brokerage partner who turned out to be a swindler, the general had lost even his sword as security for an unpaid loan, and was now engaged in a race with death to complete his *Memoirs*, hoping the proceeds would provide for his family after he was gone. He won, but only by the hardest. Re-

duced by pain to communicating with his doctor on slips of paper—"A verb is anything that signifies to be; to do; to suffer,"
one read. "I signify all three"—he managed to finish the book
within a week of his death in July, and royalties approaching
half a million dollars went to Julia and his sons. Davis had declined to comment on the career of this man whose name, in
the course of his two White House terms, had come to stand for
plunder and repression. "General Grant is dying," he replied to
the request from Boston. "Instead of seeking to disturb the
quiet of his closing hours, I would, if it were in my power, contribute to the peace of his mind and the comfort of his body."
Similarly, he had withheld comment on the passing of other former enemies, beginning with George Thomas, whose
weight rose above three hundred pounds within five years of
the end of the war, when he died on duty of a stroke in the same
year as his fellow Virginian, R. E. Lee. Henry Halleck and
George Meade, who also stayed in the army, followed him two
years later. George McClellan, after serving three years as governor of New Jersey, died three months after Grant, and was followed in turn by Winfield Hancock, who had run against Garfield in the presidential election six years back, just over three
months later.

By then it was 1886, the silver anniversary of Sumter. Memorial services and reunions were being planed throughout the
South, and Davis was pressed to attend most of them as guest
of honor. He declined, pleading frailty, until someone thought
to point out that Winnie might never know how dear he was to
the hearts of his people unless he gave them the chance to
show their love in public. That persuaded him. "I'll go; I'll go,"
he said, and accepted invitations from Montgomery, Atlanta,
and Savannah. In late April he sat on the portico of the Alabama capitol, where he had been inaugurated twenty-five years
before, and heard a eulogy pronounced by John B. Gordon, former U. S. senator and now a candidate for governor of Georgia,
who also presented Winnie to the crowd, to wild applause.
Next day Davis spoke briefly at the laying of the cornerstone

for a monument to the Confederate dead—repeating once more his contention that the seceded states had launched no revolution; "Sovereigns never rebel," he said—then set out for Atlanta, where 50,000 veterans were assembling for a May Day reunion. He was on the platform, receiving the cheers of all that host, when he looked out beyond its distant fringes and saw a man approaching on horseback, portly and white-haired, with cottony muttonchop whiskers, decked out in Confederate gray with the looped braid of a lieutenant general on his sleeves. It was Longstreet. Uninvited because of his postwar views—"The striking feature, the one the people should keep in view," he had said at the outset of Reconstruction, "is that we are a conquered people. Recognizing this fact, fairly and squarely, there is but one course left for wise men to pursue, and that is to accept the terms that now are offered by the conquerors"—Old Peter had risen that morning at his home in nearby Gainesville, put on his full uniform, come down by train, and ridden out to show the throng that he was of them, whether they wanted him there or not. Dismounting, he walked up the steps of the platform where Davis was seated, and everyone wondered what Davis would do. They soon found out, for he rose and hurried to meet Lee's old warhorse. "When the two came together," a witness declared, "Mr Davis threw his arms around General Longstreet's neck and the two leaders embraced with great emotion. The meaning of the reconciliation was clear and instantly had a profound effect upon the thousands of veterans who saw it. With a great shout they showed their joy."

One occasion of the Atlanta visit was the unveiling of a statue to the late Senator Benjamin Hill, always a loyal friend in times of crisis. "We shall conquer all enemies yet," he had assured his chief within two weeks of Appomattox, but admitted nine years later, looking back: "All physical advantages are insufficient to account for our failure. The truth is, we failed because too many of our people were not determined to win." Davis knew the basic validity of this view, yet he preferred to stress the staunchness of his people and the long odds they had faced. Northern journalists had begun to note the "inflammatory" effect of his appearances, and he tried next week in Savannah to offset this by remarking at a banquet given by the governor in his honor: "There are some who take it for granted that when I allude to State sovereignty I want to bring on another war. I am too old to fight again, and God knows I do not want you to have the necessity of fighting again." He paused to let the reporters take this down, but while he waited he saw the faces of those around him, many of them veterans like himself; with the result that he undid what had gone before. "However, if the necessity *should* arise," he said, "I know you will meet it, as you always have discharged every duty you felt called upon to perform."

Although he returned to Beauvoir near exhaustion, he recovered in time, the following year, to challenge the prohibition movement as still another "monstrous" attempt to limit individual freedom. His words were quoted by the liquor interests and he was denounced by a Methodist bishop for advocating "the barroom and the destruction of virtue." But the fact was he had mellowed, partly under the influence of strong nationalist feelings never far below the surface of his resistance. When he went back to Georgia in October, to meet "perhaps for the last time" with veterans at a reunion staged in Macon— where he had first been taken after his capture near Irwinville, more than twenty-two years ago—he spoke to them of the North and South as indivisibly united. "We are now at peace," he said, "and I trust will ever remain so. . . . In referring therefore to the days of the past and the glorious cause you have served . . . I seek but to revive a memory which should be dear to you and to your children, a memory which teaches the highest lessons of manhood, of truth and adherence to duty—duty to your State, duty to your principles, duty to your buried parents, and duty to your coming children." That was the burden of what he had to say through the time now left him, including his last speech of all, delivered the following spring at Mississippi City, only a six-mile buggy ride from Beauvoir.

Within three months of being eighty years old, he had not thought he would speak again in public; but he did, this once, for a particular reason. The occasion was a convention of young Southerners, and that was why—their youth. He did not mention the war at all, not even as "a memory which should be dear," though he did refer at the outset to the nation he had led. "Friends and fellow citizens," he began, and stopped. "Ah, pardon me," he said. "The laws of the United States no longer permit me to designate you as fellow citizens. I feel no regret that I stand before you a man without a country, for my ambition lies buried in the grave of the Confederacy." Then he went on to tell them what he had come to say. "The faces I see before me are those of young men; had I not known this I would not have appeared before you. Men in whose hands the destinies of our Southland lie, for love of her I break my silence to speak to you a few words of respectful admonition. The past is dead; let it bury its dead, its hopes and its aspirations. Before you lies the future, a future full of golden promise, a future of expanding national glory, before which all the world shall stand amazed. Let me beseech you to lay aside all rancor, all bitter sectional feeling, and to take your places in the ranks of those who will bring about a consummation devoutly to be wished—a reunited country."

Those were his last public words, and they seemed withal to have brought him a new peace, one that fulfilled a hope he had recently expressed to an old friend: "My downs have been so many, and the feeling of injustice so great, that I wish to hold on and see whether the better days may not come." A reporter who came to Beauvoir for his eightieth birthday, June 3, not only found him "immaculately dressed, straight and erect, with traces of his military service still showing in his carriage, and with the flush of health on his pale, refined face," but also observed that he retained "a keen interest in current topics, political, social, religious." He kept busy. In the course of the next year he wrote three magazine articles, a *Short History of the Confederate States*, and even got started on an autobiography, though he soon put this aside. In early November, 1889, he set out for New Orleans to catch a steamer upriver for his annual inspection trip to Brierfield, which he had lost and then recovered by a lawsuit. Usually his wife went along but this time she remained behind with guests. Exposed to a sleety rain, he came down with a cold and was so ill by the time the boat reached Brierfield Landing, late at night, that he continued on to Vicksburg. Going ashore next morning, he rode down to the plantation, only to spend the next four days in bed, sick with bronchitis and a recurrence of the malaria that had killed his bride and nearly killed him, more than fifty years before, at the same place.

Alarmed, for Davis by then was near delirium, the plantation manager got him back to Vicksburg and onto a steamer headed south. Downriver that night the boat was hailed by another coming up with Varina on board. Warned by telegraph of her husband's condition, she had set out to join him, and now she did so, transferring in midstream to claim her place at his bedside. New Orleans doctors pronounced him too ill to be taken to Beauvoir, so he was carried on a stretcher to a private home in the Garden District. He seemed to improve in the course of the next week. "It may seem strange to you," he told an attending physician, "that a man of my years should desire to live; but I do. There are still some things that I have to do in this world." He wanted above all to get back to the autobiography he had set aside. "I have not told what I wish to say of my college-mates Sidney Johnston and Polk. I have much more to say of them. I shall tell a great deal of West Point—and I seem to remember more every day." Presently, though, it was clear that he would do none of these things, including the desired return to Beauvoir. Another week passed; December came in. On December 5, within six months of being eighty-two years old, he woke to find Varina sitting beside him, and he let her know he knew the time was near. "I want to tell you I am not afraid to die," he said, although he seemed no worse than he had been the day before.

That afternoon he slept soundly, but woke at dusk with a violent chill. Frightened, Varina poured out a teaspoon of medicine, only to have him decline it with a meager smile and a faint shake of his head. When she insisted he refused again. "Pray excuse me, I cannot take it," he murmured. These were the last words of a man who had taken most of the knocks a hard world had to offer. He lapsed into a peaceful sleep that continued into the night. Once when his breathing grew labored the doctors turned him gently onto his right side, and he responded childlike by raising his arm to pillow his cheek on his hand, the other resting lightly on his heart. Midnight came and went, and less than an hour later he too obeyed Anaximander's dictum, breathing his last so imperceptibly that Varina and the others at his bedside could scarcely tell the moment of his going.

He died on Friday and was buried on Wednesday, time being needed to allow for the arrival of friends and relatives from distant points. Meanwhile, dressed in a civilian suit of Confederate gray, his body lay in state at City Hall, viewed in the course of the next four days by an estimated hundred thousand mourners. Then the day of the funeral came, December 11, and all the church bells of New Orleans tolled. Eight southern governors served as pallbearers, the Washington Artillery as guard of honor; interment would be at Metairie Cemetery in the tomb of the Army of Northern Virginia, which was crowned with a statue of Stonewall Jackson atop a fifty-foot marble shaft. "The end of a long and lofty life has come. The strange and sudden dignity of death has been added to the fine and resolute dignity of living," the Episcopal bishop of Louisiana declared on the steps of City Hall as the casket was brought out to begin the three-hour march to Metairie. After the service at the tomb, when Taps had sounded, he spoke again. "In the name of God, amen. We here consign the body of Jefferson Davis, a servant of his state and country and a soldier in their armies; sometime member of Congress, Senator from Mississippi, and Secretary of War of the United States; the first and only President of the Confederate States of America; born in Kentucky on the third day of June, 1808, died in Louisiana on the sixth day of December, 1889, and buried here by the reverent hands of his people."

Much else was said in the way of praise across the land that day, and still more would be said four years later, when his body would be removed to its permanent resting place in Hollywood Cemetery, Richmond, to join his son Joe and others who had died nearby in Virginia during the war. Lincoln by now had been a full generation in his Springfield tomb, and all he had said or written would be cherished as an imperishable legacy to the nation, including the words he had spoken in response to a White House serenade on the occasion of his reëlection: "What has occurred in this case must ever recur in similar cases. Human nature will not change. In any future great national trial, compared with the men of this, we shall have as weak and as strong, as silly and as wise, as bad and as good. Let us therefore study the incidents of this, as philosophy to learn wisdom from, and none of them as wrongs to be revenged." Davis could never match that music, or perhaps even catch its tone. His was a different style, though it too had its beauty and its uses: as in his response to a recent Beauvoir visitor, a reporter who hoped to leave with something that would help explain to readers the underlying motivation of those crucial years of bloodshed and division. Davis pondered briefly, then replied.

"Tell them—" He paused as if to sort the words. "Tell the world that I only loved America," he said.

L.Q.C. Lamar
1825–1893

Artificer of
Reconciliation

BY NASH K. BURGER AND JOHN K. BETTERSWORTH

As was the case with no few later-day Mississippians, Lucius Quintus Cincinnatus Lamar was Georgia-born. Once a part of Georgia, Mississippi was Georgia's answer to the compulsive westward movement in the youngest of Britain's thirteen colonies. For L. Q. C. Lamar the compulsive factor in bringing him from Georgia to Oxford, Mississippi, would be not land, not cotton, but the enticements of a onetime Georgian, Augustus Baldwin Longstreet, who had become president of the University of Mississippi and would make Lamar an adjunct professor at the university. Herewith was one of the few cases where pedagogical charms would be exercised by the westward movement.

As for Lamar's earliest years—the Georgia experience—it should be noted that the mobility of the roving Lamar family did not begin with Georgia. While L. Q. C. Lamar was born in 1826 at the family homestead near Satartia, Putnam County, Georgia, the Lamar family could look back to Huguenots in France, to several seventeenth century generations of Lamars first in England and finally in Maryland, from which they migrated down the Atlantic seaboard to Georgia and points west. An uncle, the redoubtable Mirabeau Lamar, even set a model for family mobility by becoming president of the Republic of Texas. Among other memorable Lamars whom Lucius knew as a boy were Gozaway B. Lamar, who had left Georgia for New York to become president of the Bank of the Republic; and Henry G. Lamar, a Georgia Congressman.

Lucius' father was a brilliant lawyer, educated for the bar in Connecticut. When he was only twenty-two, the Georgia Legislature asked him to compile the first digest of the laws of the state. At thirty-three, he was made judge of the highest court in the state, the youngest man ever to hold this office. Four years later, on July 4, 1834, this greatly respected, prosperous and successful jurist, happily married and the father of five children, returned from a public meeting, kissed his wife and children, went out into the garden and shot himself. The reason was never known. Something of his high intellectual quality, brilliance in argument and judicial interpretation, combined with sensitiveness and inner questioning, were later revealed in the personality of his famous son.

Young Lucius, the eldest of three brothers, was nine years old when his father died; his grandfather had also died less than a year before. The golden, happy plantation days were over. Removing to Georgia, where a Methodist boys' school had just opened, Lamar studied Greek, Latin, history, the natural sciences, and declamation.

As the boys approached college age, the family moved to nearby Oxford, site of Emory College, which Lamar entered in 1841. An important influence on his life was the college's new president, Augustus Baldwin Longstreet. A Georgian who had gone to school in South Carolina with John C. Calhoun, he had graduated at Yale and served in succession as lawyer, judge, Methodist minister and author of one of the South's first books of local color sketches, *Georgia Scenes*. A strong state rights advocate and a political disciple of Calhoun, Judge Longstreet's memorial to the General Conference of the Methodist Episcopal Church in 1844, split that church over the questions of slavery and state rights.

To Judge Longstreet Lamar once wrote, "I am indebted to you for ennobling influences from my boyhood up to midde age. . . . For many years I have loved you as few sons love a father." As for Lamar, no spot on earth had "so helped to form and make me what I am as this town of Oxford." He meant not only the town, but also the college, for the town was the college and the college was Judge Longstreet.

Two years after graduation Lamar was admitted to the

Georgia bar and married Judge Longstreet's daughter. They settled in Covington, but when Judge Longstreet accepted the
presidency of the University of Mississippi, Lamar and his wife
moved to Oxford, Mississippi, also. Lamar practiced law and
taught as Adjunct Professor of Mathematics at the University—a prosaic and uncongenial activity for his own imagina-
tive intelligence. "It may be a great accomplishment, that of
putting truths all in a row, 'each holding to the skirts of the
other,' " he wrote, "but in my opinion if Newton's *thoughts*
had been compelled to go through the process which is now
employed in the *demonstration* of his binomial theorem, the
world would never have heard of its discovery."

When Lamar was only twenty-six, he took his first public
part in politics. Supporting Jefferson Davis' gubernational campaign in a joint debate, he bested Davis' opponent Senator H. S.
Foote. The University students bore their young professor off in
triumph on their shoulders. Davis lost the election to Foote,
but Lamar's political future was assured.

In 1852, the family returned to Georgia. The Whigs normally
controlled the county, but Lamar was elected to the Legislature
as a Democrat. "He was then young, not more than 27," a contemporary described him, "with a handsome face, a full head of
dark hair, brilliant eyes, in figure rather below the medium of
height, handsomely dressed, with fine musical voice. . . . In a
short speech of not more than thirty minutes he captured the
whole assembly. . . . Such an excitement as was produced by
his speech I never saw in that body. . . . a remarkable exhibition of the power of the orator and the logician."

In 1855, Lamar was back in Mississippi, where he bought a
plantation, "Solitude," of more than a thousand acres, located
on the Tallahatchie River between Oxford and Holly Springs.
There he became the Southern gentleman. To his slaves, he
was at once "master, guardian, and friend." He was "loved and
petted by women folk and his children." He was frequently visited by "cultivated and attractive friends for days and even
weeks," and he visited them in turn. A planter with a feeling

for diversification, his "summers were devoted to the growing of cotton and corn, while the winters were occupied in killing hogs, curing bacon sides and delicious hams, making sausages, and trying out snowy lard." Thus his son-in-law, Edward Mayes, described the life at Solitude.

Soon Lamar was also cultivating politics. In 1857, he ran for Congress under the sponsorship of Jacob Thompson of Oxford, Secretary of the Interior in President Buchanan's cabinet and a potent figure in Democratic circles. Thompson had discovered Lamar to be "a man endowed by genius and culture with the qualities that make a politician and a statesman. . . . gifted with eloquence and of scholarly attainments, with no political or moral sins to answer for."

Lamar won, and as a young Congressman in the turbulent atmosphere of Washington he had need for all his talents. One of many who now began to despair of a peaceful solution of the slavery question, he foresaw the dissolution of the Union, and—as many did not—that a break-up of the Union meant war. "Dissolution cannot take place quietly," he wrote. "The vast and complicated machinery of this government cannot be divided without general tumult and, it may be ruin. When the sun of the Union sets, it will go down in blood."

Although Lamar was a firm supporter of state rights and of the theoretical right of a state to secede, he was not an extremist, and he worked always for honorable compromise on disputed issues. He was considered a conservative and a peacemaker. "I am no disunionist *per se*," Lamar told the Congress. "I am devoted to the Constitution of this Union; and so long as this Republic is a great tolerant republic, throwing its loving arms around both sections of the country, I, for one, will bestow every talent which God has given me for its promotion and its glory."

Writing his friend, Dr. F. A. P. Barnard, who succeeded Judge Longstreet as President of the University of Mississippi and later became President of Columbia University, he expressed regret that "the sectional war rages with unabated violence

. . . brought about by ultra party leaders and deluded fanatics." He longed for a leader capable of "rising above the passions and prejudices of the times," would "speak to both sections in a spirit at once tolerant, just, generous, humane, and national." Little did he realize that he was describing himself two decades hence.

Lamar spoke out eloquently when he felt the position of the South was threatened. He could also resort to more elementary eloquence. In February 1858, when debate over the explosive Kansas situation led to a fight on the floor of the House between Pennsylvania's Grow and South Carolina's Keitt, it was reported that "even Lamar of Mississippi and Parson Owen Lovejoy had a little set-to in the course of the passing gust."

Mrs. Clement Clay, wife of the Senator of Alabama, described Lamar as the most "affectionately held" of any Southerner in Congress. "Moody Lamar," he was sometimes called, "for he was then, as he always was to be, full of dreams and ideals and big warm impulses, with a capacity for the most enduring and strongest of friendships, and a tenderness rarely displayed by men so strong as was he."

His firm but moderate course was fully approved in Mississippi. He and Jefferson Davis had become the state's most prominent figures, and both were greatly in demand for speeches and public appearances. Even Lamar's political opponents recognized his ability and took pride in his conduct on the state and national scene. "In our judgment," said the Vicksburg *Whig*, an opposition paper, "Mr. Lamar is the ablest man in either branch of Congress from this State. . . . There is hardly a question of governmental policy on which we do not differ materially with him; but if his side is to have the Congressman, we at least feel a sort of State pride that such a man as L. Q. C. Lamar is made the recipient of the honors of his party."

Like most Southern leaders, Lamar would have preferred to avoid secession, but he had come to feel that this was impossible. Secession, said Lamar, "was the culmination of a great dynastical struggle, an 'irrepressible conflict' between two antagonistic societies. . . . This culmination was a result of the operation of political forces which it was not within the power of any individual man or set of men to prevent or postpone."

Lamar was fully convinced that the South's position was proper and constitutional. He wrote the Ordinance of Secession adopted by a State Convention at Jackson in January, 1861. The ordinance proposed that another federal union of seceded states be set up on "the basis of the present Constitution of the United States." Lamar was, in fact, ready for the Southern states to readopt the United States Constitution and all existing Federal laws, exactly as they were. It was his view, and that of many other Southern leaders, that there was nothing wrong with the Federal Union that a conscientious adherence to the laws and Constitution as written could not cure. He had become convinced, however, that such a course was not to be expected from a government dominated by Northern Republicans.

Lamar resigned from Congress in 1861, to return to Mississippi to draft his state's Ordinance of Secession. He served as lieutenant colonel and colonel of the 19th Mississippi Regiment in the Peninsula fighting before Richmond in 1862 and was three times cited for bravery and outstanding leadership. Then two attacks of a recurrent illness, a "violent vertigo . . . something like an apoplexy," put an end to his military service.

The same year he was appointed Confederate minister to Russia (though he never reached Russia) and special envoy to England and France. "Lamar struck Paris as an imposing, even picturesque personality," one writer said, "and in his broad-brimmed hat, tight buttoned coat, and hirsute luxuriance he cut a striking figure on the boulevards." A French lady praised the courtly Southerner as the only diplomat at the French court "who fully recognized and endeavored to utilize the power of the women there." He made friends also with the French poet, A. M. L. de Lamartine, who in a manner to warm the Southern heart turned out to be a distant relative.

In London Lamar stayed at Thackeray's home. Henry Adams, who was in England with his father, Charles Francis Adams, the United States Ambassador, found Lamar "quite unusual in social charm," and felt that "he would have done better in London, in place of Mason [James Mason, the Confederate minister]. London society would have delighted him; his stories would have won success; his manners would have made him loved; his oratory would have swept every audience."

Lamar spoke persuasively on the South's position to British groups. On the question of slavery he said that the South had not introduced the African to slavery, but in the South, under slavery, "the white race had been the guardians, the protectors, the benefactors of the black man; that they had elevated him in the scale of rational existence, and that they had Christianized him to a state to which he has never before attained."

To those who might say that "the South owed it to Christendom to emancipate him," Lamar replied that blacks were not ready for emancipation. "So many and so great were the boons the South had already conferred on the negro race, that the world had ample guaranty that if the time should ever come for the South to believe that liberty would be a boon, and not a curse, then she would be prepared to confer that boon upon them. . . . If that time should ever come, they would be capable of asserting their own claims; and the whites could not, if they would, withhold the boon."

Returning home, he ran the Union blockade in a ship that was pursued and wrecked. Back in Georgia, in 1864, he spoke effectively for Jefferson Davis' administration in the hostile bailiwick of stubborn Governor Joseph E. Brown and sulking Vice President Alexander Stephens.

"I shall stay with my people." With these simple words Colonel Lucius Quintus Cincinnatus Lamar, young judge advocate of the Third Army Corps, announced his decision to share the fearful consequences of what happened at Appomattox on that Sunday morning in April 1865. He would devote his life "to the alleviation, so far as in my power lies, of the sufferings this day's disaster will entail upon" the people of the South.

Lamar meant what he said. He would stay with his people

and put into their mouths the gentle words of peace. He would show Northerners that a Southerner could lead not only his own people but all the people of the nation. He would become the artificer of reconciliation.

The Civil War had already given this brilliant young man an opportunity to practice his gift of oratory. His fellow Mississippian, Jefferson Davis, President of the Confederacy, had sent him off to Georgia to battle administration critics like Alexander H. Stephens. And when he spoke in January 1865, to the tattered men of Harris' Brigade while shells crackled about him, he so stirred the desolate soldiers that they burst into cheers. The Federals "shot at the noise," but Lamar continued, though splinters flew from the stump on which he stood. Later, in Reconstruction, he would, as the lone Democrat in Congress from his home state, speak boldly on, even though some of the irreconcilable Radicals were disposed with no less success than before to "shoot at the noise."

In the War, as Lamar had foreseen, his family, like most others in the South, suffered grievously, not just financially and materially, but in the death of its members on the battlefield. Thirteen Lamars closely related to Lucius are known to have been killed. Both of Lamar's brothers were killed—one at Crampton's Gap, Maryland, in 1862; the other at Petersburg, Virginia, in 1864.

When Lamar signed his parole at Appomattox, he was attached to the First Corps, which had absorbed what was left of the old Third Corps of General A. P. Hill. He was married to Virginia Longstreet, a cousin of his new commander, James Longstreet. In the grueling postwar years that were to agitate the South and the nation, both these men played prominent and significant, but very different, roles. In the end they were to become symbols of a nation's reunification.

As Lamar made his way southward after Appomattox, through the devastated countryside to Mississippi, he fell in with another veteran, Major General Edward C. Walthall, who had distinguished himself at the battles of Chickamauga, Missionary Ridge, Nashville, and Franklin. Walthall, born in Virginia, had been reared in Holly Springs, Mississippi, where Lamar had practiced law before the War. Walthall, too, was a lawyer, and the two men decided to open an office together at Coffeeville, near Oxford. Thus began a close relationship that was to have a profound effect upon the political events of Reconstruction and after.

Lamar was soon hard at work at his law practice and in his modest home. "We keep no man servant," Mrs. Lamar wrote her mother in February, 1866. "Lucius has been working about the fences and gates and locks to his outhouses. He feeds his cows and helps cut the wood and does a great deal of work. If he can only have good health, I feel as if we would be happy under almost any circumstances." In June of that year he became Professor of Ethics and Metaphysics at the University of Mississippi and the next year Professor of Law.

During the first years of Reconstruction, Lamar believed, with General Robert E. Lee, that the best former Confederate leaders could do was to obey the law, work to rebuild the South and remain out of the limelight. "I have thought and still think," he wrote in 1870, "that all such a one can do, or should do, is not to uphold or approve, but quietly to acquiesce in, the result of the wager of battle."

Lamar "acquiesced" by giving up his post at the University after the Carpetbag and Negro regime had triumphed in Mississippi and the "Black and Tan" Constitution had been adopted in 1869. Lamar even considered leaving Mississippi. He was discouraged enough to write in May 1870: "The state of things is permanent. The Negroes have a large and increasing majority. I must take my property and family from the state." Moreover, his wife's mother had died in 1868, and Judge Longstreet a year later—two of the strongest links that had bound him to Mississippi. After some hesitation, he decided to remain, encouraged perhaps by the marriage of his daughter, Fannie, to Edward Mayes, later to become Chancellor of the University of Mississippi and Lamar's biographer.

In the years following the Radical triumph, the white Democrats of Mississippi took to the underground. Many turned to the Ku Klux Klan as a means of fighting Carpetbag and Negro rule. Federal efforts to suppress the Klan brought lawyers like Lamar into the courts to defend his accused friends and neighbors. Oxford, as a Federal court town, was the scene of many "Klan" trials, filled with Federal troops, prisoners, and a large number of government witnesses and hangers-on.

On June 22, 1871, Lamar became embroiled in a courtroom roughhouse with a disreputable government witness, a former counterfeiter, embezzler, and murderer, who interrupted and threatened him, even starting to draw a pistol conspicuously displayed at his waist. Lamar picked up a chair and declared that if the judge wouldn't make the witness sit down, he would. In the confusion Lamar knocked down and broke the jaw of a well-meaning Federal marshal who attempted to intervene. Federal troops stationed in the building were called in. Lamar spoke bitterly to the judge for permitting the situation to develop and denounced the Federal officers who were threatening to arrest him. Finally order was restored without further violence. "We never saw a better fight or heard a better speech," said one of the Federal soldiers.

Lamar apologized for his part in the disorder, especially to the marshal whom he had knocked down, but the judge temporarily disbarred Lamar from practicing in his court. The injured marshal testified for Lamar, pointing out that he had prevented a threatened riot in Oxford during the 1869 election and had always been a force for law and order in the community. The Radicals, North and South, seized on the incident as an example of Southern troublemaking, part of a Ku Klux plot.

The state was now firmly in the grasp of Carpetbaggers and former slaves. Throughout the South, the Negroes, thanks to the Thirteenth and Fourteenth Amendments and the presence of Federal troops, were now enfranchised. Many Northern states had not yet granted the suffrage even to educated Negroes, but the Radical Republicans were demanding that Federal troops guarantee the vote to the illiterate Negroes of the South. In states like Mississippi, where Negroes constituted a majority of the population, the effects of Negro voting were disastrous to the ex-Confederates except for the few who like James L. Alcorn, co-operated with the Reconstruction government.

Elected governor of 1869, Alcorn was a Mississippian who had been a member, with Lamar, of the state's secession convention of 1861 but after the War joined the Republican party. In 1869, there were thirty-six blacks in the Legislature, few of whom could read or write, and sixty-four by 1873. Taxes were so high as to be almost confiscatory; the tax money disappeared in waste, extravagance, and embezzlement. Alcorn, who as a taxpayer resisted the upward tax spiral, was subsequently kicked upstairs into the United States Senate.

From his home in Oxford, Lamar had watched what was happening with a sadness verging on despair. Late "upon almost any clement evening," wrote his son-in-law Edward Mayes, "if one should follow the plank walk until the picket fence which marked the premises of Col. Lamar should be reached, there he would be found; clad in a drab study-gown, somewhat frayed and stained with ink; his face long, massive, and sallow; bareheaded, with his long brown hair stirred by the breeze; his deep mysterious eyes fixed upon the yellowing western sky, or watching dreamily the waving limbs of the avenue of water oaks across the way; abstracted, recognizing the salutations of the passers-by with a nod half courteous, half surly, and yet obviously unconscious of all identities; a countenance solemn, sober and enigmatical."

The "grim despotism" of Radical Republican rule "glares upon us at every point," Lamar wrote to a friend. "Spies and secret detectives swarm through the country, dogging the footsteps of our best citizens . . . following up with arrests, arbitrary searches, indefinite and unexplained imprisonments, trials before vindictive and partisan juries picked for the purpose of insuring convictions." He felt that the South had laid down its arms in good faith, had submitted, indeed, to the Northern interpretation of the Constitution. "Yet the administration of President Grant . . . has never ceased to treat them with contemptuous distrust, severity, and vengeance."

So keenly did Lamar feel the ordeal of his people that he ran for Congress in 1872. He did this reluctantly, for his law practice was prospering even if his party was not. "The time has passed with me for looking to political parties, Democratic or Republican, as a means of improving public affairs." He was particularly unenthusiastic about the Democratic acceptance of the Liberal Republican nominee for President, Horace Greeley. As a former Confederate officer and public official, Lamar was disqualified for office except by special act of Congress. He was elected nevertheless—the first Democrat to be seated from Mississippi since Appomattox.

Lamar had been elected under unprecedented circumstances. He had announced before the election: "If elected . . . I will be in *one* sense a Representative according to the standard established in the purer days of the republic. Not a dollar will be spent, except for the printing of tickets in my district . . . There will not be a vote bribed . . . and no *personal influence*, will, so far as I know, be brought to bear upon anybody."

Lamar's intellectual brilliance, his power as a speaker, his gentlemanly conduct to friend and foe alike, won him not only the normal Democratic vote but considerable Republican support as well—including the vote of the Republican United States marshal whom he had knocked down in the Oxford courtroom. When the time came to ask Congress for a removal of Lamar's political disabilities so that he could take his seat, his request was supported by Republican Governor Ridgley C. Powers as well as by three Republican judges of the State Supreme Court, the Negro secretary of state, and many Federal officers stationed in Mississippi. In December 1872, Congress passed a bill permitting him to take his seat.

In 1874, a former Federal officer from Maine, Adelbert Ames, was to become governor. The fact that he was a son-in-law of

Ben Butler, whose rule as military governor of New Orleans had incurred white wrath, did not add to Ames' popularity in Mississippi.

Lamar was present when the Forty-third Congress met in December. His course as a Congressman, he declared, would be marked "by moderation and reserve. If I say or do anything it will be to give the North the assurance it wants that the South comprehends its own great necessities, and wishes to be no longer the agitating and agitated pendulum of American politics." Presently, Lamar was given an opportunity to practice these preachments.

On March 11, 1874, Charles Sumner, the Massachusetts Senator, Abolitionist and one of the chief architects of Republican Reconstruction policy, died. A few days later, before a packed gallery and a full House of Representatives, Lamar delivered a eulogy on Sumner that astounded the nation. It was an ungrudging acknowledgment of the sincerity and idealism of Sumner's career, coupled with a plea for an end to sectional bitterness and strife. "Let us hope," he said, "that future generations, when they remember the deeds of heroism and devotion done on both sides, will speak not of Northern prowess and Southern courage, but of the heroism, fortitude, and courage of Americans in a war of ideas; a war in which each section signalized its consecration to the principles, as each understood them, of American liberty and of the Constitution received from their fathers." Then he concluded with the memorable and historic phrase, "My countrymen *know* one another, and you will *love* one another." So moving, so brilliantly delivered were Lamar's sentiments that Congressmen and spectators wept. In helping to heal the wounds of a war that had rent the nation and desolated much of it, here was probably the most important single speech ever delivered in the House.

"It must begin to dawn upon even the most inveterate rebel haters in Congress, and the press," said the Springfield (Mass.) *Republican*, "that the war is indeed over." The speech "is instinct with the patriot's pride and faith," said the Boston *Ad-*

vertiser. "Evidence of the real restoration of the Union," was the verdict of the Boston *Globe.* Two Boston papers, the *Transcript* and the *Herald,* thought Lamar's generosity and tolerance proved that Republican policy in the South had erred in not following a more moderate course and working with such natural leaders as Lamar.

Southern papers praised Lamar no less. As Lamar himself said, "I never in all my life opened my lips with a purpose more single to the interests of our Southern people. . . . I wanted to seize an opportunity, when universal attention could be arrested, and directed to what I was saying, to speak to the North in behalf of my own people."

Congressman James G. Blaine of Maine, the Speaker of the House, later gave a shrewd and realistic, but no less complimentary evaluation of Lamar's achievement: "It was a mark of positive genius in a Southern representative to pronounce a fervid and discriminating eulogy upon Mr. Sumner, and skillfully to interweave with it a defense of that which Mr. Sumner . . . believed to be the sum of all villainies. Only a man of Mr. Lamar's peculiar mental type could have accomplished the task. . . . There is a certain Orientalism in the mind of Mr. Lamar, strangely admixed with the typical Americanism. He is full of reflection; seemingly careless, yet closely observant; apparently dreamy, yet altogether practical."

Lamar was henceforth listened to with respect and consideration by all members of the House, including those of the dominant Republican party. In June 1874, he reviewed before the House the Reconstruction scandals in Louisiana relating to a contested election for governor, and at the same time coupled the Louisiana scandal with a general survey of Radical Republican activities in the South. "No party supported by the moral sentiment of the American people," he said, "can long bear the responsibility of the infamy and disgrace which these grotesque caricatures of government have brought upon the very name of Republicanism."

Every one of these state governments, continued Lamar, "depends every moment of its existence upon the will of the President. That will makes and unmakes them. A short proclamation backed by one company determines who is to be the governor of Arkansas; a telegram settles the civil magistracy of Texas; a brief order to a general in New Orleans wrests a State government from the people of Louisiana." This speech, "though listened to by all the Republican leaders," reported one observer, was "neither answered nor contradicted and could not be, because the facts were indisputable."

Members of the House crowded around Lamar, however, to congratulate him after his speech, and newspapers, North and South, praised the address almost as highly as they had the one on Sumner. The Boston *Advertiser* declared that the "generous temper, the nobility of sentiment, and the moving eloquence of the present representative from Mississippi are doing more than anything else could to dispel unpleasant feeling and to promote good offices between sections of the Union." In Mississippi the Jackson *Clarion* called the address "a most triumphant vindication of a wronged people, executed in a style so knightly as to disarm opposition and compel attention and respect."

By the close of the session, Lamar had become in the eyes of his fellow Congressmen and of the nation, one of the leaders of the House. He had answered to his own cry of the 1850's for a statesman who could "rise above the passions and prejudices of the times." He was concerned only with the extent to which his efforts might serve to promote national harmony and hasten the end of the Reconstruction regimes in the South. He knew that in eulogizing Sumner, in speaking in conciliatory terms to the North and publicly accepting the political and constitutional results of the Northern victory, he was risking repudiation by the South, but he took this risk. On the whole, the people of his state supported him.

To a constituent who wrote urging that Lamar speak out to "expose the villainy and corruption" of the national administration and "the outrages upon our liberties," he replied that such an attack would only stir up sectional bitterness and strengthen the hold of the Radical Republicans. The Radicals, said Lamar, would gladly "raise a purse of $50,000" to reward any Southern leader who would so help their cause by making an intemperate and public attack on President Grant. The dominant party, he pointed out, "has even yet the power to inflict upon our defenseless people suffering or oppression which awakened resentments may invent. . . . The only course I, in common with other Southern representatives, have to follow, is to do what we can to allay excitement between the sections, and to bring about peace and reconciliation. That will be the foundation upon which we may establish a constitutional government for the whole country, and local self-government for the South."

"My recent speeches," he wrote a member of his family, "have not been prompted by self-seeking motives. It was necessary that some Southern man should say and do what I said and did. I knew that if I did it I would run the risk of losing the confidence of the Southern people. . . . Yet I loved my people more than I did their approval. I saw a chance to convert their enemies into friends, and to change bitter animosities into sympathy and regard. If I had let the opportunity pass without doing what I have, I would never have got over the feeling of self-reproach."

Republican rule in the South, the scandals of the Grant Administration and—it is not too much to say—Lamar's own words and deeds, all contributed to a great victory for the Democrats in the national elections of November 1874. The House of Representatives went Democratic for the first time since the war. Papers in all parts of the country enthusiastically suggested Lamar for Speaker of the House, even for Vice President in the next Presidential campaign. Lamar declined to be considered for either post, believing that it was not appropriate or wise for a Southerner to hold such offices as yet.

He worked busily, however, to counteract a serious threat in the House from the lame-duck Republican majority, which sought to pass various bills giving wide powers to President Grant to continue Republican Reconstruction in the South even after the Democrats took control of the House. Particularly obnoxious was the so-called "Force Bill," that would give the President dictatorial powers to control elections in Arkansas, Alabama, Louisiana, and Mississippi, states as yet under Carpetbag rule, thereby helping to guarantee not only continued Republican control of those states but also the continuation of Republican occupancy of the White House after the next Presidential election. The Force Bill was so extreme and its constitutionality was so doubtful that some Republicans, including Speaker Blaine, gave support, open or tacit, to Lamar's extraordinary efforts to defeat it. In the end by parliamentary maneuvering and delaying tactics Lamar prevented the passage of the bill.

Lamar was also able to cause some modification of a civil rights bill, a legacy from Charles Sumner. On many occasions he had avowed his acceptance of the postwar constitutional amendments granting full rights to the Negro and had urged his constituents to do the same. However, he felt that attempts to spell out by legislation in Washington the exact details of these rights was a mistake. Such a move would only create tension and imperil normal race relations—as, indeed, experience in the Reconstruction years had already proved. The Federal government, said Lamar, "by constituting itself as the Negro's sole protector in the State drives him to trust only its agents and partisans, often men of the vilest character, and rarely men who have any material relation to the State or to society among us. The Negro is thus isolated from the white people among whom he lives." And Lamar knew in the 1870's, just as many Southerners did nearly a century later, how disastrous this isolation could be for the black man.

After the adjournment of Congress, Lamar made several speeches in New Hampshire at the request of the Democratic party, a move designed to convince Northern voters that the Democrats were truly a national party and that Southern Democrats were fully reconciled to the verdict of Appomattox. No better choice could have been made. He spoke to large audiences, made up of members of both parties, who turned out to hear this former Confederate officer and diplomatic envoy. Lamar spoke frankly of the "corruption, cupidity and graft, peculation and embezzlement, intimidation of voters, bribery, waste of public treasure, loss of public credit, fraudulent balloting, intimidation by the Federal military, taxation in all its grinding and diversified forms" prevailing in the South under the Reconstruction regimes. But he assured his hearers of the South's acceptance of the results of the war, including the rights granted the freed slaves, and he pleaded for understanding and justice. Lamar also spoke in Boston, taking as his topic Daniel Webster and John Calhoun and praising both as men who loved and revered the Constitution, though they agreed to disagree on interpreting it.

The famous Southern newspaperman and inventor of the New South movement, Henry W. Grady, wrote of him at this time: "Mr. Lamar has all the physical characteristics of his knightly and illustrious family—the peculiar swarthy complexion, pale but clear; the splendid gray eyes; the high cheek bones; the dark brown hair; the firm and fixed mouth; the face thoroughly haughty and reserved when in repose, and yet full of snap and fire and magnetism. Added to these was that indefinable something which all great men carry about them."

At home in Mississippi, Lamar threw himself into the political campaign of 1875. He was a candidate for re-election, and public opinion in the state and nation were alike in demanding his return to Washington. But affairs in Mississippi had gone from bad to worse. The carpetbag governor, Adelbert Ames, was a favorite target of Democratic ire. T. W. Cordoza, the Negro superintendent of education, was under indictment in New York for larceny. At all levels of government—municipal, county, and state—charges of corruption were commonplace. Taxes had been increased 1,400 per cent in five years, with the result that in 1874, a total of 6,000,000 acres of land were forfeited for taxes—more land than there was in the states of Massachusetts and Rhode Island combined.

The bonded debt of the river town of Vicksburg (population 12,443) had increased from $13,000 in 1869 to $1,400,000 in 1874. In 1864, a Taxpayer's League was organized to wrest control from the Negroes. A riot followed. Many former Federal soldiers in the town fought with the whites against the armed blacks. Sixteen persons were killed. There was another bloody riot during the following summer at Clinton, near Jackson, the state capital, and there were constant threats of outbreaks at other towns in the state.

In May 1875, representatives of the "white citizens" assembled at Jackson and issued a memorial to the nation written by Lamar, listing their grievances. Lamar, aided by James Z. George, a rising leader in state politics, who had become chairman of the State Democratic Committee, mapped a strategy whereby organizations were set up in each county to work during the full elections "by legitimate means to regain control of our public affairs, and thus secure to all classes, white and black, the blessings of a just and honest government."

Lamar constantly decried the forming of parties on racial lines, but the whole policy of the Radical Republicans had been to pit the freedman against the native white man. Governor Ames had even tried to reorganize Lamar's Congressional district so that it would be predominantly black, hoping thereby to defeat him. Before the State Democratic Convention in August, Lamar strongly opposed setting up the Democrats as a white man's party, and he urged that the rights of "the newly enfranchised race" be respected. In speeches all over the state, sometimes two or three a day, Lamar continued to appeal for and to the Negro, and the Democrats confidently expected to win over a sizeable black vote.

If a really serious conflict in Mississippi had forced Grant to send in Federal troops, this would, of course, have strengthened the Republican position. "The blood of twenty-five or thirty Negroes," said Governor Ames, "would benefit the party in the

State." Ames did indeed call on Grant for troops and used the black state militia to buttress his position. But Grant refused; the country, he said, was weary of these continued calls for Federal troops. There is no doubt that Lamar's speech on Sumner and his other speeches, notably in New Hampshire and Boston, had helped to convince the rest of the country that the ex-Confederate whites were safely back in the Union. Of Ames, the New York *Herald* said: "He has corrupted the courts, has protected criminals, and has played even with the lives of the blacks in a manner that, if this fall a good legislature should be elected, ought to procure his impeachment."

The election campaign, which had begun with both sides arming themselves to the teeth, ended in a somewhat less trigger-happy fashion. The contenders tacitly agreed to refrain from the use of bullets and to limit their attention to the ballot. Democrats wearing the characteristic red shirt that came to be symbolic of the "Redeemers" all over the South, did not necessarily abandon their sidearms. Rallies were noisy, excitement was unbounded, but shooting was generally into the air. Undoubtedly, the white Democrats, though they carefully avoided riots and incidents, engaged in a considerable degree of intimidation and economic pressure to frighten away or at least control the Negro voters. This policy of keeping the lid tightly sealed on the powder keg came to be known as the "Mississippi Plan," and it was imitated elsewhere, especially in South Carolina in the following year. Much of this strategy was conceived by Lamar.

The 1875 elections brought a resounding victory for the Democrats. The new legislature forthwith began to clean house. The Negro lieutenant governor, A. K. Davis, was immediately convicted of bribery and removed from office. The black superintendent of education, Cordoza, resigned to escape impeachment. In February, twenty-three counts of impeachment against Governor Ames were presented in the Legislature, but he agreed to resign if the charges were not pressed. His offer was accepted, and Ames left the state.

In the showdown of 1875, Lamar was indisputably the dominant figure. He had made clear his state's acceptance of the results of the War. At the same time he restrained extremists in his own party who would have resorted to violence and extraordinary measures that might have brought down new forms of punishment on the state. His wise and moderate stand won support even from the opposition, including many Negroes.

The Forty-fourth Congress, meeting in December 1875, brought a number of prominent white Southerners and former Confederate leaders to Washington. Lamar declined to be considered for Speaker of the House, but did serve as chairman of the Democratic party caucus, declaring the aim of his party to be "to restore the Constitution to its pristine strength and authority, and to make it the protector of every section and of every State in the Union and of every human being of every race, color, and condition in the land." To which the New York *Evening Post* replied: "A more genuine, conservative, comprehensive, sound politico-economic, and above all, Union speech could not have been made by Thomas Jefferson himself."

The good will and loyalty expressed by Lamar and other Southern leaders in the new Congress were well received in the North. Nationwide revulsion against the scandals of the Grant Administration endangered Republican control of the government. With a scarcity of things about which the party might boast, except that it had "won the war," Republican Congressional leaders were soon reduced to waving the bloody shirt in an effort to stir up for their own benefit the sectional animosities Lamar had tried to allay. One such occasion was a violent interchange in the House between Blaine, who had Presidential ambitions, and Ben Hill of Georgia over a bill that would have provided amnesty to all ex-Confederates. By an impassioned and unusually effective speech, designed to counteract Blaine's manuever, Lamar pleaded for harmony and "a restored and fraternal Union," thereby doing much to avert serious damage to the cause of reconciliation.

Meanwhile there were occasional outbreaks of violence in

the South, caused by extremists on both sides. One such incident occurred in Hamburg, South Carolina, in July 1876, where several persons were killed. There was an attempt to make political capital out of the incident in the House, but here again Lamar's words had a calming effect.

Meanwhile there had been a growing demand that Lamar be advanced to the Senate to succeed James Alcorn. The movement grew so strong that a party caucus in Mississippi in January 1876, nominated Lamar unanimously, and a few days later a joint session of the two houses of the legislature elected him with only a scattering of opposing votes. He was to take his seat in 1877.

Lamar took a leading part in the Presidential campaign of the summer and fall of 1876 that found Democratic Governor Samuel J. Tilden of New York running against Republican Governor Rutherford B. Hayes of Ohio. It was the first opportunity since the war for Mississippi to participate freely in a Presidential election without the supervision of Federal troops. In Mississippi the Democrats scored a complete victory, winning all six Congressional seats and casting the state's electoral votes for Tilden.

In the contested Presidential election, Lamar, as a member of the House, did what he could to assure justice for Tilden. He voted to set up the nonpartisan Election Commission, but when its actions became obviously partisan, he voted against accepting the Commission's report in favor of Hayes. In the crisis that followed, Lamar was the leading Southern negotiator in drafting the bargain that saved the day for the nation—and for the South.

The diary and papers of Rutherford B. Hayes have shed considerable light on the origin and nature of the "Bargain of '77" and of Lamar's dominant role in it. In December of 1876, Hayes wrote that he and Colonel William H. Roberts, a New Orleans editor, had discussed the matter. Roberts called upon Hayes to give him "the views of Lamar of Mississippi, Walthall, ditto, Wade Hampton of South Carolina, and probably General Gordon of Georgia." Then Roberts came to the point. "You will be President," he said. "We will not make trouble. We want peace. We want the color line abolished. We will not oppose an administration which will favor an honest administration and honest officers in the South." Not the least intriguing feature of the Roberts declaration is the statement that the color line in Southern politics was invented by the Northern Republicans as a means of discriminating against the Southern whites.

In February 1877, in the final, critical stages of the bargaining, Hayes invited Lamar to a private meeting at his Ohio home, where mutual commitments were made. Lamar's support of the compromise and Hayes' acceptance of it created difficulties for both with their respective supporters. It was soon obvious in Mississippi, however, that Lamar had taken the best possible course for the South. Shortly after his election, Hayes, not without some sharp reminders from Lamar, was true to his promises. Federal troops were recalled from Florida, Louisiana, and South Carolina, and the Carpetbag politicians were retired to private life, or at least to political offices in other states.

Even after Hayes was inaugurated, there still remained the question of whether Lamar would be seated in the Senate. No former high-ranking Confederate had yet become a Senator. Georgia's Alexander Stephens, elected earlier to that body, had been denied his seat. Some Republicans were charging that the Mississippi elections had been marked by intimidation. Lamar, however, had strong support, both in Mississippi and in Washington, from blacks as well as whites, Republicans as well as Democrats. Many Negroes had voted the Democratic ticket, and Hiram R. Revels, a former Negro Senator from Mississippi, had written to Grant and told him so. In the end, after a brief dispute, Lamar was permitted to take his seat. Worthy of note is the fact that the Senator from Mississippi was aided by the timely parliamentary maneuvering of James G. Blaine, now a Senator from Maine and traditionally a Republican waver of bloody shirts.

Lamar spent the summer of 1877 resting at his Oxford home.

In August he attended, as a delegate from his county, the Democratic State Convention at Jackson. His efforts, as usual, were directed toward party harmony, state and national, and he advised the party to permit Negro participation.

One of Lamar's greatest speeches offended many people in his own state. In 1873, Congress had suspended the coinage of the silver dollar, which had been out of circulation for forty years, thanks to a scarcity of silver. By the late seventies, the silver supply had greatly increased, and a restoration of the silver dollar would have resulted in the coining of dollars containing less than a dollar's worth of silver. This would have created inflation—something the debtor classes wanted. Such doings seemed to many, including Lamar, dishonest; it would have permitted the redemption of obligations in a devaluated currency. Times were hard, however, and many persons seized on the device as an inflationary, antidepression step.

The Mississippi Legislature requested the state's senators and representatives in Congress to support the bill for silver inflation. Lamar's speech came when he informed the Congress of his instructions and then proceeded to state his reasons for not following them. While his vote against the bill drew an implied rebuke from the Legislature, which passed a resolution praising the Negro Senator, Blanche K. Bruce, for his support, there was general admiration for Lamar's integrity. There was irony in the fact that he endangered his political career to support payment in gold of Federal war debts incurred in defeating the South, while many Northern Senators, with an eye on the ballot box, heeded popular clamor and pushed the bill through to passage. Already the "Redeemers" seemed to be turning into "Bourbons," as the conservative pro-industrial element in the South soon came to be called.

Lamar did not find his course easy. In a letter to a friend he wrote, "It is indeed a heavy cross," he said, "to lay upon the heart of a public man to have to take a stand which causes the love and confidence of the constituents to flow away from him. But the lilberty of this country and its great interests will never be secure if its public men become the mere menials to do the biddings of their constituents instead of being representatives in the true sense of the word, looking to the lasting prosperity and future interests of the whole country." Nearly two decades later, Lamar's party was going to heed another leader who spoke of a cross—"a cross of gold." He was young William Jennings Bryan, who had gone all the way from free silver to the horror of the Southern conservative element but to the delight of the rising Southern demagogues.

The South was slowly regaining its position in the government and the nation, but there were periodic flare-ups in Congress of sectional feeling, often as a cloak for political scheming. Lamar stood firmly for his section but worked for harmony. His ability to think on his feet in extemporaneous Congressional debate frequently enabled him to repulse fierce attacks. He defeated an attempt by Maine's Republican Senator Blaine to revive the question of Negro voting and Southern election practices. Blaine's action arose from a Northern uneasiness at the emergence of the Solid South—solidly Democratic, that is. The blame, of course, was correctly laid at the door of the Republican party and its Radical Reconstruction policies. In a fierce barb directed at the Radicals, Lamar observed that Blaine would have done the race problem service had he and the Republicans proposed "some well-devised scheme of public education by which this newly enfranchised race may be fitted to exercise their great duties as freemen and citizens and as participants in the sovereignty of Commonwealths."

In March 1879, Lamar reacted swiftly to a bloody-shirt speech by Senator George F. Hoar of Massachusetts comparing Jefferson Davis to Aaron Burr and Benedict Arnold. "Jefferson Davis," said Senator Lamar, "stands in precisely the position that I stand in, that every Southern man who believed in the right of a State to secede stands. The only difference between myself and Jefferson Davis is that his exalted character, his pre-eminent talents, his well-established reputation as a statesman, as a patriot, and as a soldier, enabled him to take the lead in a cause to which I consecrated myself. . . . Jefferson Davis is honored among the Southern people. He did only what they sought to do; he was simply chosen to lead them in a cause which we all cherished. . . . The people of the South drank their inspiration from the fountain of devotion to liberty and to constitutional government." Later in the same debate Lamar expressed his gratitude for the generosity "of the victorious section in its treatment of the section that was conquered." The reunited nation was a "great, imposing and inspiring spectacle." Shrewd Southern orators like Lamar had long ago learned that the best answer to the waving of the bloody shirt was the waving of the flag.

Later in a bitter senatorial debate on a military appropriation bill to forbid use of Federal troops in controlling Southern elections, Lamar tangled with Senator Roscoe Conkling of New York. Conkling replied angrily, "Should the member from Mississippi, except in the presence of the Senate, charge me, by intimidation or otherwise, with falsehood, I would denounce him as a blackguard, as a coward, and a liar." To this Lamar answered, "I have only to say that the Senator from New York understood me correctly. I did mean to say just precisely the words and all they imported. I beg pardon of the Senate for the unparliamentary language. It was very harsh; it was very severe; it was such as no good man would deserve, and no brave man would bear."

"In the dead silence that followed Lamar's subtle and fatal stab," reported the Washington *Capital*, "Conkling was to the last degree unnerved and confused. . . . The point to the whole affair, however, is the fact that the terrible thrust came from the coolest, politest, and most self-controlled member of the Senate. Lamar, of Mississippi, has been noted for his courteous bearing in both public and private life." Lamar was indeed slow to anger, but under attack he could be deadly. No longer did he wave aloft pieces of furniture, as he had done in the Oxford courthouse during a Klan trial in 1871. He had now learned to flail with words.

Yet Lamar could still go beyond verbal combat. On one occasion Senator O. D. Conger of Michigan made an insulting personal reference to him in a speech. The next day Lamar walked over to Conger, looked him straight in the eye, and said, "Conger, you are always talking about fighting, but never fight; that's where you and I are a good deal unlike. I don't talk about fighting, but I am ready for it any time." Conger said nothing and Lamar walked back to his seat. Senator Conger's subsequent references to Lamar were remarkably temperate.

While Lamar was vigilant in the Senate in upholding the position of his state and region in a restored Union, he labored in Mississippi when Congress was not in session to keep peace among the divergent elements in his party and to create national as well as sectional unity. In 1879 there was real danger that some of the "unreconstructed" Bourbon Democrats would not only precipitate a split in the party (with the result that the Republicans might regain control) but provoke a revival of sectional feeling. In many respects Lamar was a Bourbon of the Bourbons, but he parted company with them when they forgot their moderation of '76. The Bourbons, he said, "unwisely invite upon themselves and the State a restoration of the evils from which, since Democratic supremacy was established, we have been slowly recovering by means of conservatism and moderation." For the time being, his influence was strong enough to keep his party united and the conservative faction in control of the state.

In 1879 the strain of a summer of campaigning and speech making, followed in October by the death of his mother in Macon, Georgia, caused Lamar to suffer from one of his periodic apoplectic attacks. He did not take his seat in the Senate until February 1880. Even then he wrote his wife, "I am easily fatigued, and writing makes my head swim. My arm is heavy and weak, but I have thrown aside my crutches and walk with a stick."

In Washington the artificer of reconciliation had an opportunity to launch an attack on an attempted revival of the racial issue, specifically in a speech by Senator William Windom of Minnesota. Lamar's rebuttal Senator Hoar of Massachusetts called "the very best speech that could possibly be made on that side of the question." A Washington correspondent observed:

> The influence wielded in Congress by Colonel Lamar is peculiar and wonderful, and it is fair to say that no man's utterances are so attentively regarded and considered by the members of all parties in both Houses. . . . If it is known that he is to speak, the galleries are crowded; every official of the capitol deserts his office for the Senate Chamber; while all the members of the House of Representatives who can get away from their own hall are found on the floor of the Senate . . . each man feeling that, in the remarks that are falling from the lips of the distinguished Mississippian, his peculiar political faith or belief is receiving the strongest possible support, or is being entirely undermined and crushed.

That summer Lamar rested at Oxford. His health was poor. "I am so liable to attacks of vertigo that I cannot prepare a detailed speech. I cannot study documents without a painful swimming in the head, nor bend over to write without a rush of blood to the brain."

More serious, his wife was quite ill with tuberculosis. "I have been in the room of my invalid wife for twenty-one days," he wrote "scarce an hour of which she has spent in freedom from pain." Yet he took part in the election campaign of 1880, in which the Democratic Presidential candidate, W. S. Hancock of Pennsylvania, was defeated by James A. Garfield of Ohio. Whatever the fortunes of his party, Lamar, as a Mississippi newspaper observed, stood as "a great, central, conservative power in himself, able to repel force with force when the attack is directed against his people, able to restrain impolitic impetuosity when his own people rush to the attack. In heart, in interest, in high commission, a Mississippian, he is a great national conservator of the peace, whose sphere and influence are almost limitless."

Yet Lamar had some opposition, especially from extremists who opposed his moderate attitude toward the North. These hotheads still remembered his active role in the Bargain of '77 that had made Hayes President and his conservative stand in the silver coinage controversy. In 1881, he voted to give a pension to General Grant. In fact, Lamar was the only Southern Democratic Senator to speak in support of the bill. In the state legislative elections of that year Lamar's Senate seat was at stake. Had he alienated his Mississippi constituents? The answer came in unmistakable terms. His supporters were swept into office, and Lamar was re-elected when the Legislature convened in January, 1882. Among the legislators who voted for him was the black Republican, J. A. Shorter.

Lamar returned to the Senate to become embroiled in the first sustained Democratic attack on the protective tariff since the hegemony in national affairs of the prewar Democrats. In the sixties the Republicans had risen to power in the industrial east with promises of a high protective tariff. Once levied, the tariff not only remained, it increased; for Big Business would not hear to a curtailment.

By 1883, when the Democrats won control of the House of Representatives, Lamar was ready to launch a vigorous attack. The New York *Evening Post*, reporting the substance of Lamar's first oratorical assault on the tariff, pointed out how Lamar had sarcastically observed that the United States was "probably the only country in the world whose people were severely and superfluously taxed . . . because their rulers were unable to devise a mode of reducing that taxation." Lamar also denounced the practice of "paying bounties to certain business interests" in the form of the tariff, thus making American industry "dependent for existence, not upon the natural development of resources and the natural growth of industries, but upon taxation by the government."

Perhaps no less fateful than the tariff speech in its significance was Lamar's forthright defense of Federal aid to public education in an address on March 28, 1884. It is startling to note that the South, which in the ante-bellum period and again in the troubled mid-twentieth century would have few words of favor for Federal aid to education, should produce vigorous affirmation of such a policy in the 1880's by a supposedly conservative leader. Lamar spoke enthusiastically for a bill to permit temporary aid to public schools, mostly in the South. Constitutional objections he cast aside in welcoming what he felt would bring "unspeakable benefits" to the entire population of the South, white and black.

Prior to the Civil War the South's system of private colleges, schools, and academies had made public education a sometime thing. But the double economic blows of War and Reconstruction had pulled the financial rug from under private schooling in most parts of the South. When Carpetbag governments brought public schools to the South, there was at first bitter resistance. Schools were burned and schoolmasters driven out of town, for the public schools set up by the Radicals were largely for Negroes and the white taxpayer had to foot the bill. Then, when Reconstruction was ended, the destitute Southerner suddenly realized that if he were to educate his children at all, the task had to be performed at public expense. Not always were these schools, either for Negroes or whites, given adequate financial support, for money was lacking. But public schools were almost universally accepted, and became the educational novitiate for Southern whites of all classes: the tenant farmer and the planter, the worker and the industrial leader.

Probably never before in the turbulent history of American public schooling had democracy in education come nearer achievement among the whites. In the eighties a Massachusetts educator described the Southern public school as "the most favorable, the most persistent, the most devoted public school now in any part of the world." The first school integration ever to be known in the South was not a racial one but a social one. Wherever else the Southerner maintained his sense of class, he lost it in the public school as few Americans ever had before.

Not many Southerners were conscious of what was really happening. As much as anything else it was a matter of an economic determinant known as "impoverishment"; but it happened. Certainly L. Q. C. Lamar must have understood. "Now," he observed in his remarks to the Senate, "the common school system has become the indispensable factor in diffusing education generally throughout the South." And Lamar felt that universal schooling could do for the Negro what it was doing for the white. While his support of the Federal subsidy was predicated largely upon the aid it could give the white man in the financial support of Negro schools, Lamar observed that "this bill is a decided step toward the solution of the problem of race."

Back in Mississippi, Lamar's personal affairs were complicated by the worsening condition of Mrs. Lamar. She died at Oxford in December 1884, before Lamar could reach home. He wrote to his sister: "The present is a dark period of my life. The pale face of my wife is ever before me, and my grief seems to have fixed itself in my heart." Two years later, in January 1887, Lamar was married to Henrietta Holt, widow of General William S. Holt, former president of the Southwestern Railroad Company. The second Mrs. Lamar, wealthy and socially prominent in Washington, was a native of Macon, Georgia and Lamar had known her since boyhood.

Lamar returned to Washington in 1885, to find he might be appointed to the Cabinet by the incoming President, Grover Cleveland, the first Democrat elected to the office since the Civil War. Lamar did not seek the post—that of Secretary of the Interior—and he accepted it with some reluctance, knowing full well that President Cleveland by appointing a Southerner would probably join Jeff Davis on the "sour apple tree." But Cleveland was not a man to be deterred by fear of public reaction.

Lamar wrote Davis:

> I hope that the step I am about to take will meet your approval. It certainly proceeds from no motive of ambition; but when pressed by my friends in the Senate and in the House, and through the country, and by those nearest to the President-elect, to take a posi-

tion in his Cabinet, I have hardly felt at liberty to decline. If, by conducting the affairs of the executive department prudently and honestly and fairly to all sections, I may serve the interests of a common country, I may do more good than I have ever yet been able to accomplish. . . . Recent events have crushed out all ambition in my heart, and I now have no other desire connected with public affairs except to serve to the best the interests that our people have entrusted to me so often. . . . I am inclined to think I ought to have retired when I saw the South restored to her Constitutional position in the Union. . . . I have always though it was a serious blemish, or rather a defect, in our American statesmen, that they always cling to office too long.

The Senate confirmed Lamar as Secretary of the Interior, despite some opposition, and most Northern newspapers approved, with the New York *Times* commending Lamar's "original and thoughtful mind, conservative habit, and sobriety of judgment," and it observed that in the new Cabinet member "the President secures a good adviser and an administrative officer whose deep-rooted aversion to such doubtful and devious ways as have of late caused the Interior Department to be made the subject of unfavorable comment cannot fail to have a wholesome effect."

Lamar soon impressed the nation with the efficiency of his administration. He had the Southern Redeemer's sense of economy. He even cut down sharply on the numerous horses and carriages maintained for the use of Department employees. Lamar was conscientious in the administration of public lands, and he vigorously pushed civil service reform. He scrupulously backed the actions of his subordinates, even if he questioned their judgment. The Mississippi Negro Ex-Senator Bruce later recalled how Lamar for some time paid from his own pocket the salary of a black cleaning woman who had been discharged by the Department and for whom Bruce interceded. Lamar did not want to interfere in the handling of the incident by a Department official, but he was anxious that the woman should not be in want.

Lamar's administration of the Interior Department received

national acclaim. The Washington *Post* called him "the brainiest, most logical, and clear-headed" Secretary ever to fill the post. The Augusta (Georgia) *Constitutionalist* described him as "the most fascinating member of the Cabinet, the most active, hard working and industrious. So far he has completely put to the sword all predictions that he would be a scholastic dreamer and moody talker."

One of Lamar's best known addresses was made in April 1887, at Charleston, South Carolina, on the occasion of the unveiling of a monument to John C. Calhoun. Into the speech Lamar poured all of his lifetime study of the Southern viewpoint on the American political system as enunciated by Calhoun, together with the conclusions appropriate to the facts of American history since Calhoun's death. It was, in a way, Lamar's valedictory political speech. It was heard and applauded by thousands and read by other thousands over the nation. In his address Lamar paid tribute to the accomplishments of the "lion-hearted" Wade Hampton and felt that old John C. Calhoun would be happy to see South Carolina restored to "dignity and equality in the Union." South Carolina would sacrifice no principle and falsify no sentiment "in accepting the verdict" and would "henceforth . . . seek the happiness of her people, their greatness and glory, in the greatness and glory of the American Republic."

In December, President Cleveland nominated Lamar to the United States Supreme Court. It was an honor that had been rumored for some months and had at first been almost universally applauded. A small group of Republican politicians and newspapers, however, sought to make political capital of the matter and gained some support from party members. Lamar did not wish to continue in the Cabinet while his nomination was being considered, lest it be thought he was in position to influence Senators about to vote on his confirmation; so he resigned.

The Republican Cincinnati *Commercial Gazette* declared that "the Supreme Court is in danger as well as the Senate of the

United States." Similarly, the Cleveland *Leader* argued: "Little ground now remains for the South to win back in order to regain all its lost prestige and posts of honor and emolument. The Army and Navy will doubtless soon be attacked by the Democrats in behalf of the ex-Confederate officers." Some of the opposition to Lamar came from extremists in his own party. The Jackson *New Mississippian*, an unyielding paper, complained of "the extraordinary conservative course which he had pursued at Washington, the preference which he has shown to the Grand Army of the Republic, and the tenderness with which he has dealt with the negro Republicans from Mississippi."

The Richmond *Whig* characterized Lamar as "the peer of any man upon the Supreme Bench," despite the "silly charges that have been made against him by malignants." He was "equal to any of them in patriotism and devotion to the Union and the Constitution." When Lamar was finally approved in January 1888, a few Republicans actually joined the Democratic minority in order to make the confirmation possible.

Nevada's Senator William M. Stewart was one of the Republicans who voted for Lamar's confirmation. "The beneficial results of that action of the Senate," said Stewart, "were immediately felt both North and South. Confidence, respect and good fellowship were increased in every section of our common country. It was an object lesson for the world. It marked the contrast between the methods of despotic governments, which never forgive a fallen foe, and our own free government, which, entertaining malice toward none, has charity for all."

Lamar's characteristic modesty caused him to write his son-in-law that he hesitated to accept the nomination, feeling unequal to the position. "I had no more idea of it than I had of the dukedom of Argyle. . . . I have been too long out of the atmosphere of practical jurisprudence, and my misgivings are so painful that I have sleepless nights."

From the day in January 1888, when he assumed his place on the Court at the age of sixty-three, Lamar took an active part in its work. He early attracted attention by the courage and wisdom of his opinions and the force and clarity with which they were expressed. Chief Justice W. M. Fuller said Lamar's was "the most suggestive mind that I ever knew, and not one of us but has drawn from its inexhaustible store." For two years Lamar applied himself vigorously to this new role, and even after 1890, when he was increasingly troubled by illness and failing strength, he conscientiously continued to serve.

In December 1892, Lamar and his wife set out to visit Pass Christian on the Mississippi Gulf Coast. Enroute he suffered a heart attack. At the home of Captain W. H. Virgin, a son-in-law of Mrs. Lamar, in Macon in his native state of Georgia, among friends and relatives, he died quietly on January 23, 1893. He was buried in Macon. Later his body was moved to the cemetery of St. Peter's Episcopal Church in Oxford, Mississippi.

To the grave he bore in his right hand a copy of the United States Constitution he had carried with him for many years. To many that document had been a holy thing. Some had worshipped it; some had called it, as to a saint, to do their special bidding; some had presumed to interpret it as they would Scripture; and some had considered it entirely capable of working miracles. Perhaps all were right. Certainly Lamar's veneration for it was something more than a lawyer's quest for ultimate law or a politician's last resort for winning arguments. For Lamar it could work miracles—miracles of reconciliation. It was itself a "bundle of compromises," as any student of the founding of the Republic knows. It had been begotten in reconciliation of faction with faction; and there its strength and its inspiration to Americans, North and South, would lie. Lamar had lived with this Constitution for years, carrying it as it were, next to his heart, as soldiers do Testaments to ward off bullets. When the Union was sundered in '61, he would have no new constitution, only the old one kept inviolate like a cherished relic. When the Union was restored in '65, he could see no other course but a rigid adherence to the ancient gospel which had reconciled a disunited Republic in 1787 and must become the only workable basis for the reconciliation of a divided Union scarcely a century later.

Lamar had not only *lived* with this Constitution; he had become like it. "Until the hour of his death," said the New York *Illustrated American*, "Lamar meant to the South the voice that had stilled faction, restored Constitutional right; to the North the intellect that had penetrated the darkness of Northern doubt. . . . It is as the inspired pacificator that Lamar will stand out unique, almost incomprehensible, to other times . . . ." Like his beloved Constitution, he had become the artificer of reconciliation.

SUGGESTIONS FOR FURTHER READING

Cate, Wirt Armistead. *Lucius Q. C. Lamar: Secession and Reunion.* New York: Russell and Russell, 1969.

Mayes, Edward. *Lucius Q. C. Lamar: His Life, Times, and Speeches.* Nashville, Tenn.: Publishing House of the Methodist Episcopal Church, South, 1896.

Murphy, James B. *L. Q. C. Lamar: Pragmatic Patriot.* Baton Rouge: Louisiana State University Press, 1973.

Sibley, Samuel Hale. *Georgia's Contribution to the Law: The Lamars.* New York: Newcomen Society of England, American Branch, 1948.

William Alexander Percy
1885–1942

Mississippi's
Renaissance Man

BY LOUIS DOLLARHIDE

The ideal of the Renaissance Man was set forth by early humanists as a goal toward which educators and rulers alike pointed their charges. This ideal gentleman is aptly summarized by Ophelia after her harrowing experience with the antic Hamlet:

O, what a noble mind is here o'erthrown!
The courtier's, soldier's scholar's eye, tongue, sword;
Th'expectancy and rose of the fair state,
The glass of fashion and the mould of form,
Th'observed of all observers, quite, quite down!

Sir Philip Sidney, in the public mind, approached this ideal, but he died young, before his mettle was really tested. Sir Walter Raleigh and the Earl of Essex both decorated Elizabeth's court; but one let his own vanity and his philandering, and the other, his ambition lose them the great queen's favor. One remained in the Tower long enough to write a history of the world; and the other ended his tumultuous life, quite young, on the chopping block on Tower Hill.

Sir Thomas More, who helped project this ideal of the gentleman with his humanist colleagues, with backward glances at the Romans Cicero and Quintillian and the Italian Castiglione, has himself been called a Man for All Seasons. And in many ways he represents supremely well the ideal of the humanist scholar-gentleman, even standing against his king on a matter of principle and faith and forfeiting his life thereby. The fact remains, however, that the Renaissance Gentleman, the creation of these early English humanists, the star for them and later generations to aspire toward, was an ideal, and as such never existed, fullbodied, in one single individual. But it has remained an ideal, perpetuated by centuries of educators, playwrights, poets, novelists and philosophers. And this image of the complete man has persisted to this day, especially in American and English schools as the aim of a liberal arts education. In fact, until very recently the requirements for the Rhodes Scholar, for example, might have been written by Dean Colet and Sir Thomas More themselves. With his characteristic self-deprecation, William Alexander Percy might well have smiled if someone had called him a Renaissance Man; but in his relatively short life of fifty-six years, he lived above the ordinary for those verities like honor and honesty, truth, courage, duty, love of learning, the hallmarks of the ideal humanist-gentleman.

By the time young William Alexander Percy could remember, both branches of his kin were reckoned "good family," so securely placed there was little reason to question the fact, never proud in an arrogant sense of the parvenu but assured, with nothing that really needed to be proved. Born on May 14, 1885, he was the only child of Camille Bourges and Senator LeRoy Percy of Greenville, Mississippi, the home he was to leave so often in order to return. The Bourges grandparents were French from New Orleans, but just as French "as if they had landed the day before yesterday from Lyon or Tours." Mère, the grandmother, lorded it over Père, who was merely "bon bourgeois," because she claimed descent, her grandson thought on small evidence, from an extravagantly romantic Générelly de Rinaldi. The Percys themselves, by the time young Will was in the line of descent, were also established as "good family," part French from a great, great grandmother, whose flamboyant husband, called Don Carlos, arrived below Natchez with his own ship, a load of slaves, and a Spanish land grant. Mystery, never resolved by an older Will Percy, lay behind this first Percy.

Searching for the qualifications for admission into this "post-Civil-War aristocracy" Will was later to rule out pedigree and wealth, and to consider, perhaps, an established way of life for several generations, a tradition of living, a style and pattern of thinking and feeling not acquired but inherited. "No matter how it came about the Percys and the Bourges were nice people—" he wrote, "and that is what I breathed in as a child, the certainty I was as good as anyone else, which, because of the depth of the convictions, was unconscious, never talked of, never thought of."

In many ways he lived a charmed and golden childhood, loved and watched over by two sets of grandparents, a loving and careful mother and father, and family retainers, who spoiled him terribly. Sheltered by a warmth of family, he was surrounded with music and reading and infinite time to play with the children of servants and his cousins. Perhaps his independence of mind and character first asserted itself most noticeably when, at fifteen, he was taken by his mother and father to enter the preparatory school at Sewanee. After the departure of his parents, he took one look at the military uniforms the prep boys had to wear, and hating everything military, he decided the prep school was not for him. He took and passed the college entrance examination to the University of the South. There followed four enchanted years in the mountains of Tennessee, as he grew in knowledge, friendships, and vision, if not in physical stature and age. Always a small man, he compensated for physical size and vigor with courage, great charm, and friendliness. To those who knew him, he always stood taller than he knew.

After he graduated from Sewanee "with good grades," his father and mother, thinking he looked overworked and thin, accompanied him to Paris, where they secured him a modest flat furnished with a piano and less than modest furnishings. Then they departed, leaving him alone for his year in Europe. He was nineteen, an American with a modest stipend to live on, who spoke little French, and who didn't know a soul in Europe. But he learned and he listened and he explored every detail of Paris. Mary Garden sang Melisande and Louise. Bernhardt was still doing Tosca and Phèdre. And Rejane was appearing "with exquisite style," in plays on "the eternal French theme," which were a trifle "disturbing to his American Puritanism." He visited Italy and even made his way to Egypt. In fact, he was to write years later, ". . . for a year I ate and walked and lived and slept with loneliness, until she was so familiar I came not to hate her but to know whatever happened in however many after years she alone would be faithful to me. . . and would always return. And that perhaps is the only important thing I learned that year. What must be learned at last had as well be learned early."

Back home, confronted with the uninteresting prospect of earning a livelihood, he chose without any great enthusiasm the family profession, the law; but again he asserted his independence by not going to the University of Virginia. With no deeper motive than the fact that Boston was close by, he asked his father to send him to the Harvard Law School. There for three years he performed what was expected of one to receive a law degree, but his cherished memories were of Caruso, Geraldine Farrar, Louise Homer, and the "divine Fremstadt with her head high . . . as though she had just stepped from the porch of the Erechtheum." And the great Boston Symphony. Law was for him "a dash of cold water, a first film of nacre for a very shell-less oyster." And as for his going north, his primary motive from the beginning was that he wanted "to be near Boston with its music and theaters, which he would miss the rest of his life in his future Southern home."

He returned to Greenville in 1909.

In the years that followed, Will Percy settled uneasily, if obediently, predestinately, into the social milieu of his river town. Joining his father's law firm, he worked steadily, if without great enthusiasm, and considered himself a distressing social failure. His best moments were spent taking long walks along the "high levee," loving the dark river and its mysteries, observing at different seasons the willows growing down to the water's edge on the Arkansas side, a state almost as familiar to him as Montana. In these long walks he was joined by three friends who also liked to walk the levee, Will Francis, Lynne Starling, and George Roth, about whom he was to write years later they "are with me still." And about this time he began to work seriously at poetry partly because of the influence of a lonely teacher, Miss Caroline Stern, and partly because he felt the need of some private form of self-expression. Because he had been literary editor of the school magazine at Sewanee some of his early verses came back to haunt him, and one poem, to his surprise, was accepted by *McClure's*. He had even given a small thought to becoming a writer, but could not face his father with such an outlandish idea. And so the law. He wrote his poetry in his lone times because he was always "aware in the act of putting words to paper" that what he felt and thought" had been felt and thought by thousands in every generation." "Only that conviction," he wrote, "would have permitted me to publish without feeling guilty of indecent exposure." Miss Carrie and other friends, his long walks along the high levee, his poetry sustained him during the lonely years after 1909.

But the lonely years—and all of his years were, in a way, lonely—but they were not empty years, not for Will Percy. When United States Senator from Mississippi McLaurin died suddenly while on a bird hunt in Arkansas, the selection of a successor fell to an election in the State House of Representatives. With the encouragement of friends and family, LeRoy Percy was persuaded to stand against James K. Vardaman, whom Will described as "a kindly, vain demogogue, unable to think and given to emotions he considered noble." Through various maneuvers, the old process of divide and conquer, LeRoy Percy emerged as the new senator, a position he filled with dignity and statesmanship. But when he stood for re-election, once more he was faced by the Great White Chief, James K. Vardaman, who had made a good governor for the state and "craved public office because the spot-light was his passion and because, eternally in need of money, he abhorred work." The race was emotionally harrowing for all concerned. For the first time the issue of race was was inserted into Mississippi politics as a major issue. Vardaman stood for the "poor whites against the 'nigger'—these were his qualifications as a statesman."

After this bad experience Will, his mother and his father made a trip to Europe, which took them, among other places, to Greece. When war broke out in Europe in 1914, Will joined Herbert Hoover's Commission for Relief in Belgium; and despite his customary self-deprecation and irony, served two years with distinction, getting food and medical supplies to the Belgians and placating the invading Germans. Back home in 1916 he faced his being turned down for officers training for being thirty-five pounds underweight with his usual determination. He went on a crash diet of rich foods for a month, then on the day of his re-examination filled himself with bananas and water. He tipped the scales at the required weight and thus entered officers training at Leon Springs, Texas, where he was relegated to the pee-wee squad, the smallest men in the training program. Because he spoke French, most of his work was liaison, but before the war ended he saw service in Flanders. And again despite his customary demurrers, he returned home a captain with a Croix de Guerre with a gold and a silver star. Whatever he did, he seemed to feel, was never quite enough or brilliant enough, or even sufficient.

Two of the real tests of his courage, will power and leadership came in the decade after the war. First, in 1922, the creeping poison of bigotry and malice emerged in Atlanta in the form of the revival of the Ku Klux Klan. The Percys and other Delta folks, reading about it, felt as though it was happening in a foreign country. It could never happen in their own town. One day, however, it was announced abroad that a "Colonel" Camp was to speak in their own courthouse. What should they do? Close the courthouse to him? Instead, the town leaders, including Will Percy and his father attended the meeting. On the appointed night, the Colonel, instead of attacking Negroes and Jews, the most popular targets, chose to turn his vitriol against

Catholics. This, Will thought, was strange since there were only a handful of Catholics in the town, including him and his mother. But according to the Colonel, there was a Popish Plot to take over the country. "It was an example," Will wrote, "of Nazi propaganda before there were Nazis." After the Colonel had been listened to with "courtesy" Senator Percy, to the Colonel's great surprise, answered him. "I never heard a speech that was so exciting and so much fun," Will Percy later recounted. "The crowd rocked and cheered. Father's ridicule was amusing but bitter; and as he continued it wasn't funny, it was terrifying." At the close of the Senator's speech the crowd "went quite mad, surging about and shouting and cheering, and thoroughly dangerous." A resolution was passed condemning the Klan. The terrified "Colonel" Camp "scuttled" out a side door and appealed to a deputy, a genial Irish Catholic, for protection and was escorted to his hotel. But the Klan, like a seeping poison, persisted, never openly in Greenville, but its presence was felt. Catholic employees were fired, and several Catholic merchants were boycotted. There were never hooded marches, never cross burnings; but across the river at Mer Rouge in Louisiana atrocity murders were committed. And the body politic of the once united town disintegrated.

As the Senator spoke and wrote against the Klan, speaking as far north as Chicago, and becoming head of the Protestant anti-Klan committee, he was singled out, to his son's deep distress, for special hatred. One rainy night what proved to be an attempted kidnapping by the violent crowd across the river was foiled by the timely arrival of the Senator's three "bridge-playing cronies." The real struggle came to a head when the Klan tried to elect a sheriff, an effort defeated by a hectic campaign and the election of George B. Alexander. Years later an old Klansman was to ask Will Percy why he had never forgiven him. His answer was: "Forgiveness is easy. I really like you. The trouble is I've got your number and people's numbers don't change."

The other great trial of strength and courage was the great

flood of 1927, a "torrent ten feet deep the size of New Jersey." It was "thirty-six hours coming and four months going; it was deep enough to drown a man, swift enough to upset a boat, and lasting long enough to cancel a crop year." It was the greatest flood in the country's history. In 1973 the river rose higher, but by then the protection of the levees had become a duty of the Army Corps of Engineers. But in 1927 there was no such thing as a national flood control program. And the Delta was almost totally unprepared for the months of flooding ahead. With his experience as a relief agent in Belgium, Will Percy was appointed by the Greenville mayor as Chairman of the Flood Relief Committee and the Red Cross. He was charged with rescuing, housing, and feeding sixty thousand human beings and thirty thousand head of livestock. Appeals to friends in the North brought in ten thousand dollars, and to the nation, millions, and tents, bedding, and food. And with the Red Cross moneys came Red Cross personnel from Washington, "trained, patient, and easy to work with." In tribute to the help received, Will Percy wrote, "Whenever you are just about to decide that Americans are selfish, unpatriotic, and unintelligent, they prove themselves the most liberal and lovable people in the world. You just can't stay disgusted with them."

June was looked forward to as a respite in the flood. The river always fell in June. But this time it fell a foot, reversed itself and rose higher. And only during the last week of August did the river "crawl back to its bed through the trail of slime and desolation." At this point an exhausted Will Percy left things in the hands of Fleetwood Farish, his future law partner, and the Red Cross and sailed for Japan. But his conclusions on the effect of the flood were characteristically acute. God Almighty had used an extreme way of uniting their town again. "If out of the 1927 flood our people learned mutual helpfulness instead of the tenets of the Klan, our farmers learned the cultivation of alfalfa [suggested by Hoover as a fall feed crop], our Negroes learned how to avoid pellagra [by eating cheap salmon brought in by the Red Cross], and our government learned the necessity of flood control, we Delta folks will have to pronounce that flood an unqualified success."

Two years after the flood, "mercifully" within a few weeks of one another, his mother and then the Senator died, leaving Will an unencumbered plantation of over 3,000 acres and a continuing law practice. He might have continued his bachelor's life of making the plantation a model farm, of writing his poetry, taking his long walks on the high levee, and travel had it not been for the fact that two years after his father's death his "favorite cousin" LeRoy Percy and his wife died, leaving three orphaned boys, Walker, 14; LeRoy, 13; and Phinizy, 9. With no hesitation, a matter of family duty, Will Percy brought the boys into his home, adopted them, and, wholly unaccustomed to dealing with young people, set about giving them the best chance in the world he was capable of. His house turned from a quiet retreat, though often a stopover for friends going north or south, into a place overrun by young people. For them he gave up largely his love of travel, the writing of poetry, and most of the other perquisites of a bachelor's life. To give them some foundation "out of his own darkness," he placed in their hands the Gospels "because even though written by simple men writing about events they did not witness they threw more light than darkness on the heart-shaking story they told"; and the *Meditations* of Marcus Aurelius because the self-communing of the Emperor "convince a man he never need be less than tight-lipped, courteous, and proud, though all in pain." But according to Walker Percy, now an eminent novelist and essayist, Uncle Will, as the boys called him, taught them much, much more. He taught them how to see, to read, to see colors, hear music, in short, to value every good thing in life. "About him," Walker Percy writes in the Introduction to the 1973 re-printing of *Lanterns on the Levee*, "I will say no more than that he was the most extraordinary man I have ever known and that I owe him a debt which cannot be paid."

During his relatively brief lifetime, William Alexander Percy travelled the world over, an inveterate traveller, partly going

.away because the best part, he said, was returning home, to Greenville. And he left as a kind of legacy the largest body of poetry published thus far by a Mississippian, and an extraordinary autobiography, *Lanterns on the Levee*. The poetry was his own, written, he said, for himself and published because he sensed in what he wrote sentiments common to all men in all times. Of his poetry, he wrote, "When you feel something intensely, you want to write it down—if anguish, to staunch the bleeding; if delight, to prolong the moment. When after years of pondering you feel you have discovered a new truth or an old one which suddenly for you has the excitement of a new one, you write a longish poem. To keep it free of irrelevant details you set it in some long-ago time, one, of course, you love and perhaps once lived in." He tried to make it "sound beautiful" and as "fitting" as possible. In all, he published four long volumes of poetry—*Sappho in Levkos*, 1915; *In April Once*, 1920; *Enzio's Kingdom*, 1924; *Selected Poems*, 1930; and after his death his executor, his "nephew," LeRoy Percy, brought together his poems, unedited, in *Collected Poems*, 1944. Interestingly, the young William Faulkner, reviewing the second volume, *In April Once*, for the University of Mississippi student paper, *The Mississippian*, came directly to the greatest weakness of the poems: they were old-fashioned. Whatever good qualities the poetry had, it belonged, Faulkner judged, among the Victorians. A reader today might even push them further back in time, say, to the early Romantics, particularly Wordsworth, except for the fact (and the young Faulkner detected this, because he was also being touched by the same influence) that some of them are as ardently sensuous as anything Swinburne ever wrote. Swinburne in a Wordsworthian form. Even when the first volume appeared in 1915, at the last gasp of the genteel tradition, the poems were already old-fashioned in diction and texture; and read today one can hardly believe Will Percy could have been as aloof from the poetic ferment of his own time. He numbered among his friends many poets, but he seems deliberately to have remained untouched by what was going on in the world of letters. He wrote little poetry after 1930. But T. S. Eliot had already published "Ash Wednesday." But, Percy maintained, he wrote the poetry for himself.

Lanterns on the Levee, Recollections of a Planter's Son was a different matter. If the poetry were written for himself, a form of self-expression, the autobiography was his Letter to the World, and as fate would have it, his envoi, for he lived only long enough to know that the book had been well-received by press and readers alike. He died the year after the publication of *Lanterns,* but he had already been struck down by a crippling stroke. Reading the book now, one cannot fail to apprehend that Will Percy rounded off the book intuitively, as an obituary, his own. The last chapter, entitled "Home," is a description of the old cemetery where family and friends had been laid to rest. Not knowing the state of Percy's health, another Mississippian, Herschel Brickell, in the *New York Times Book Review,* wondered at the fact that Percy was writing his autobiography at the age of 55. Brickell called the book "a work of exceptional merit and importance. The high quality of the prose would entitle it to consideration for a permanent place in our literature, and it has numerous other virtues as well." He felt that its "real significance . . . lies in the candor and completeness of the revelation of the Southern aristocrat's point of view." The very word "aristocrat," which appears so often in the pages of the book, was to turn critics away from the book then as it does now. But if it does so, the reader has not understood what William Alexander Percy stood for. His was not an aristocracy of wealth or what Walker Percy calls "genealogical games," but an aristocracy of the intellect, of taste and judgment, of honor and responsibility, closer to the concepts of a Plato than to any social register or order. Walker Percy puts this in other words: Will Percy's own aristocracy was a "meritocracy of character, talent, performance, and quality of life." To know his "uncle" was "to encounter a complete, articulated view of the world as tragic as it was noble." He speaks also of the "over all pessimism" of the book. And indeed Percy concludes the quotation above concerning the response of the American people to calamities with a sentence which undercuts the optimism of the praise: "What a pity they are not disciplined enough to survive!"

The book is melancholy, but it is a melancholy tempered by Aurelian acceptance. "Half a century," he writes near the close of his book, "is a long time, specially in a world as lovely as ours, as starred with brave and pitiful people with honey at their hearts and on their lips. No use remembering the ugly and the evil, they were never real anyway and nothing came of them. Evil is for the sunny side, to test the strength of the climbers, I suppose. It is easier to remember the good."

And he closes the book with his own kind of benediction. "Of all the hours of happiness granted to me, none has been so keen and holy as a few unpredictable moments alone. . . . As one comes beneath the tower, the High God descends and faces the wayfarer. He speaks three slow words: 'Who are you?' The pilgrim I know should be able to straighten his shoulders, to stand his tallest and to answer defiantly: 'I am your son.' "

William Alexander Percy was a man out of his time simply because he was, as Walker Percy calls him, "one of a kind." Small of stature, frail most of his life, he managed to embody in a time in which such virtues were not greatly cherished those of a Philip Sidney, a Thomas More, or a Hamlet before the fall. He was intelligent, courageous, dutiful, a lover of the true and the beautiful. We shall not often see his like again.

SELECTED BIBLIOGRAPHY

Percy, William Alexander. *Collected Poems.* New York: Alfred A. Knopf, 1943.
———. *Enzio's Kingdom and Other Poems.* New Haven: Yale University Press, 1924.
———. *In April Once.* New Haven: Yale University Press, 1920.
———. *Lanterns on the Levee: Recollections of a Planter's Son.* New York: Alfred A. Knopf, 1941.
———. *Of Silence and Stars.* Foreword by Hodding Carter. Greenville, Mississippi: Levee Press, 1953.

――――. *Sappho in Levkas and Other Poems*. New Haven: Yale University Press, 1915.

――――. *Selected Poems*. Preface by Llewellyn Jones. New Haven: Yale University Press, 1930.

――――, ed. *Poems of Arthur O'Shaughnessy*. New Haven: Yale University Press, 1923.

――――. *Birds and Beasts of the Greek Anthology* by Norman Douglas. New York: Jonathan Cape and Harrison Smith, 1929.

――――. *An Address Delivered Before the Friends of the Howard-Tilton Memorial Library of Tulane University in 1923*. San Francisco: The Ward Ritchie Press, 1944.

――――. *The Little Shepherd's Song*. Music by Wintter Watts. New York: Riccordi, 1922.

About William Alexander Percy

Carter, Hodding. "The Most Unforgettable Character I've Met." *Reader's Digest*, 61 (August 1952), 21–25.

Cohn, David. "Eighteenth Century Chevalier." *Virginia Quarterly Review*, 31 (1955), 561–575.

Percy, Walker. Introduction. *Lanterns on the Levee* by William Alexander Percy. Baton Rouge: Louisiana State University Press, 1973.

Richardson, Thomas. *William Alexander Percy: Lanterns on the Levee*. Jackson: Mississippi Library Commission, 1977.

Spalding, Phinizy. "Mississippi and the Poet: William Alexander Percy." *The Journal of Mississippi History*, (February 1965), 63–73.

Martin Sennett Conner
1891–1950

Governor Mike Conner and the Sales Tax, 1932

⟨ornament⟩

BY WILLIAM WINTER

EDITORS' NOTE

Martin Sennett Conner, governor of Mississippi from January 19, 1932, to January 21, 1936, exerted capable and heroic leadership in helping Mississippi to survive the Depression. He was born in Hattiesburg in 1891 and was educated at University of Mississippi (B.S. and L.L.B) and at Yale (L.L.B.). After practicing law at Seminary, he served in the Mississippi House of Representatives.

"Beginning his term as Governor during the greatest depression in history, he found Mississippi's treasury empty. In less than two years he cut down the debt of the State, balanced the budget, restored Mississippi's credit, and placed its revenues on a sound basis by procuring the passage of the general sales tax. This new source of revenue aroused nation-wide interest" (JACKSON TIMES, *January 30, 1964, p. 3). Governor Conner died in 1950.*

The winter rains had temporarily subsided, but the great flatlands of the Delta were in flood—the worst since the spring of 1927. The morning of Tuesday, January 19, 1932, dawned clear and cold. There was a faint trace of fog rising out of the lowlands along the Pearl River. It was Robert E. Lee's birthday. It was also the day appointed by Mississippi Constitution for the inauguration of the state's forty-fourth governor.

At noon in front of the New Capitol, Martin Sennett "Mike" Conner, the Piney Woods boy who at the age of fifteen had gone to the University of Mississippi and then to the Yale Law School, would stand before 15,000 of his fellow Mississippians, and, after the smoke of the nineteen-gun salute had drifted into the magnolia trees by the Confederate monument, he would speak of his plans and hopes. The squarely built new governor, although only forty, was no novice in state politics. He had come home from Yale to Covington County to practice law, and at the age of twenty-four had been elected speaker of the Mississippi House of Representatives. That was in the first administration of Governor Theodore G. Bilbo (1916–1920), and Bilbo had supported his fellow South Mississippian against the legislative veteran, Oscar Johnston of Clarksdale.

Another term as speaker followed and then there were two unsuccessful races for governor. In 1923 it had been Conner and Bilbo in a race that Henry Whitfield won over both, and in 1927 it was Bilbo winning a second term, with Conner running a distant third. The speculation then was that Conner was through—a has-been at thirty-six—an intensely able man who was too shy and too honest to make it at the polls.

And now here he was—victor in the 1931 primaries over Tupelo lawyer George Mitchell, former Congressman Paul B. Johnson, Sr., of Hattiesburg, and Columbia lumberman Hugh L. White. The preceding four years under Bilbo had been turbulent ones. Scandals rocked the State Tax Commission and other departments of government; impeachment proceedings were directed at some of Bilbo's closest political associates; massive dismissals of university presidents and professors had cost the accreditation of the state's only university and most of its colleges; the budget was badly out of balance; and to make matters almost desperate was the fact that the entire country had plunged into its most disastrous depression.

It was not a reassuring state of affairs, therefore, that faced the new governor on this January day. Some seventy banks had closed their doors throughout the state, and more were closing every week. In many cities such as Gulfport no banks remained open for business. In his final address to the legislature the previous week, the irrepressible Bilbo himself had taken note of that unhappy situation:

> Every man and woman in Mississippi is demanding that this legislature do something to make the banks of Mississippi safer and stronger. . . . In China, it is said that when a bank fails all the officials of the bank are led out into the public square of the city in which the bank failed and the heads of said bankers are promptly cut off, and I am also informed that there hasn't been a bank failure in China in over a thousand years. Suppose you try this in Mississippi.[1]

But Bilbo, for all of his brashness, was leaving office in general disfavor. Only 31 of the 189 members of the preceding legislature had been returned by the voters. Confidence in the political system was at a low ebb. On the very morning that he left office Bilbo had pardoned 101 convicts from the state penitentiary.[2]

The financial condition of the state was unbelievably bad. According to the published report of the state auditor, on January 1, 1932, there was a total of $1,326 in the State Treasury and outstanding warrants had been issued against that amount in the sum of almost $6,000,000.[3] There were many school districts in the state where teachers had not been paid in full for almost a year. Equally as serious was the impending failure of the state to meet its payments on its full faith and credit bonds. In a word, the state of Mississippi was broke.

When the legislature convened for the 1932 session, one of its first acts was the passage of a concurrent resolution authorizing the chairman of the State Tax Commission to borrow $750.00 with which to purchase postage stamps so as to be able to mail out income tax notices.[4] The members of the legislature themselves could not cash their salary warrants imme-

---

[1]House Journal, 1932 Regular Session, 56.
[2]Jackson *Clarion Ledger*, January 20, 1932.
[3]House Journal, 1932 Regular Session, 105.
[4]Senate Concurrent Resolution No. 12, 1932 Regular Session.

diately, and many stayed at the Edwards Hotel and other places in the city through the tolerance and generosity of those establishments.

The newspapers carried notices of public auctions for the sale of entire stocks of merchandise of stores that had been plunged into bankruptcy.[5] The list of lands to be sold for delinquent ad valorem taxes filled almost the entire edition of some papers. In the *Clarion Ledger* that inauguration week the Dyer Feed and Grocery Company of Jackson was advertising "White help only" and among others the following items: "Yard eggs—every one guaranteed—per doz. 15¢" and "Kansas City Stamped Chuck Roast—17¢ per lb."[6]

Such was the setting for the beginning of the Conner administration—an administration that would have a unique and unparalleled imprint on the history of Mississippi. The keynote was sounded in the Governor's inaugural address:

> The state's credit is like a woman's virtue. It is the "immediate jewel of her soul," and those to whose keeping it is entrusted should hold the duty of safe-guarding it as a sacred obligation, the full discharge of which is the highest form of public service. . .
>
> There is but one means whereby the state's credit may be properly protected and its obligations to its citizens properly discharged. That is through the legislature provision of sufficient revenue to meet legislative appropriations and standing commitments of whatever character. The short phrase for this operation is "balancing the budget."[7]

The new governor went on to portray in specific detail the grim facts of the state's fiscal plight. He pointed out that in the preceding four years the bonded debt had increased 227 per cent—from $15,000,000 on January 1, 1928, to more than $50,000,000. Conner reminded his audience that in the twelve-year period since 1920 only twice had the budget been in bal-

---

[5] Jackson *Clarion Ledger*, January 31, 1932.
[6] *Ibid.*, January 17, 1932.
[7] House Journal, 1932 Regular Session, 103.

ance at the end of a fiscal year, and that there was an accumulated deficit for that period of almost $15,000,000. A further depressing statistic that the governor cited was that while appropriations in the preceding administration had increased by $9,500,000, general fund receipts had increased by only $3,500,000. A special session called the year before by the outgoing governor to deal with the problem had authorized the issuance of current expense bonds in the amount of $6,000,000, but, as Conner wryly pointed out, nobody was willing to buy the bonds.[8]

As if those figures were not grim enough, the governor injected an additional note of distress. Because of the general economic depression, tax collections in every category were down significantly. The eight-mill state property tax was the bellwether revenue source, and there was a shrinkage of some $80,000,000 in property assessments. The bottom line on all of this was that the legislature could expect a current operating deficit of $7,500,000. Added to that was the obligation to honor the $6,000,000 in currently unpaid warrants and to pay debt service on outstanding bonds in the coming biennium of almost $9,000,000.[9]

Finally the governor got to the obvious answer. It appeared necessary that taxes would have to be increased. Just how to do it was for the legislature to decide. One thing, however, was clear. Taxes on property, particularly land, must not be raised. He cited what was happening in other states. California, for example, had just mandated "relieving the present excessive burden on real property."[10] Then he dropped a more specific suggestion in the form of a quotation from the chairman of the Iowa State Tax Commission: "Tax policies of the states from Maine to California and from Washington to Florida are all being modified to raise less revenue from the general tax upon real and personal property, and more from taxation of incomes,

---

[8] *Ibid.*, 104–106.
[9] *Ibid.*, 106.
[10] *Ibid.*, 107.

levies upon intangibles, such as securities and investments, or from selective or general sales taxes."[11]

The reminder of the address was almost a textbook presentation on governmental reform—consolidation and reorganization of agencies, county unit system, centralized purchasing, consolidation of schools, elimination of political interference in college administration, natural resource conservation, and industrial development. One melancholy footnote of the past was down in the fine print. In a routine recitation of appropriations for various services of government, the figure for Confederate pensions was greater than that for all of the state's colleges and the university combined. Neither amount was very large.[12]

While Conner had not presented a specific tax proposal to the legislature, it was obvious where his thinking lay. But in those first days after his inauguration he resembled the proverbial engineer charged with draining the swamp but who at the moment was up to his waist in alligators. Banks were continuing to close, teachers were working without contracts and without pay, short-term notes were due, and the governor found himself meeting around the clock to find solutions to the myriad problems.

On the weekend following the inauguration the Senate Finance Committee and the House Ways and Means Committee began a series of sessions designed to develop a revenue program. Conner met several times with both committees, and it was reported the following week that a package involving a retail sales tax plus an increased income tax was in the works.[13] A few days later hints of disagreement between the two committees began to circulate. The Senate, it appeared, was going to be more amenable than the House to a higher sales tax and an accompanying property tax reduction. Finance Committee chairman and ex-Rhodes Scholar John Kyle of Sardis announced plans to introduce a sales tax bill at a rate possibly as

[11] *Ibid.*, 107.
[12] *Ibid.*, 116, 118.
[13] Jackson *Clarion Ledger*, January 31, 1932.

high as three per cent. This, he explained, would permit a reduction in the property tax from eight to six mills. Ways and Means Committee chairman Torrey McCallum of Laurel in the meantime scheduled a public hearing on the sales tax issue.[14]

On February 5, the *Clarion Ledger* reported that the Finance Committee was leaning toward a three per cent sales tax, and that Conner wanted it high enough to permit a reduction of the property tax.[15] The following day there was editorial speculation in the same newspaper that an eventual agreement would be reached on a two per cent tax. That article took note, however, of the growing opposition, particularly from the retail merchants, to any type of sales tax levy: "But while the dove of peace held forth in the legislative halls, solons were reminded that it is an eagle which perches on the dome of their capitol, as the corridors rang with the battle cries of opponents to the general sales tax."[16] This opposition began in Natchez, when the local Chamber of Commerce called for a statewide meeting at the Edwards Hotel in Jackson. Meanwhile Senator Luther Whittington of Natchez, along with Representative George Smith of Gulfport, introduced resolutions opposing any new taxes until expenses had been reduced. The same day United States Senator Pat Harrison addressed a joint legislative session and, blaming all of the state's and country's problems on "Republican extravagance and profligacy," he predicted a "sweeping Democratic victory in November." He flayed the Washington bureaucracy that "burdens the people with millions of useless expense" even as he urged increased taxes at both the state and federal level.[17]

The *Clarion Ledger* in a major editorial the following Sunday attempted to put it all into perspective:

It is generally understood that the legislature has not yet seen the full prescription of the bitter dose that is to come. Governor

[14] *Ibid.*, February 3, 1932.
[15] *Ibid.*, February 5, 1932.
[16] *Ibid.*, February 6, 1932.
[17] *Ibid.*, February 11, 1932.

Conner's attitude indicates that if anything the medicine is going to be all the stronger. There is no question that the state must accept a dose of medicine far from pleasant before its ailing budget is corrected, but right now the physicians are going to have plenty of trouble with a patient who insists upon rejecting some of the medicine offered him if not actually prescribing his own tonic. One thing stands out in all this and that is that there is a rapidly growing sentiment in favor of a gross income tax and against a sales tax.[18]

The governor now began to take off the gloves. Faced with increasing dissension in the legislature and a growing taxpayer revolt outside, he requested permission to address a joint session. At the same time he agreed to meet the protestors face-to-face at their statewide meeting. Dr. J. C. Rice of Natchez was in charge. Unable to get into the Edwards Hotel because of their number, the crowd had marched down Capitol Street to the City Auditorium, where they heard the embattled Conner lay it on the line: "This problem is as serious as though an armed force were beating on the gates of our state, and it must be met as patriotically and heroically. . . . A protest never solved any problem. You have adopted resolutions. Instead of giving us your resolutions, give us your plan."[19]

Later that afternoon he was presented to the joint session of the legislature by Lieutenant Governor Dennis Murphree. Making no reference to the sales tax as such, he again referred to the gravity of the state's financial situation and called for prompt action to balance revenues and expenditures. He cited particularly the need for governmental reorganization as an essential part of that process and laid before the legislators a far-reaching series of recommendations for the restructuring of state and local government.[20]

In spite of the statewide protest activity which now included full-page advertisements in the state's newspapers, the follow-

[18] *Ibid.*, February 15, 1932.
[19] *Ibid.*, February 18, 1932.
[20] House Journal, 1932 Regular Session, 275.

ing days were relatively good ones for the governor. The Senate
Finance Committee reported favorably a two per cent sales tax
bill along with a gross-income tax bill, while the Ways and
Means Committee came forth with a one per cent levy.[21] Conner's emphasis on reorganization and economy in government
touched an especially responsive chord. The Calhoun City
Monitor Herald put it in the following manner:

> The situation is being handled with common sense and courage.
> Let those who have been drawing large salaries and playing golf
> work for their money. Let salaries be reduced, budgets lopped off to
> the quick, needless employees find themselves something else to
> do. Then let's pay for the folly of our last administration through
> the noses—by selling our coats and doing without our snuff, by
> storing up our rattle traps, by developing a taste for speckled peas
> and turnip greens instead of apple pie a la mode.[22]

The first week of March brought the emerging drama to center stage. First the Senate in a dizzying series of maneuvers reduced the rate to one per cent after turning down attempts at
five and three per cent, and then in utter disarray defeated the
entire bill at one per cent after Conner let it be known that he
would veto a one per cent tax.[23] Two days later Representative
Walter Sillers led a successful floor fight in the House to raise
the rate to three per cent, but, to the administration's dismay, a
subsequent amendment was adopted giving the counties one
per cent of the desperately needed revenue.[24]

With a climactic House vote on final passage scheduled for
the following day, Conner again requested permission to address a joint session. On the morning of March 8, the determined chief executive, in what may have been the finest address of his career, put it squarely to the legislature. Reminding
them that every elected state official had publicly endorsed a
sales tax bill, the governor recounted once again the state's des-

[21] Jackson *Clarion Ledger*, February 17, 1932.
[22] *Ibid.*, February 16, 1932.
[23] *Ibid.*, February 27, 1932.
[24] *Ibid.*, March 2, 1932.

perate plight and denounced with increased fervor the "inequitable and oppressive tax burden which rests most heavily upon land." He went into a history of the sales tax in other countries, invoking in that connection the name of Adam Smith. It was for the most part a scholarly and reasoned argument for a three per cent retail levy, but toward the end of his speech the governor turned on all of the appeal of which he was capable. He reminded the members of their duty: "Our public officials are not chosen by mass meetings, and a relatively small percentage of the electorate attend such gatherings. Again I remind you that the great masses have no one here to speak for them except you who have been elected to represent them and guard their welfare."[25]

That evening after more than five hours of debate the House gave the governor its answer. By a vote of eighty-one for to fifty-eight against, the sales tax bill fell three votes short of the three-fifths majority required by the Constitution for the passage of revenue measures. Both sides had rolled out their heaviest oratorical guns. In addition to Chairman McCallum, the proponents were led by Sillers, Fielding Wright, and, as their surprise final gunner, House Speaker Tom Bailey, who, in a highly unusual move, left the chair and took the floor of the House to plead for passage. However, the tax foes were not to be denied on this day at least, and, with the Ways and Means Committee decimated by defections of the "one percenters," one by one they plodded up the aisles to denounce the three per cent levy and some, any levy at all. Hilton Waits of Leland, later to serve for twenty years as chairman of the committee, told his colleagues, "I have always supported Mike Conner for governor, but I cannot follow him this far."[26]

Held on a motion to reconsider, the bill was called up the following day by Sillers and on final passage was defeated once again by almost the identical vote of the day before. The fol-

[25] House Journal, 1932 Regular Session, 380.
[26] Jackson *Clarion Ledger,* March 9, 1932.

lowing morning the *Clarion Ledger*, now fully committed along with the *Daily News* against the sales tax, printed the names of the House opponents of the tax in a box on the front page under the heading, "Sales Tax Honor Roll."[27] Waits predicted a hopeless deadlock and called on the governor to compromise. Conner, however, was undaunted, and, after a frantic night of calls and cajoling, on the following afternoon, with the eighty-one identical "Aye" votes standing fast through a third roll call, but with six of the original "Nays" failing to vote, the magic three-fifths was achieved by one vote, and the "three percenters" had their victory. The same edition of the *Clarion Ledger* that announced the result devoted ten full pages to delinquent tax notices.[28] The next day a full-page ad called for a massive statewide meeting of the opponents at the City Auditorium. The war had just begun.

Critics of the sales tax were becoming increasingly shrill. The Mississippi Merchants Association sponsored a newspaper spread which proclaimed: "Augustus Caesar who ruled the Roman Empire, feudal lords in the Middle Ages, Louise [*sic*] the Eleventh of France, and Isabella of Spain all levied a sales tax in their time and all with the same result. In each case they were forced to abandon it because of the almost open rebellion of the people."[29]

On the day of the protest meeting most of the stores in Jackson closed at noon, and a crowd estimated at more than 5,000 moved down Capitol Street to the Auditorium. There those who were able to get inside heard speaker after speaker denounce the governor and his revenue program. The gloves had come off. Conner was not invited to be on the platform for this one. Dr. Rice again presided, but the cast had been strengthened, and the rhetoric had escalated.

Jackson merchant R. E. Kennington fired the first blast: "The governor evidently thought his inauguration was a coronation.

[27] *Ibid.*, March 10, 1932.
[28] *Ibid.*, March 11, 1932.
[29] *Ibid.*, February 29, 1932.

He acts as though he was crowned king of Mississippi." Editor T. M. Hederman, Sr., of the *Clarion Ledger* predicted the direct consequences: "If a sales tax is passed, it will be the darkest day Mississippi has ever known. Sherman's invasion was not more disastrous." The progressive young editor of the McComb *Enterprise*, Oliver Emmerich, thought that "the administration had overestimated the gullibility of Mississippians."[30]

Following the meeting there assembled what must have been one of the most ludicrous and bizarre marches ever staged in the Capital City. Led by an improvised fife-and-drum corps consisting of three young black men along with two other men, one in a yellow shirt and purple trousers leading a little donkey wearing a blanket on which was printed, "This is what the sales tax will make of Mississippi," the crowd moved from the auditorium up Congress Street to the Capitol. The mood for the most part was good-humored, but then, as some of the marchers surged into the Capitol and filled the corridors leading to the governor's office, the demeanor changed. There was a demand to see the governor, but a cordon of security personnel and some members of the legislature stood in front of the closed doors.

Representative Sam Lumpkin, who was later to be elected speaker and lieutenant governor, was one of those self-appointed to protect the governor. Afterwards he would record what happened:

> Our blockade was thrown up none too soon. Minutes after we took our positions several hundred yelling men surged through the corridor to confront us. One red-faced man thrust himself forward, pulled a pistol from his belt and pointed it through the door.
>
> "Stand back," the gunman yelled. "I'm coming in."
>
> Then Dr. E. T. Brock, a physician of McComb, was lunging between to strike the man's arm upward. The gun clattered to the floor and slid away. The crowd opened, swallowed the gunman, then closed again.
>
> Sight of the pistol had sobered the crowd. Quiet descended. The

[30] *Ibid.*, March 17, 1932.

men shifted from foot to foot and started avoiding each other's eyes. By one and two's and three's, as they regained their individuality, they began breaking away to drift silently down the stairs and out of the Capitol.

Our small group went back into the office. Governor Conner was dictating a statement to his secretary, reaffirming his stand for the sales tax measure. The secretary read the statement aloud and Conner nodded approval. Then he stood up and smiled.

"Gentlemen," he said. "I think it's time to call it a day."

I went out of the Capitol by a side entrance into the gathering dusk. Under a street light I saw the last straggler of the crowd of tax protestors. It was the little jackass, his blanket gone, nibbling spring grass on the Capitol lawn.[31]

The next day the House unanimously adopted a resolution by Sillers protesting the group's intemperate attacks on the governor, and the Senate passed a similar measure with only one dissenting vote. Senator John Culkin of Vicksburg abstained, explaining that he thought the governor was perfectly capable of taking care of himself without any resolutions from the legislature.[32] In the meantime state Superintendent of Education W. F. Bond was rallying the school forces for the tax, and a few days later a crowd estimated to be as large as that of the protestors converged on Jackson to voice their support.[33]

In the Senate the Finance Committee reported the House bill but with an amendment dropping the levy to one per cent.[34] The Senators debated the bill for three days the following week after adopting a floor amendment raising the levy back to three per cent. The day before the vote, Conner had sent a special message to the legislature again saying that he would veto a one per cent bill and further emphasizing the state's desperate financial plight. Only sixty-four per cent of the previous year's ad valorem taxes had been paid, he pointed out, and 45,000 farms were then being sold for taxes. Finally, before packed gal-

[31] Malley Byrd, "The Day of the Jackass," *The New South*, May, 1973, 19.
[32] Jackson *Clarion Ledger*, March 18, 1932.
[33] W. F. Bond, *I Had a Friend* (Kansas City, 1958), 117.
[34] Senate Journal, 1932 Regular Session, 468.

leries which spilled into the corridors and even onto the floor of the chamber itself, the Senate voted. The bill lost by five votes.[35] A week later they tried again. The debate was increasingly bitter. The result was the same but by a smaller margin. The time for compromise was at hand.

John Kyle met frequently with the governor. Conner did not think two per cent was adequate. Kyle, who had voted against the three per cent levy himself, insisted that it was two per cent or nothing. Slowly the accommodations were worked out. The bill was set for special order on April 5.[36] The courtly Senator L. C. Andrews of Oxford assured his colleagues that he had the governor's pledge to call a special session to repeal the tax if it proved unworkable.[37] The two per cent amendment was adopted, and the bill passed thirty to seventeen.[38]

The undaunted Walter Sillers, House floor leader for the bill, the next day announced that the House would not concur on the two per cent figure,[39] and now the action shifted to a conference committee. When three days later the conferees reported that they were unable to agree and requested to be discharged, the corridors buzzed with predictions of a hopeless deadlock. The governor's forces appeared split between those who insisted on a three per cent levy and those who felt that two per cent was all that could possibly be enacted.[40]

The next week after new conferees had been named, the committee brought in its report with the two per cent figure still in the bill. It was promptly called up in the Senate and adopted by the smallest possible margin of one-fifth of a vote.[41] Victory for the pro-sales tax forces now seemed to be in sight, but the stage was simply set for the most stirring and improbable scene of all.

[35] *Ibid.*, 508.
[36] Senate Journal, 1932 Regular Session, 572.
[37] Jackson *Clarion Ledger*, April 6, 1932.
[38] Senate Journal, 1932 Regular Session, 620.
[39] Jackson *Clarion Ledger*, April 7, 1932.
[40] *Ibid.*, April 12, 1932.
[41] Senate Journal, 1932 Regular Session, 703.

The following day, in front of overflowing balconies, the conference report was presented to the House. Sillers told his fellow representatives that he was not at all happy with less than a three per cent levy, but that he would vote for the report as being the best that could be obtained.[42] While he did not quote the governor, he was undoubtedly expressing Conner's views as well. But when the day's debate had ended, the conference report failed to be adopted by two votes.[43] The opponents were jubilant. Scrap Woolfolk of Tunica and Joe Patterson, later to be attorney general, thought it was all over. Since a conference report could not be amended, it therefore could not be reconsidered. Speaker Bailey thought otherwise. Representative Lamar of Pittsboro entered a motion to reconsider, but it was agreed by everyone that there could be only one reconsideration.

The report was set for special order four days later. Everything was on the line. It was a tumultuous session. The accumulated tensions and pressures of more than two months of almost continuous stuggle could not be concealed. Sillers was at the podium defending the report when Representative Denson of Prentiss County assailed him with torrents of verbal abuse. The Deltan appealed to the chair for order so that he might proceed, but before the presiding officer could act, seventy-six-year-old Dr. J. S. Austin, fiery representative from Warren County, who, it was said, carried a pistol most of the time, came at Denson with fists flying. The melee was halted before any serious physical damage was done, but a short time later the acid-tongued George Smith felt that his honor had been challenged by Harvey Mason of Wayne County, and it appeared that another fight would erupt.[44] But now the clerk was directed to call the roll.

It was generally agreed beforehand that, based on the number of members expected to be present, eighty-one votes would be needed to adopt the report. But minutes before the roll call be-

[42] Jackson *Clarion Ledger*, April 16, 1932.
[43] House Journal, 1932 Regular Session, 676.
[44] Jackson *Daily News*, April 19, 1932.

gan, Representative L. O. Smith of Chickasaw, an opponent who was reported to be stranded in Vicksburg, arrived breathlessly in the chamber. The numbers were now changed. It would take eighty-two votes. The governor's forces could count only eighty-one at best. The roll call commenced: Allen of Desoto—"Nay," Anderson of Washington—"Aye," Armstrong of Copiah (at twenty-one the youngest member of the legislature)—"Aye," and on down the list of the 140 members.[45] When the final name had been called, Sillers, who had been keeping tally, saw to his dismay that the supporters of the tax were one vote short. The bill was dead. And then it happened. Just as the clerk was preparing to announce the result, a voice was heard from near the center of the chamber:

"Mr. Speaker."

"For what purpose does the gentleman from Bolivar rise?"

"Mr. Speaker, I desire to change my vote from "Nay" to "Aye.""

Oscar Wolfe of Bolivar County would later explain that in those agonizing seconds of decision he saw financial chaos for the state and a hopeless deadlock in the legislature if the tax issue was not resolved at that point, and therefore he laid aside his own personal feelings to vote for the bill. After almost three months of struggle, the deed was done. The conference report had been adopted by two-fifths of a vote.[46]

Conner was as magnanimous in victory as he had been persistent in the struggle. He said simply, "It has been a long, hard fight. I hope everyone will forget about the scrap."[47] He signed the bill a few days later, and at midnight on May 1, 1932, it went into effect. Alfred H. Stone, newly appointed chairman of the State Tax Commission, called for cooperation from the merchants and from the people. For the most part he got it, although Dr. Rice promised to continue to fight through the

---

[45] House Journal, 1932 Regular Session, 697.
[46] Ibid.
[47] Jackson Clarion Ledger, April 20, 1932.

courts. Stone would be a key man in the success of the tax, and his long and successful tenure under six governors was largely attributable to his own characterization of his technique of tax administration. "The secret," he later said, "is to get the greatest amount of feathers with the least amount of squawking from the goose."

The tax bill as passed in 1932 was styled the "Emergency Revenue Act" and carried an automatic repealer of June 30, 1934. So effective was it, however, in stabilizing the state's fiscal problems, that in 1934 the legislature reenacted it with certain refinements as a permanent part of the revenue structure. One month after Conner's term as governor had expired, the Mississippi Supreme Court held the tax constitutional.[48]

In its first full year of collection, the new source of revenue produced $2,673,000, or just over $1,000,000 for each per cent of levy. It should be noted that the per capita income of Mississippi that year was $131.[49] With the tax now levied at a five per cent rate, it is interesting to compare recent collection figures. In calendar year 1978, the sales tax produced $526,000,000, or more than $100,000,000 for each per cent. The per capita income figure was $5,590. Mississippi had come a long way, and it must be finally recorded here that a significant share of the credit for that record of economic recovery and financial stability will forever rest with the shy but determined young man from the Piney Woods by way of Ole Miss and the Yale Law School, who seemed to live up to the closing words of his own inaugural address: "And if in this hour we shall set the public welfare as the only goal of our ambition, if we shall make it the supreme object of our effort and dedicate to its achievement the best endowment of our lives, we need not fear for the results of our labors nor for the future of the state."[50]

---

[48] V. B. Wheeless, "The Sales and Use Tax," 1965, 24. This is an excellent account of the background, enactment and administration of the sales tax by the official who served for many years as chief of the Sales Tax Division of the State Tax Commission.

[49] *Ibid.*, 30.

[50] House Journal, 1932 Regular Session, 130.

SELECTED BIBLIOGRAPHY

Conner, Martin Sennett. *Mississippi's Fiscal Problems*. Jackson, Mississippi: Hederman Brothers, 1917. A speech in which Conner, a representative in the state legislature, gives a general survey of what the legislature has done and what needs to be done.

———. Inaugural Address, January 19, 1932. Mississippi Collection, University of Mississippi.

———. Message of Governor Martin Sennett Conner Delivered before the Senate and House of Representatives, January 3, 1934. Mississippi Collection, University of Mississippi.

House Journal, 1932.

Senate Journal, 1932.

Senate Concurrent Resolution No. 12, 1932.

Jimmie Rodgers
1897–1933

Jimmie Rodgers:
Father of Country Music

BY JACK CROCKER

During his professional career Jimmie Rodgers was tagged with two labels: "The Singing Brakeman," which reflected his railroad background, and "America's Blue Yodeler," which referred to his unique style of singing. This background and style eventually led to his being crowned with a glorious third title: "Father of Country Music." From his first recording session in 1927 until his death in 1933, Jimmie Rodgers became a hero to millions who bought his records and flocked to see him perform. In the process he ushered in a new era in American music.

Rodgers's life follows the American dream, rags-to-riches pattern of a hero. His father, Aaron Woodberry Rodgers, born in Choctaw County, Alabama, moved to Meridian, Mississippi, as a young man, added the "d" to Rogers and got a job on the Mobile & Ohio Railroad. There he met and married Eliza Bozeman, whose father, Samuel, was a fairly well-to-do farmer from the Pine Springs Community near Meridian.

After two sons were born, Walter in 1886 and Talmage in 1890, Eliza's health deteriorated with advancing tuberculosis. The disease was probably contracted in the rough, primitive conditions of the various railroad camps where she lived with Aaron as he traveled about being a foreman of section crews. Finally, because of Eliza's illness, the family moved to the house at Pine Springs that Samuel Bozeman had built for them as a wedding gift. There, on September 8, 1897, James Charles Rodgers was born.

The death of his mother in 1903 began a nomadic existence for Jimmie Rodgers that was to be characteristic of the rest of his life. Although the folklore depicting the young Rodgers as a homeless waif is inaccurate, it is true that he was shuttled about from his father to the Bozeman family to staying with an uncle who ran a barber shop in Meridian. For a while he lived with his Aunt Dora Bozeman on the farm in Pine Springs. Accomplished in music and well-educated, she was very fond of the playfully mischievous James and insisted on schooling for him. Although Aunt Dora remained one of his favorite people, school was not one of Jimmie's favorite pursuits, despite her efforts; consequently, between sojourns with Aunt Dora his formal education was sporadic.

Jimmie's street education, however, was constant and thorough. At the turn of the century Meridian was a bustling trade and transportation center offering a universe of excitements for adventurous scamps like Jimmie. Rail yards, pool rooms, barber shops, Negro joints, and, most of all, the shows—carnivals, circuses, street players—these became, as Nolan Porterfield points out in his superb biography *Jimmie Rodgers: The Life and Times of America's Blue Yodeler*, "the foundation of both his art and his life, and served him well."

Porterfield relates several episodes that reveal Jimmie's dream of becoming a famous entertainer apparently began very early in his life, a dream buttressed by steadfast faith and obsessive determination. Rather than a railroad man who incidentally became a renowned entertainer, he was an entertainer from the beginning who out of necessity became a high rail rider until he could make his music pay. In one escapade, Jimmie, already a street clown and cut-up, organized a group of his running mates into a "carnival," stole sheets from his sister-in-law for a tent, and traveled to several towns before being caught and returned. Another time he pulled the same stunt, but for a "big top" he bought an expensive camping tent and charged it to his father without his father's knowledge. The end result was the same. Still once more, after winning an amateur talent contest sponsored by the Elite Theater in Meridian he joined a medicine show and ended up a hundred miles from home before quitting. He was thirteen years old at the time.

These impulsive excursions into the heady world of entertainment came to a halt when at the age of fourteen Jimmie accompanied his father to Macon, Mississippi, to become a railroad man. Starting as a flunky, learning to line and surface track with his father's section gang, he eventually worked as flagman, baggage master, and brakeman. His genial, gregarious, free-spirited nature made adaptation to the rough and rowdy ways of railroad life relatively easy. He enjoyed the camaraderie of railroad camps and the kibitzing of section crews. Furthermore, the young Jimmie Rodgers was an avid and apt student of the railroad lore that would provide images and language for later songs. Also it was during this period that he absorbed the music of the black gandy dancers—the wailing, gutsy, tender, defiant, bawdy, jubilant, mournful blues. Although the itinerant nature of railroading matched his rambling spirit, the frequent exposure to inclement weather and raw working conditions exacerbated Jimmie's susceptibility to colds and pleurisy. He was often sick during the winter months; already the insidious disease that killed his mother was stalking him.

Jimmie, who had a winning smile and amiable manner, made friends easily, especially with girls. In 1917 in Durant, Mississippi, he met a dark-haired beauty named Stella Kelly. After a furious courtship of several months the two were married. Soon, however, the romance succumbed to reality. Money problems (Jimmie's lack of it), Jimmie's apparent lack of ambition and irresponsible behavior, Stella's parents, Stella's independent spirit, all seem to have played a part in the inevitable separation and ultimate divorce. Stella left for Oklahoma pregnant with a child Jimmie was not to see, or apparently to know about, until 1930 when in a highly melodramatic moment Stella brought little Kathryn Rodgers backstage after a show to meet her daddy. Despite the awkwardness, Jimmie accepted her enthusiastically.

After the break with Stella, Jimmie advanced his reputation as a carefree rounder by indulging his appetite for girls, drinking, taking in every show and carnival he could, and singing and playing every chance he got. It was not long, however, before one particular girl caught his eye. She was Carrie Williamson, a Methodist preacher's daughter. Not with the Williamson family's blessings, Jimmie and Carrie were married on April 7, 1920. After the fact, however, Carrie's family accepted her choice of husband, even one with a smudged reputation, and always came to the aid of the young couple in hard times.

Carrie stayed with Jimmie through the good times and the bad, as a country song would say. Two daughters were born—Carrie Anita and June Rebecca. The latter died in infancy. Carrie wrote an affectionate account of her life with the Blue Yodeler in *Jimmie Rodgers, My Husband.*

For seven years after his marriage to Carrie, sporadically employed, drifting across the country taking any railroad job he could get, at other times resorting to any odd job available, Jimmie seemed to be fulfilling the prediction made by some family and friends that he was a shiftless rambler who would never amount to anything. His guitar picking and singing were interpreted as useless—stalled on a directionless sidetrack, Jimmie had missed the mainline train.

But the powerful will and implacable drive to sing and entertain that had prompted him to run off with a carnival when he was only thirteen had not abated. His singing and playing for various functions, in pool halls, for dances, might have been frivolous escapades to some, but to Jimmie Rodgers it was necessary experience and practice in dedication to a dream. He listened to records. He hawked vaudeville shows. He absorbed what he needed, slowly transmuting the material he heard and learned into his own inimitable style. By 1927 he was professionally ready. All he needed was a break. And although he had stubbornly shunted aside a doctor's diagnosis of tuberculosis, being determined to keep active in his musical pursuits, he could not deny the daily fever and the blood flecks in his handkerchief. He knew the lucky break had to come soon.

The opportunity Jimmie had been waiting for came on August 4, 1927, when man and moment met in the unlikely location of Bristol, Tennessee. The previous winter Jimmie had left Meridian for Asheville, North Carolina, ostensibly to check on a railroad job, but more likely to try to relieve his ailing lungs in the clear, lighter air of the mountains. It was not long before he had organized a band. A group called the Tenneva Ramblers joined him to become the Jimmie Rodgers Entertainers. Meeting with slim success, they hustled one-night stands in high school auditoriums and small-town theaters. The best job they had, playing at a summer resort near Asheville, was abruptly canceled when Jimmie learned of a recording session scheduled by Ralph Peer in Bristol.

Ralph Peer had become a pioneer in the field recording of traditional American singers and their music while with Okeh records. Later, hired to develop a "Hillbilly" and "Race" repertoire for the Victor Talking Machine Company, he set out to search for new talent and struck gold in Bristol. On one serendipitous week he recorded a trio called the Carter Family and an outwardly brash, confident Mississippian, Jimmie Rodgers.

After a quarrel with the Tenneva Ramblers as to what name would be used on their records, Jimmie decided to record alone. On August 4, 1927, he entered the makeshift studio in Bristol to audition for Peer with only his guitar, raw talent, and an unquenchable desire to succeed as an entertainer. That afternoon he made recording history. It took seven tries, but he finally got wax masters for two sides. One song was the sentimental "The Soldier's Sweetheart," the other a lullaby, "Sleep, Baby, Sleep."

His recording career launched, Jimmie with typical flamboyant confidence believed grand success was at hand. Released on October 7, 1927, the record sold reasonably well for a new artist with meagre promotion. But the whole process was too slow for Jimmie, his impatience surely fired by his awareness of the tightening squeeze of TB on his body. When neither Peer nor anyone else from Victor called within the time he thought they should, Jimmie set out for New York and casually offered himself for another recording session. Agreeing, Ralph Peer arranged a session at the Victor factory in Camden, New Jersey.

At this session Jimmie recorded his first "Blue Yodel" ("T for Texas"), an event that, as Porterfield says, "led to a sequence of recordings which altered and shaped the patterns of emerging hillbilly music, materially contributing to the legitimization of the genre in the canon of American culture." The two songs that had been recorded at Bristol were traditional fare, pale and maudlin compared to "Blue Yodel No. 1." It was a driving, zestful, rowdy song sung with immaculate clarity and emotional force punctuated by the rippling yodel that was to become a permanent fixture in Rodgers's music, a musical tattoo that would thrill and excite millions of fans. This record backed with "Away Out on the Mountain" thrust Jimmie into the bright lights of national prominence.

Jimmie reveled in the glow of success. Not only did it validate his unwavering faith in himself, but it also showed the homefolks that he was not doomed to failure. Within a year of his second recording session he had a weekly radio show in Washington, D.C., where he also got star billing at the first-class Earle Theater, headlined the prestigious Loew Circuit Southern tour, and was making over $2,000 a month. Thus he could now make a triumphant return to Meridian, get a hero's welcome, and pay old debts, for the erstwhile railroad drifter was finally riding the high rails of fame and fortune.

And the ride was fast and thrilling, the way Jimmie liked and wanted it. Knowing his time was short, he shoved hard against the limits. He loved the applause whether he was headlining a big-time vaudeville bill in major city theaters or playing in small tent repertoire companies in the hinterlands of the South and Southwest. When there were no tent companies or vaudeville tours, he made independent bookings, seizing on every opportunity to hit the road.

Meanwhile, Ralph Peer kept him busy with recording sessions. Usually hard-pressed for song material, Jimmie compiled songs from various sources, often from the welter of blues lyrics that seemed to float around to be picked up by different artists. He used numbers ranging from tunes by hacks of Tin Pan Alley to songs written by his sister-in-law, Elsie McWilliams, in Meridian. Eventually he would record at least 110 songs for the Victor company.

Forty-four of the recordings feature just Jimmie and his guitar. The others have various back-up musicians, sometimes one or two, at times a house band or a group such as Lani McIntire's Hawaiians. One of the most historically and musically memorable tunes was cut in a Hollywood session when Jimmie recorded "Blue Yodel No. 9" ("Standin' on the Corner") with Louis Armstrong on trumpet and Lillian Hardin Armstrong on piano. The combination is a sound testament to his kinship with blues and jazz.

The record sales were tremendous—between 1927 and 1933 perhaps as many as 20,000,000. In addition to the records there was a movie short made for Columbia in 1929 called *The Singing Brakeman* that met with national success. A highlight for Jimmie occurred in 1931 when he joined Will Rogers on a tour to raise money for the Red Cross. According to Will Rogers, Jr., the two men were mutual admirers.

Indeed the frail Mississippi drifter with the big grin and easy manner was riding high. Success meant money and money meant that Jimmie could indulge in an extravagant lifestyle. Like another Mississippi singer who would head up a musical revolution in the 1950s, he lavished many dollars on fancy automobiles, jewelry, and clothes, and he was generous with hand-outs to cronies and friends. For Jimmie, money was made to be spent, especially if one knew time to spend it was growing short. In 1929 he began building his mansion, "Blue Yodeler's Paradise," in Kerrville, Texas, having moved there because the climate was kinder to his ravaged lungs. The high-living years, from 1929 through 1931, came to an end when the effects of the

Great Depression crunched the record business. Jimmie was forced to sell "Blue Yodeler's Paradise." Once again, though famous this time, he had to hustle for paying jobs.

If the Depression caught up with him, tuberculosis was inexorably overtaking him. As it caused frustrating interruptions in performances, he more and more turned to alcohol and other pain killers to assuage the suffering. The disease never became an issue with his fans though it was apparent what was wrong. Perhaps his quietly heroic struggle was best reflected in the ominously ironic "T. B. Blues" when he sang that though he knew he would probably lose he would go out fighting like a lion.

Certainly it was with lionheartedness that he approached his last recording session. Knowing he did not have long to live, needing money, and wanting to leave as healthy an estate as he could for Carrie and his daughter, Anita, the Blue Yodeler embarked by boat with a private nurse from Galveston and arrived in New York on May 14, 1933. Severely weak and in almost constant pain, he recorded twelve numbers over several strenuous days, often having to rest on a cot in the studio between songs, and at one time even forced to sit in a chair propped on pillows before the microphone. But he made it and with neglible loss of quality to his voice. The feisty spunk of his youth had matured and culminated in this magnificent exhibition of courage and will.

On May 26, 1933, two days after the final song was recorded, Jimmie Rodgers died in a room of the Taft Hotel in New York. He was thirty-five years old. In a lily-covered casket the body was borne back to Meridian by train. A long, moaning whistle announced its sad return to thousands of sorrowing friends and fans. The Singing Brakeman, America's Blue Yodeler, was dead, but his influence on American music was just beginning to live.

Pre-eminent in giving form and direction to the emerging "Hillbilly" genre, later to be called "Country and Western," Jimmie Rodgers did exert a vital influence on the course of

American music. With the image of a hard-drinking good-ole-boy up from poverty and a hardscrabble life, constantly on the road performing for the common folks, singing suggestively about love gone bad or good, yearningly for home or far away places, endearingly of mother and pals, knowingly of trains and departures, assuming a pose of arrogant defiance, or mournful heartbreak, or down-and-out but hanging on, performing with a wink, tongue-in-cheek, or mostly with a massive anguish in the voice, he became the prototypical Country Music Star.

Yet, Jimmie conceived of himself as essentially a popular entertainer in the mainstream of commercial music. On the other hand, some of his records are prized by jazz aficionados, and of course many of his songs possess a blues structure which he rendered in the best tradition of that idiom: that is, like the great blues singers, no matter the grave anguish or moaning desperation expressed in the lyrics, the method of delivery, the quality of voice, always projected an underlying, irrepressible affirmation of life, a masterful balance of the tragic and comic dimensions of our basic emotions.

Jimmie Rodger's great achievement then was an act of synthesis: To the Anglo-Saxon folk tradition he welded the gut-essence and heartbeat rhythm of the Delta blues and burnished it now and then with jazz phrasings. In creating such a rich musical concoction, he originated a unique personal style and, moreover, made it supremely commerical.

Perhaps above all he was an artist for the common man and woman. The direct, genuine clarity of his voice and the acrobatic curls and jumps of his yodel, always true and controlled, that could go from sweet to raunchy, touched the hearts of the people. (His fondness for the Hawaiian steel guitar, a staple instrument of Country music, must have stemmed partly from the affinity of his voice with it. The controlled manipulation of the metal slide over the strings can create shouts, whines, cries, and yodels—can run the scale of human emotions from unleashed elation to black-hole depression.) And he controlled the stage with the radiant charisma all great performers have.

Usually wearing a light-colored suit, spiffy bowtie, and a straw boater cocked at a rakish angle on his head (only occasionally did he wear the railroad uniform), standing with a leg propped on a straightbacked chair, offhandedly spinning a humorous tale, projecting a curious paradox of frail vulnerability and command, he would sing the songs the people came to hear, the trademark voice establishing command, the guitar often in peculiar, unorthodox timing (sometimes seeming to assume a separate existence) but always complementary and ultimately joining to make a metaphysical whole, sending the people away feeling they had heard and seen themselves.

The man's music, his ability to relate to an audience, his courage in the face of great odds, made him a hero to millions and enshrined his memory in the folk consciousness of American culture. Other shrines and honors have followed. In 1976 the Jimmie Rodgers Memorial Festival, Inc. built in Meridian the Jimmie Rodgers Museum and Monument. The Museum houses many of Rodgers's personal belongings as well as railroad artifacts from the 1920s and 1930s. Also a Country Music festival featuring top country entertainers is held annually in Meridian during the week of May 26th in honor of "The Blue Yodeler." Another honor was bestowed in memory of the man and his music on May 24, 1978, when the U. S. Postal Service issued a commemorative stamp. It pictures Jimmie in a railroad cap and coat (but sporting a bowtie) flashing the jaunty thumbs-up signal. In May of 1980 Bristol, Tennessee, officially opened its Country Music Museum where Jimmie's historic first recording session is prominently noted. And of course a signal honor came in Nashville when Jimmie Rodgers was enshrined as the first member of the Country Music Hall of Fame and designated the "Father of Country Music." But perhaps the greatest tribute still comes from the people, those who continue to buy his reissued records and listen to the magic.

In Jimmie Rodgers the state of Mississippi has a hero. From the Delta blues singers, such as John Hurt, John Lee Hooker, James Thomas, to the king of rock-and-roll, Elvis Presley, the state's musical heritage is indeed rich and dynamic. But for singular influence on music styles and massive popular appeal there is no greater legacy than that left by "The Singing Brakeman," "America's Blue Yodeler," the "Father of Country Music," Jimmie Rodgers.

BIBLIOGRAPHY

Barra, Allen. "The Singing Brakeman." *Horizon*, 22 (September 1979), 70–73.

Gentry, Linnell. *A History and Encyclopedia of Country, Western, and Gospel Music.* St. Clair Shores, Mich.: Scholarly Press, Inc., 1972.

Hemphill, Paul. *Nashville Sound: Bright Lights and Country Music.* New York: Simon and Schuster, 1970.

Malone, Bill C. *Country Music, U.S.A.: A Fifty-Year History.* Austin: University of Texas Press, 1968.

Malone, Bill C., and Judith McColloh. *Stars of Country Music.* Urbana: University of Illinois Press, 1975.

Pleasants, Henry. *The Great American Popular Singers.* New York: Simon and Schuster, 1974.

*Porterfield, Nolan. *Jimmie Rodgers: The Life and Times of America's Blue Yodler.* Urbana: University of Illinois Press, 1979.

Rodgers, Carrie. *My Husband, Jimmie Rodgers.* Nashville: Ernest Tubb Publications, 1935.

Shelton, Robert, and Burt Goldblatt. *The Country Music Story: A Pictorial History of Country Music.* New Rochelle, N.Y.: Arlington House, 1971.

Stambler, Irwin, and Grelun Landon, eds. *Encyclopedia of Folk, Country, and Western Music.* New York: St. Martin's Press, 1969.

*This book is by far the most nearly accurate, best written account of Jimmie Rodgers's life. It also contains a complete discography.

William Faulkner
1897–1962

William Faulkner

William Faulkner:
Transcending the Place Mississippi

BY WILLIAM BOOZER

William Faulkner was a storyteller. One of the stories he liked to tell was that he was a Mississippi dirt farmer who wrote on the side. Another was that he was a failed poet who wrote like he did because he couldn't write like Shakespeare and Shelley.

In truth, he put on paper some of the world's great literature. Genius and talent carved from him what he was, a sculpted sum of observation and imagination and experience. He was a remarkable individualist, an American original.

He was a little man. At five feet five-and-a-half inches, he might go unnoticed when he entered a crowded room. If he found a corner, or a wall to stand against and prop a foot, where he could practice his art of observation, he might for awhile go unnoticed, taking his own measure of the things he saw and heard. But he was distinctive. His courtly manners and the piercing dark eyes exposed the uniqueness of the mind and heart and muscle housed in the slight shell of him. The mind, the intellect, he did not trust. The heart he did, and his advice to writers was that they write from the heart and not the glands. Something else in this little man made him into what he wanted people to think he was—a farmer, a simple country-man; a man who, while in residence at Charlottesville, Virginia, could decline John F. Kennedy's invitation to a White House dinner for Nobel Prize winners because one hundred miles was too far to go for supper.

But his art betrayed him.

He had some things to say at Charlottesville and in Stockholm about universal verities, about courage and honor and hope and pride and compassion and pity and sacrifice. He had some things to say about responsibility in an unsung Delta Council speech in Mississippi that ranks with his finest achievements. And for forty-five years of a published career in which his prose was laced with poetry that will live because the people who populate the prose breathe and cast shadows, he lived and breathed and wrote about these things of the heart, the spirit.

As a storyteller, he was a fibber with few peers who knew early in life what he would someday be. "I want to be a writer like my great-grandfather," he told his third grade teacher. Years later, on the threshold of old age, he would write author Joan Williams that he now realized "what an amazing gift I had: uneducated in every formal sense, without even very literate, let alone literary, companions, yet to have made the things I made. I dont know where it came from. I dont know why God or gods or whoever it was, selected me to be the vessel." He wasn't being humble or falsely modest, he said. "It is simply amazement."

He was a fictionist in real life, as well as on paper. When *Forum* magazine accepted the short story "A Rose for Emily" for its April, 1930 issue, the editors asked the still relatively unknown Faulkner for a biographical account of himself. Faulkner replied:

"Born male and single at early age in Mississippi. Quit school after five years in seventh grade. Got job in Grandfather's bank and learned medicinal value of his liquor. Grandfather thought janitor did it. Hard on janitor. War came. Liked British uniform. Got commission R.F.C., pilot. Crashed. Cost British gov't £2000. Was still pilot. Crashed. Cost British gov't £2000. Quit. Cost British gov't $84.30. King said, 'Well done.' Returned to Mississippi. Family got job: postmaster. Resigned by mutual agreement on part of two inspectors; accused of throwing all incoming mail into garbage can. How disposed of outgoing mail never proved. . . Met man named Sherwood Anderson.

Said, 'Why not write novels? Maybe won't have to work.' Did. . . . Age 32. Own and operate own typewriter."

It was one of the first of many attempts at saying the work is the important thing, and never mind who wrote it.

He was even less accommodating during the same period to H.L. Mencken's *American Mercury*, which wanted a biographical blurb to run with "Honor" in the July, 1930 issue. "Dont tell the bastards anything," Faulkner wrote his friend and agent Ben Wasson. "It cant matter to them. Tell them I was born of an alligator and a nigger slave at the Geneva peace conference two years ago."

Thus did he build a barrier around himself, throwing a smokescreen about the privacy he longed for but which his art abdicated. It was the sort of pedigree, a mixture of lies, half-truths and tall-tale humor, that invited more knocks at the door, more mail and telephone calls, endless invasions of his private life.

There would come a time, at age forty-six, when he would welcome an essay proposed by Malcolm Cowley which the critic suggested might "redress the balance between his worth and reputation." Faulkner's seventeen books were all but out of print, he was doing hack writing in Hollywood to pay bills, and he was thinking that he had worked too hard at his trade "to leave no better mark on this our pointless chronicle than I seem to be about to leave." But forget the biography part, Faulkner implored Cowley. "If what one has thought and hoped and endeavored and failed at is not enough, if it must be explained and excused by what he has experienced, done or suffered, while he was not being an artist, then he and the one making the evaluation have both failed."

Five years later, Cowley's essay having grown into the Viking *Portable Faulkner* and sparked a revival of interest and recognition that would be followed soon by the Nobel Prize for literature for Faulkner, the shy Mississippian was still at it. "It is my ambition to be, as a private individual, abolished and voided from history, leaving it markless, no refuse save the printed books; I wish I had had enough sense to see ahead thirty years and, like some of the Elizabethans, not signed them. It is my aim, and every effort bent, that the sum and history of my life, which in the same sentence is my obit and epitaph too, shall be them both: He made the books and he died."

What manner of man was this, a high school dropout who dabbled at poetry in the mode of Swinburne and Housman and at drawings in the style of Aubrey Beardsley, left odd jobs at home in Oxford, Mississippi, to work briefly in New Haven before enlisting in the Royal Air Force Canada, moved restlessly around Oxford and the University of Mississippi campus and Memphis before moving on briefly to New York and New Orleans, and went to Paris to sit on park benches and watch the pigeons and to a cafe to look at James Joyce but apparently not to Sylvia Beach's Shakespeare & Co. bookstore where Pound and Joyce and Hemingway and Fitzgerald and Gertrude Stein and Ford Madox Ford and less notable people were aspiring to become famous writers, as Janet Flanner recalls, "as soon as possible." Who wrote two inferior novels, learning how to write, left New Orleans for Oxford again and home, his own "little postage stamp of native soil," to realize that it was so rich in material that he would never live long enough to write it all down, created a mythical land called Yoknapatawpha County in his third novel, *Sartoris*, and went on, in Cowley's words, to tell its story from Indians days to what he regarded as the morally disastrous present, "a sustained work of the imagination such as no other American writer had attempted."

What nature, this man, who could publish such masterpieces as *The Sound and the Fury, As I Lay Dying, Sanctuary, Light in August,* and *Absalom, Absalom!* in a seven-year period, the greatest burst of creativity in our literature, and go on to write masterpieces like *The Unvanquished* and *The Hamlet* and *Go Down, Moses,* "The Bear" and "Spotted Horses" and other great long and short stories, publish in all nineteen novels, six volumes of collected stories, and two of poetry, and be puzzled over why people would be interested in the man behind the work, his likes and dislikes, the experience out of which the work grew?

With the half-truths and fiction about himself, it was natural that legends would flourish about this man who encouraged them in his efforts to discourage the invasions of privacy.

There are the legends about his drinking, for which John Faulkner, himself an accomplished artist and writer, said his brother Bill got more credit than he deserved. There are the legends about Faulkner's period as Ole Miss postmaster, about his being, in his friend Phil Stone's words, "the damndest postmaster the world has ever seen," being too busy reading or writing or drinking or playing cards or golf to put up the mail or send it out, being relieved of his duties and glad of it because, in Faulkner's words, he would never again have to be "at the beck and call of every son of a bitch" who had two cents to spend on a postage stamp.

There are the stories with no substance of his combat flying and crashing His Majesty's airplanes and coming home with a silver plate in his head, of the years of bondage, painfully true, as a Hollywood script writer and writing potboilers for the magazines to make money to pay bills, of returning home to Mississippi from Hollywood on one occasion pulling a horse in a trailer because he didn't want any mare of his to throw a foal in California. And the time he asked a studio boss if he could work on a certain script at home, the boss thinking he meant across town at his apartment, asking later where Faulkner was, learning that he was home in Oxford, naturally, working on the script.

And the legends grow.

A Memphis newspaper reporter who admires Faulkner is in the basement of Sears when he spots Faulkner coming down another aisle. The reporter does a double-take, breaking stride.

Their eyes meet, Faulkner's saying "Here is somebody who has recognized me and is fixin' to move in on me." The reporter relents, going on to look at lampshades.

The same reporter is told one evening by the night city editor to call William Faulkner down at Oxford and ask him about something to do with a sheriff in Panola County who was waging war on beer, raiding picnic tables and looking in back seats and trunks of cars, searching for sin. "He doesn't answer the telephone," the reporter says. "Call him anyway," the editor barks. The reporter hears the operator tell the lady who answers the phone that there is a long distance call for Mr. Faulkner, hears the lady say "Just a moment," and in a moment is talking to Faulkner, who is courteous and accommodating, calling the young reporter "sir." One legend destroyed.

The reporter, while a college student, had gone to Ole Miss for a Southern Literary Festival, finding luminaries there like John Crowe Ransom, Stark Young, Elizabeth Spencer and Harry Harrison Kroll, but not Faulkner. He drove out to Faulkner's home, thinking he'd get more out of an afternoon visit with Faulkner than the festival program. Faulkner's daughter Jill answered the knock at the door, saying her father was at Sardis Lake in his boat. Strange literary man, the student thought, who preferred his boat to a literary festival in shouting distance of his house.

And so the reporter decides to read this man. He is dumbfounded as he reads *The Sound and the Fury*, which he can't even understand except to recognize something of the dignity and strength of Dilsey. He racks the Faulkner books at home, reading them with growing astonishment, in time having more of Faulkner's books and books about Faulkner than Faulkner had.

And the children. From their cradles on, they hear the name Faulkner spoken; growing, they stand and look at the books, even read one or two. So it is a natural enough response the reporter's daughter has on that February 22 when she is four years old.

"Good morning, Charlotte. Know whose birthday it is today?"

"Who?"

"The father of our country."

"Today's William Faulkner's birthday?"

"No, darling. George Washington's."

"Oh."

It is this father of unique literature—a complex yet simple man who masqueraded as just another Mississippian but whose work unmasked him—whom we honor here as one of Mississippi's heroic sons. He wrote his way to such stardom that Mississippi now shares with the world this genius whose work is universal, transcending the place Mississippi. His heart beat a Mississippi tempo, but his pen wove a stark legend of mankind, of the human heart in conflict, which in words that Faulkner used to describe the writer's duty, "uplifts men's hearts and helps them endure . . . prevail."

> "He was born of it and his bones will sleep in it. . .Loving all of it even while he had to hate some of it because he knows now that you don't love because: you love despite; not for the virtues, but despite the faults."
> —— "Mississippi"

William Cuthbert Faulkner was born in New Albany, Mississippi, on September 25, 1897, the first of four sons of Murry C. Falkner and Maud Butler Falkner. Faulkner said his ancestry goes back to Inverness, Scotland, the name Falkner having been corrupted from Falconer. Faulkner put the "u" in (or back in; the accounts vary) when he went to Toronto for flight training with the Royal Air Force Canada in 1918.

The modern family history dates paternally to Col. William Clark Falkner, who was born in Knox County, Tennessee, in 1825 while his family was migrating from North Carolina to Ste. Genevieve, Missouri. He left home in his early teens to live with a schoolteacher uncle, John Wesley Thompson, in Ripley, Mississippi. The young Falkner grew up to fight in the Mexican and Civil Wars, was with Stonewall Jackson's left at 1st Manassas, became a lawyer, built a narrow gauge railroad from Middleton, Tennessee to Ripley and on to Pontotoc, was a successful and wealthy landowner and businessman, authored a romantic novel, *The White Rose of Memphis*, and five more books of fiction, travel and epic poetry, and was elected to the Mississippi Legislature. He was gunned down on the streets of Ripley on November 5, 1889, by the man he beat in the legislative race, his former partner in the Ripley, Ship Island and Kentucky Railroad ("The Doodle Bug," it would be called). He died the next day.

Colonel Falkner would become the prototype of John Sartoris in the fiction of the great-grandson who wanted to be a writer like the great-grandfather. The Old Colonel was by nature heroic, "a considerable figure in his time and provincial milieu," Faulkner would say, who had come to town a barefoot waif of fourteen and built a dynasty of his own.

More important to William Faulkner than his great-grandfather's literary output, Michael Millgate writes, "were those qualities in Colonel Falkner and those aspects of his active and often violent life which provided the basis for the figure of Colonel John Sartoris in books like *Sartoris* and *The Unvanquished*."

"Faulkner must have been attracted above all by the Colonel's determination to leave his mark on the world, by his considerable success in doing so, and by the part he played in the Civil War and its aftermath. The building of the railroad, in particular, seized Faulkner's imagination: he referred to it many times in his early fiction and used it as the main axis of his legendary Yoknapatawpha County."

Faulkner's grandfather, John Wesley Thompson Falkner, the family's "Young Colonel," was president of the short-line railroad until it was sold in 1902, founded and was president of First National Bank of Oxford, and was the prototype for Colonel Bayard Sartoris in his grandson's fiction.

William Faulkner's father, Murry C. Falkner, had a varied career. He worked for the family railroad at New Albany and Ripley before moving his family to Oxford the year the railroad was sold. In Oxford, he operated a cottonseed oil mill, an ice plant, a livery stable, a Standard Oil agency, and a hardware business before becoming secretary and business manager of Ole Miss. He died in 1932 at age sixty-two, disappointed that his eldest son, if he had to write, was writing things like *The Sound and the Fury* and *As I Lay Dying* instead of mysteries.

Faulkner's mother, Maud Butler Falkner, would survive her husband by almost three decades and know joy and heartbreak as only a mother can. She excelled at the art of raising four boys, and as an oil painter prolific in her output of landscapes and florals. Uplifted and sustained by the achievements of each of her sons, she would see her eldest win the coveted Nobel Prize and be forever diminished by the tragic death of her youngest in his prime of life. She was eighty-nine when she died in 1960.

Faulkner's parents moved with him in late 1898 or early 1899 to Ripley, where his brothers Murry C. Falkner, Jr., who would be called Jack, and John Wesley Thompson Falkner III (Johncy) were born. Five years after the 1902 move to Oxford, the fourth of the Falkner boys, Dean Swift Falkner, was born.

Their growing up in the small university town of Oxford would spawn more legends of a time when life was simpler, when family ties were stronger, and when the world was at peace with itself.

Jack Falkner would fight in two world wars, join his brothers in their passion for flying, serve as a special agent for the Federal Bureau of Investigation, and write family memoirs including articles and one book, *The Falkners of Mississippi.*

John Faulkner was in many respects more in touch with the homefolks and in harmony with the Mississippi of their time than big brother William, whose more liberal stand on race was a cross borne well by family and friends. More Oxonians may have read John than William; they could understand what John was writing about, some said. A civil engineering graduate of

Ole Miss, John worked for a time as Oxford city engineer, was employed by the Mississippi Highway Department, and flew professionally. He was an accomplished artist who would not sell the original of a painting (a number of them depicting scenes from William's fiction) but would make a "copy" of an original, promising that it would be better because he had had the practice. It was while managing William's farm in Lafayette County's notorious political subdivision, Beat Two, in the late 1930's that John began writing fiction. Among his eight novels are *Men Working* (1941), *Dollar Cotton* (1942) and *Chooky* (1950). His other work includes *My Brother Bill: An Affectionate Reminiscence* and a number of short stories and articles.

Dean Swift Falkner excelled at anything to do with sports, the outdoors, and flying, from high school football to Ole Miss baseball, golf, hunting and barnstorming. He carried on the family's artistic heritage with promise, but more than anything he was an accomplished aviator, the best of the four flying Falkners. He died in 1935 at age twenty-eight in a crash during an air show at Thaxton, Mississippi.

William Faulkner's life and work are superbly documented in such sources as the two-volume *Faulkner: A Biography* by Joseph Blotner, Michael Millgate's *The Achievement of William Faulkner*, published work of Cleanth Brooks, Carvel Collins, James B. Meriwether, Robert Penn Warren, Elizabeth M. Kerr, Warren Beck and other scholars, Malcolm Cowley's *Portable Faulkner*, and family chronicles. (See Bibliography.) Faulkner Studies through the years have focused valuable scholarship on the man and the work, correcting earlier errors and helping illuminate the experience out of which the work grew.

Faulkner's was a largely typical Mississippi experience, save for the modicum of family squirearchy and of course the genius that set him apart and which leaves us with a picture larger than life. He was a complex man who shunned limelight, vigorously defended his private life, wrote stories and novels in order to rid himself of "demons," and seemed not to care, once they were on paper, whether they were liked or disliked, read or unread. And he was a simple man, a "Mississippi dirt farmer," with the same foibles and warts and strengths of his neighbors. He personified his complex/simple nature by being a liberal conservative in politics, a loving father who could tell his child Jill when she complained once about his drinking that "Nobody remembers Shakespeare's child," a husband whose marriage lost its sheen but who met his obligations and responsibilities and made work what didn't. He was a compassionate man, years ahead of his time on race relations, and a patriotic provincial who could say in February of 1956 that he preferred a middle road but that if he had to choose between the United States government and Mississippi he'd choose Mississippi even if it meant going into the streets and shooting Blacks— and then meet the furor by saying that no sober man would make such statements nor any sane man believe them. He liked to hunt but not to kill, and rode horses he was always falling from. He smoked cheap tobacco and expensive blends in costly English Dunhill pipes and wore Johnston & Murphy or mismatched shoes along with a ragged Harris tweed jacket that the Salvation Army wouldn't have had, a white handkerchief in the breast pocket and another tucked in a sleeve in the British manner. He drank bourbon whiskey to excess, and admired moderation in all things. He could write a simple sentence like "It was Saturday morning, about ten oclock." And he could write nonstop sentences that ran on for pages. Grown weary over complaints about the length of them, he said once that he thought that in his next book he'd have the publisher put a whole page of periods at the back so the reader could cut them out and paste them in wherever they were wanted. He was a profoundly religious man who rarely went to church.

He was short of formal education, jumping from the first to the third grade and dropping out in the eleventh (at that time, final) year without taking a high school diploma. His only other classroom experience as a student was that of a flying cadet and as a student at Ole Miss under a special arrangement for returning World War I veterans, withdrawing in the second year.

If no classroom could hold him, his education went on. He read voraciously, and was a peerless observer of the language and life of his people and place. He was reading Conrad and Shakespeare and Balzac in the fourth grade, was writing and illustrating his own stories by the fall of 1909 when he was twelve, and poetry at age thirteen.

In all of Oxford, there were two people who seemed to notice that there was among them a rare talent, genius perhaps. One was Maud Butler Falkner. The other was Phil Stone, who had a law degree from Ole Miss and another from Yale University. Stone, four years Faulkner's senior, was as versed in poetry and literature as law. He loaned Faulkner books to read, and encouraged him at his writing. He would come to be called "mentor," and be instrumental in Faulkner being first published.

Faulkner mostly floundered. He "failed" at poetry. He failed to stick with jobs in his grandfather's bank and in his father's livery stable and hardware store. He did odd jobs, house painting among them. He failed as a war hero, the war ending before he could get there. His boyhood girl friend married someone else and went to live in China. He failed as Ole Miss postmaster. He wandered about Mississippi and Memphis and New Orleans, and took six months to tramp around Europe.

But he was being published—the first time with a drawing of a couple dancing, in the 1917 Ole Miss yearbook, the first time outside Oxford with a poem, "L'Apres-Midi d'un Faune," in the August 6, 1919 *New Republic*, and in the New Orleans *Double Dealer* and New Orleans *Times-Picayune*. He became friends in New Orleans with Sherwood Anderson. His first book, *The Marble Faun*, was published in December, 1924. Then came *Soldiers' Pay* and *Mosquitoes*, those first two novels in which he learned to write.

On January 21, 1929, Harcourt, Brace and Co. published *Sar-*

toris, and the town of Jefferson and the county of Yoknapatawpha were founded. Faulkner would spend the rest of his life spinning yarns about his mythical Yoknapatawpha, a 2,400 square mile kingdom populated by 6,298 whites and 9,313 Blacks. The only time he would get in trouble as a writer was when he infrequently stepped outside Yoknapatawpha, as in *A Fable*, an allegory of Passion Week that is a critical failure despite having won the National Book Award and a Pulitzer Prize. (Faulkner had won the National Book Award in 1950 for *Collected Stories*, and would win a second Pulitzer in 1963 for *The Reivers*.)

The year 1929 was marked in two other major respects for Faulkner. On June 29, he married Estelle Oldham Franklin, who had returned from China with two children and a divorce. As children, Blotner tells us, Billy Falkner and Estelle Oldham had wanted to grow up and raise chickens. On October 6 that year, Jonathan Cape and Harrison Smith published *The Sound and the Fury*, which Faulkner years later would call his favorite not because it was his best but because it was his "most splendid failure," the one he had worked at the longest and hardest, "anguished the most over." Many see it today as his masterpiece.

With a wife now and two step-children, Faulkner had another job: firing the boilers in the power plant at Ole Miss, where he wrote *As I Lay Dying* in six weeks, mostly between midnight and 4 a.m. while the student population was asleep.

He would begin publishing stories in national magazines in 1930, the year he bought an antebellum house and four acres on the outskirts of Oxford, naming it Rowan Oak after the Scottish mountain ash that he couldn't get to grow in Mississippi red clay.

Faulkner was thirty-two, half his life behind him. Biographers paint him at midpoint as very warm and human. If not the best postmaster Ole Miss ever knew, he had been one of the best scoutmasters in Oxford's history until being drummed out of the troop by a pulpit outcry over his drinking. He loved chil-

dren and captivated them by his storytelling. He was serious
about his work, but did not take himself too seriously. He possessed a rare humor.

A daughter was born prematurely to the Faulkners, living
only nine days. Two-and-a-half years later, Jill Faulkner was
born.

Recognition of Faulkner's work was slow coming, and his income insufficient to support his family and others dependent
wholly or in part upon him with the death of his father.
Faulkner in 1932 turned to Hollywood and script writing, a
mostly unhappy alliance that would occupy him off and on for
the next twenty-two years and sap his creative energies, in the
early Hollywood years, when they were still strong. Some of his
best work was behind him when he first went to Hollywood.
But ahead were *Absalom, Absalom!*, which many call his
finest novel, *The Unvanquished, Go Down, Moses*, the Snopes
trilogy, six lesser novels and five collections of short stories. He
spent one seven-year period under contract bondage with War-
ner Brothers, for a time getting $300 a week when other script
writers were earning as much as $2,500 a week. Jack Warner
would boast that he had America's greatest writer under contract for peanuts. Faulkner would work on forty-nine films during his Hollywood era.

With the Hollywood years came "farming," flying lessons at
age thirty-five and the purchase of his own plane, and the revival of interest in his work following the *Portable Faulkner*
when all except *Sanctuary* was out of print. And financial security for the first time in his life with sale of *Intruder in the
Dust* to Hollywood in the late 1940's for $50,000, and big pub-
licity hullabaloo at Oxford during the filming and premiere.
Then the acclaim that came with the Nobel Prize and other
honors. Something strange happened to Faulkner. Like many
writers a reticent and poor speaker, he suddenly began accepting speaking engagements and agreeing to interviews. He made
trips to Greece, Japan and South America as a goodwill ambas-

sador for his country. He spent several years as writer in residence and Balch lecturer at the University of Virginia.

The honors had begun in 1920 when he won a $10 poetry prize offered by an Ole Miss professor. Twenty years later he would be elected to membership in the National Institute of Arts and Letters. In succession would come election to the American Academy of Arts and Letters, the Academy's Howells Medal for Fiction, the 1949 Nobel award, the French Legion of Honor, the Silver Medal of the Greek Academy, the Gold Medal for Fiction of the National Institute of Arts and Letters, the two National Book Awards, and the two Pulitzers.

The honors, at last the recognition, mellowed him. His daughter Jill and her husband, Paul D. Summers Jr., presented the Faulkners with three grandsons, further mellowing him.

He was sixty-four years old now, an aging patriarch. The writing well was running dry, he feared, if the pencil was unbroken. On January 3, 1962, he was injured in a fall from a horse at Charlottesville. In April, he met for two days with cadets and faculty at the U.S. Military Academy at West Point, where his son-in-law had graduated. On May 24, he was in New York to receive the Gold Medal for Fiction. *The Reivers* was published on June 4, Faulkner calling it the funniest book he had ever read. Back home in Oxford, he hurt his back in a fall from a horse on June 17. He entered a hospital at nearby Byhalia on July 5. At 1:30 a.m. on July 6, he died.

Novelist William Styron was among those who gathered in Oxford for the services in the parlor at Rowan Oak, and burial in St. Peter's Cemetery. He told in a *Life* magazine tribute of having joined novelist-historian Shelby Foote in a search in the Faulkner library for an anthology containing a Faulkner poem. They found it in the writer's "office," a work room at the rear of the house, along with Henry Kyd Douglas's *I Rode With Stonewall*, which Faulkner had been reading when death came. The 1924 poem had been called "Mississippi Hills: My Epitaph" when he gave it late that year to Myrtle Ramey, a friend since the third grade. The poem has had six variant printings, the most recent in 1979 in its original, longer version in *Mississippi Poems*, a facsimile printing by Oxford's Yoknapatawpha Press of typescripts given Myrtle Ramey and now owned by Faulkner collector Louis Daniel Brodsky. The poet Faulkner sang:

> If there be grief, let it be the rain
> And this but silver grief for grieving's sake,
> And these green woods be dreaming here to wake
> Within my heart, if I should rouse again.
>
> But I shall sleep, for where is any death
> While in these blue hills slumbrous overhead
> I'm rooted like a tree? Though I be dead,
> This soil that holds me fast will find me breath.

At some point in time, Faulkner had a vision. *Sartoris* would announce the vision: his apocryphal Yoknapatawpha County. One book followed another, in small printings customary of the day, and the stories, and the literary world took faint notice. Critics who thought they knew what he was doing were a long time recognizing the creation of a mythical kingdom, the evolution of a legend, a saga, not of Oxford and Lafayette County but of the whole South, and beyond the South because people everywhere have the same frailties, the same verities he wrote and talked about. He was telling the story of the South's decay, they said. He was writing bad things about his town and his people, debasing and defiling his native state, some homefolks decided, and should be ashamed. Some people wouldn't speak to him on the streets of home. Sometimes, when they'd speak, he wouldn't speak back, his mind in Yoknapatawpha County or elsewhere. Uppity man. Count No 'Count, they called the "arrogant" young man when he came home from the war that had cheated him, moving about town and campus "putting on airs."

Faulkner went on writing. If at any time he read the critics, the reviewers, he stopped. He would write Malcolm Cowley that he thought he had "written a lot and sent it off to print before I actually realised strangers might read it." Cowley would note that the man's early novels were overpraised, usually for the wrong reasons, and the later better novels had been condemned or neglected.

Faulkner was indeed writing about the decay of the Old South, the deep cicatrices from the curse of slavery, but he was also writing about the moral confusion and social decay of the present everywhere; like sinister Snopesism which carries the germs, they are so creeping as to go unseen and unknown. Faulkner would prescribe an antidote: eternal vigilance.

"Essentially he is not a novelist," Cowley wrote of Faulkner, "in the sense of not being a writer who sets out to observe actions and characters, then fits them into the architectural framework of a story. For all the weakness of his own poems, he is an epic or bardic poet in prose, a creator of myths that he weaves together into a legend of the South."

Cowley focuses our attention on the parallels of Faulkner and Hawthorne, two solitary writers who had a voice to listen to and ears to hear, and the poetic nature and raw genius to put on paper what the voice said. Cleanth Brooks perceives for us the parallels and affinities of Faulkner and Yeats—their view of man on its positive side aristocratic and heroic, the provincial cultures in the American South and the Ireland that nourished their genius. The Irish poet's local resources, says Brooks, "became important only as he brought them to bear upon the crucial issues of the twentieth century and so joined the mainstream of international literature. The same should be said of Faulkner. It would have been stupid to praise him as a superb local colorist, just as it was stupid to praise him for conducting an alleged exposé of Southern degeneracy. His fiction was not designed either to congratulate or to scold his fellow Southerners. What he succeeded in doing was to use the experiences that he knew best in order to interpret universal issues. His cultural heritage proved to be ultimately important in providing him with a special and most valuable perspective on Western civilization as a whole."

The English novelist Arnold Bennett was less scholarly in his early assessment of the man from Mississippi. Faulkner "writes generally like an angel," said Bennett in a London review of Faulkner's first novel.

One of the finest estimates of Faulkner came from Hamilton Basso, who knew Faulkner slightly in their New Orleans days. In "William Faulkner: Man and Writer," in the July 28, 1962 *Saturday Review*, Basso looked back on those years and to his reading of the man he had called "the Little Confederate."

"There are a few things in the South that, as far as intellectual comprehension is concerned, I 'know' almost as well as anybody. So when I read Faulkner. . . I begin, so to speak, from the inside looking out. But then something happens. What I 'know' begins to lose its hold. It fades and grows dim. And soon, instead of being on the inside looking out, I am on the outside looking in. It wasn't the South that Faulkner was writing about: it was his vision of the world. Those who read him as a 'realistic' novelist might just as well read Dante as a Baedeker to the nether regions, and Milton as a Michelin going in the opposite direction."

But no one, of course, could speak with more certitude of Faulkner than Faulkner. In some things he was uncompromising. He was a compassionate man with an unrelenting devotion to fidelity and courage and honor. They were traits poignantly reflected in his remembrance of Ned Barnett, who served four generations of Falkners back to the Old Colonel, and Caroline Barr (Mammy Callie), whose funeral he preached in the parlor at Rowan Oak and to whom he dedicated *Go Down, Moses*: "Who was born in slavery and who gave to my family a fidelity without stint or calculation of recompense and to my childhood an immeasurable devotion and love." He wrote about each of them in "Mississippi" in the April, 1954 *Holiday* magazine, at middle age remembering Uncle Ned, who had been born in a back yard cabin in 1865. "And Caroline too, whom the middle-aged had inherited too in his hierarchal turn, nobody knowing any more exactly how many more years than a hundred she was. . ." Who in the sunset of her long life would have but one need: that "Miss Hestelle" should make for her a fresh clean cap and apron to lay in.

"Two days after Christmas the stroke came that was the one; two days after that she lay in the parlor in the fresh cap and apron she would not see, and the middle-aging did indeed lay back and preach the sermon, the oration, hoping that when his turn came there would be someone in the world to owe him the sermon owed to her by all who had been, as he had been from infancy, within the scope and range of that fidelity and that devotion and that rectitude."

In that speech to the Delta Council in the heart of Faulkner country's vanishing wilderness, at Cleveland, Mississippi, on May 15, 1952, the man who in his Nobel acceptance in Stockholm two-and-a-half years earlier had declined to accept the end of man, believing that man "will not merely endure: he will prevail," had some things to say about freedom and liberty and independence and responsibility. He read a statement that John Curran, the Irish statesman, had made two hundred years before: "God hath vouchsafed man liberty only on condition of eternal vigilance; which condition if he break it, servitude is the consequence of his crime and the punishment of his guilt." Faulkner declined to believe that man had forgotten this. Nor would he accept what the economists and sociologists were saying, that the reason for man's present condition, a mishmash of too much government and bureaucracy and lost initiative, all of it masquerading as progress, was too many people.

He declined to believe, he said, that man's crime against his freedom is that there are too many of him, because that would be to believe "that man's sufferance on the face of the earth is threatened, not by his environment, but by himself: that he cannot hope to cope with his environment and its evils, because he cannot even cope with his own mass.

"Which is exactly what those who misuse and betray the mass of him for their own aggrandisement and power and tenure of office, believe: that man is incapable of responsibility and freedom, of fidelity and endurance and courage, that he not only cannot choose good from evil, he cannot even distinguish it, let alone practice the choice. And to believe that, you have already written off the hope of man, as they who have reft him of his inalienable right to be responsible, have done, and you might as well quit now and let man stew on in peace and in his own recordless and oblivious juice, to his deserved and ungrieved doom.

"I, for one, decline to believe this. . . I believe that the true heirs of the old tough durable fathers are still capable of responsibility and self-respect, if only they can remember them again. What we need is not fewer people, but more room between them, where those who would stand on their feet, could, and those who won't, might have to. Then the welfare, the relief, the compensation, instead of being nationally sponsored cash prizes for idleness and ineptitude, could go where the old independent uncompromising fathers themselves would have intended it and blessed it: to those who still cannot, until the day when even the last of them except the sick and the old, would also be among them who not only can, but will."

It was a Mississippian talking to Mississippians. But more than that, it was an uncommon man talking to mankind. It spoke better than anything except his fiction of the heroic nature and the abiding faith in man's capacity to prevail that qualify him as an honored member of the human race, which he would call the best honor. In the fiction, in "The Old People" in *Go Down, Moses*, McCaslin Edmonds said it best of all:

"Think of all that has happened here, on this earth. All the blood hot and strong for living, pleasuring, that has soaked back into it. For grieving and suffering too, of course, but still getting something out of it for all that, getting a lot out of it, because after all you dont have to continue to bear what you believe is suffering; you can always choose to stop that, put an end to that. And even suffering and grieving is better than nothing; there is only one thing worse than not being alive, and that's shame. But you cant be alive forever, and you always wear out life long before you have exhausted the possibilities of living. And all that must be somewhere; all that could not have been invented and created just to be thrown away. And the earth is shallow; there is not a great deal of it before you come to the rock. And the earth dont want to just keep things, hoard them; it wants to use them again. Look at the seed, the acorns, at what happens even to carrion when you try to bury it: it refuses too, seethes and struggles too until it reaches light and air again, hunting the sun still."

BOOKS BY WILLIAM FAULKNER

1924 *The Marble Faun* (poetry)
1926 *Soldiers' Pay*
      Sherwood Anderson & Other Famous Creoles: A Gallery of Contemporary New Orleans (with William Spratling; 250 numbered copies)
1927 *Mosquitoes*
1929 *Sartoris*
      The Sound and the Fury
1930 *As I Lay Dying*
1931 *Sanctuary*
      These 13 (stories)
      Idyll in the Desert (400 signed, numbered copies)
1932 *Salmagundi* (525 numbered copies)
      Miss Zilphia Gant (300 numbered copies)
      Light in August
1933 *A Green Bough* (poetry)
1934 *Doctor Martino and Other Stories*
1935 *Pylon*
1936 *Absalom, Absalom!*
1938 *The Unvanquished*
1939 *The Wild Palms*
1942 *Go Down, Moses*
1946 *The Portable Faulkner* (Malcolm Cowley, ed.)
1948 *Intruder in the Dust*
1949 *Knight's Gambit* (stories)
1950 *Collected Stories*
      Notes on a Horsethief (975 signed, numbered copies)
1951 *Requiem for a Nun*
1953 *Mirrors of Chartres Street* (1,000 numbered copies)
1954 *The Faulkner Reader*
      A Fable

1955　*Jealousy and Episode: Two Stories* (500 numbered copies)
　　　Big Woods (stories)
1957　*The Town*
1958　*New Orleans Sketches* (Carvel Collins, ed.; rev. edn. 1968)
1959　*Requiem for a Nun: A Play* (from the novel, adapted to the
　　　stage by Ruth Ford)
　　　The Mansion
1962　*Selected Short Stories of William Faulkner* (Modern Library)
　　　The Reivers
　　　Early Prose and Poetry (Carvel Collins, ed.)
1965　*The Marble Faun* and *A Green Bough* (first joint publication)
1966　*Essays, Speeches and Public Letters* (James B. Meriwether, ed.)
1967　*The Wishing Tree* (children's book)
1973　*Flags in the Dust* (original version of *Sartoris*; Douglas Day,
　　　ed.)
1975　*Marionettes: A Play in One Act* (facsimile edn. of 510 num-
　　　bered copies of 1920 work which Faulkner lettered, hand-
　　　bound and illustrated in six copies; issued with "A Memory of
　　　Marionettes," by Ben Wasson)
　　　The Marionettes (facsimile edn. of 100 numbered copies)
1976　*Mayday* (facsimile edn. of 125 numbered copies of an allegori-
　　　cal tale which Faulkner lettered, hand-bound and illustrated in
　　　one gift copy in 1926; accompanied by "Faulkner's *Mayday*,"
　　　by Carvel Collins)
1977　*Selected Letters of William Faulkner* (Joseph Blotner, ed.)
　　　The Marionettes (Noel Polk, ed.)
1979　*Uncollected Stories* (Joseph Blotner, ed.)
　　　Mississippi Poems (facsimile edn. of 500 numbered copies
　　　with Introduction by Joseph Blotner and Afterword by Louis
　　　Daniel Brodsky)
1980　*Mayday* (first trade edn.; Introduction by Carvel Collins)

Interviews

1956　*Faulkner at Nagano* (Robert A. Jelliffe, ed.)
1959　*Faulkner in the University* (Frederick L. Gwynn and Joseph L.
　　　Blotner, eds.; rev. edn. 1965)
1964　*Faulkner at West Point* (Joseph L. Fant III and Robert Ashley,
　　　eds.)
1968　*Lion in the Garden* (James B. Meriwether and Michael Mill-
　　　gate, eds.)

William Faulkner

SELECTED BIBLIOGRAPHY

Beck, Warren. *Faulkner: Essays by Warren Beck*. Madison: University of Wisconsin Press, 1976.

Blotner, Joseph. *Faulkner: A Biography*. 2 vols. New York: Random House, 1974.

———. *William Faulkner's Library: A Catalogue*. Charlottesville: University Press of Virginia, 1964.

Brooks, Cleanth. *William Faulkner: The Yoknapatawpha Country*. New Haven: Yale University Press, 1963.

———. *William Faulkner: Toward Yoknapatawpha and Beyond*. New Haven: Yale University Press, 1978.

Campbell, Harry Modean and Ruel E. Foster. *William Faulkner: A Critical Appraisal*. Norman: University of Oklahoma Press, 1951.

Cofield, Jack. *William Faulkner: The Cofield Collection*. Introduction by Carvel Collins. Lawrence Wells, ed. Oxford: Yoknapatawpha Press, 1978.

Coughlan, Robert. *The Private World of William Faulkner*. New York: Harper & Brothers, 1954.

Cowley, Malcolm. *The Faulkner-Cowley File: Letters and Memories, 1944–1962*. New York: The Viking Press, 1966.

Duclos, Donald Philip. *Son of Sorrow: The Life, Works, and Influence of Colonel William C. Falkner, 1825–1889*. Ph.D. Thesis, University of Michigan, 1961. Ann Arbor: University Microfilms.

Falkner, Murry C. *The Falkners of Mississippi: A Memoir*. Baton Rouge: Louisiana State University Press, 1967.

Faulkner, John. *My Brother Bill: An Affectionate Reminiscence*. New York: Trident Press, 1963.

Franklin, Malcolm. *Bitterweeds: Life with William Faulkner at Rowan Oak*. Irving, Texas: The Society for the Study of Traditional Culture, 1977.

Hamblin, Robert W. and Louis Daniel Brodsky. *Selections from the William Faulkner Collection of Louis Daniel Brodsky: A Descriptive Catalogue*. Charlottesville: University Press of Virginia, 1979.

Hoffman, Frederick J. *William Faulkner*. New York: Twayne Publishers, 1961.

Howe, Irving. *William Faulkner: A Critical Study*. New York: Random House, 1952.

Kawin, Bruce F. *Faulkner and Film*. New York: Frederick Ungar, 1977.

Kerr, Elizabeth M. *William Faulkner's Gothic Domain*. Port Washington, N.Y.: Kennikat Press, 1979.

———. *Yoknapatawpha: Faulkner's "Little Postage Stamp of Native Soil."* New York: Fordham University Press, 1969.

Massey, Linton R. *William Faulkner: "Man Working," 1919–1962.* A Catalogue of the William Faulkner Collections at the University of Virginia. Introduction by John Cook Wyllie. Charlottesville: Bibliographical Society of the University of Virginia, 1968.

Meriwether, James B. *The Literary Career of William Faulkner: A Bibliographical Study.* Authorized reissue. Columbia: University of South Carolina Press, 1971.

Millgate, Michael. *The Achievement of William Faulkner.* New York: Random House, 1966.

Miner, Ward L. *The World of William Faulkner.* Durham: Duke University Press, 1952.

O'Connor, William Van. *The Tangled Fire of William Faulkner.* Minneapolis: University of Minnesota Press, 1954.

Petersen, Carl. *Each in its Ordered Place: A Faulkner Collector's Notebook.* Ann Arbor: Ardis, 1975.

———. *On the Track of the Dixie Limited: Further Notes of a Faulkner Collector.* LaGrange, Ill.: The Colophon Book Shop, 1979.

Tuck, Dorothy. *Crowell's Handbook of Faulkner.* New York: Thomas Y. Crowell, 1964.

Vickery, Olga W. *The Novels of William Faulkner: A Critical Interpretation.* Rev. edn. Baton Rouge: Louisiana State University Press, 1964.

Waggoner, Hyatt H. *William Faulkner: From Jefferson to the World.* Lexington: University of Kentucky Press, 1959.

Wagner, Linda Welshimer, ed. *William Faulkner: Four Decades of Criticism.* East Lansing: Michigan State University Press, 1973.

Warren, Robert Penn, ed. *Faulkner: A Collection of Critical Essays.* Englewood Cliffs: Prentice-Hall, 1966.

Webb, James W. and A. Wigfall Green, eds. *William Faulkner of Oxford.* Baton Rouge: Louisiana State University Press, 1965.

Wilde, Meta Carpenter and Orin Borsten. *A Loving Gentleman: The Love Story of William Faulkner and Meta Carpenter.* New York: Simon and Schuster, 1976.

Medgar Evers
1926–1963

Medgar Evers

Medgar Wylie Evers:
The Civil Rights Leader As Utopianist

BY CLEVELAND DONALD, JR.

At 12:00 midnight Medgar Wylie Evers drove his car, which had aged another 40,000 miles during the year, from the Masonic Temple on Lynch Street toward his home. The monotonal hum of the eight-cylinder Chevy engine and the nocturnal silence cocooned him so that unmolested he enjoyed a fleeting glimpse of the peaks and valleys of his life. The usual thoughts came to mind. A child of nature he again had found peace in a machine's lullaby; a man of the people he had discovered once more the safety of a deserted street.

Medgar was thirty-seven. He was tired. And, as always, he reacted with ambivalence to the thought that he was a tired, thirty-seven year old man. By the standards of a black world, where the bodies of men died long before they lost the will to live, he could be thankful. In this world his aching muscles reminded him of life and his fatigue of that of the Mau Mau warrior fresh home from an heroic conquest. Yet, by the standards of the white world, where men were promised at birth three score and ten years, there was reason for concern. However, the slowing of the car just before it turned into the driveway of his home, stopped under the carport, and went mute caused him to forget standards and instead to remember his family, his wife Myrlie and his three children. He had gotten out of his car and turned toward his house, when suddenly an unbearable pain clawed his body while simultaneously the "thunderous roar" of a high-powered rifle echoed in the noiseless night. Repeatedly, he heard himself screaming "Turn me loose; turn me loose." By 12:30 a.m. he was free.[1]

[1]Observations of fatigue are taken from, and the phrase "Turn me loose" is quoted in, John R. Salter, *Jackson, Mississippi: An American Chronicle of Schism and Change*

A simple recounting of his life does not readily show that it took the full thirty-seven years for Medgar Evans to lock himself into the circumstances that occasioned his untimely death. He was born in 1926 in Decatur, Mississippi, in Newton County. In 1944 he entered the army and was sent to Normandy. After the war he returned to Mississippi, where he attended and graduated from Alcorn A&M, at the time one of two black state-supported four year colleges. He worked briefly as a Delta insurance agent before the National Association for the Advancement of Colored People appointed him in 1954 to the position of field secretary for the state of Mississippi. By 1963 he had established dozens of local chapters of the NAACP and made the civil rights organization a major force in the state. He had earned respect from blacks for his courage and leadership long before, but in 1960 he began a boycott of merchants in Jackson, Mississippi, that brought him to the attention of all Americans. Yet, partly because he had subordinated the use of voter registration and legal remedies to the need for direct action to solve systemic injustice and racial bigotry, his leadership was increasingly questioned and challenged by three groups: the white political and economic elite in Jackson, as well as their supporters in the state and national governments; a large and conservative number of the Afro-Jacksonian middle sector; and elements in the national headquarters of the NAACP. He lived until June 12, 1963, when, according to the district attorney who prosecuted the case, one Byron de la Beckwith lurked behind bushes to murder him.[2]

(New York, 1979), pp. 58, 69, 153, 183; and "thunderous roar" in Myrlie Evers, "Why I Left Mississippi," Ebony, March 1965, 25–28; others' comments on his death are James Jackson, At the Funeral of Medgar Evers in Jackson: A Tribute in Tears and a Thrust for Freedom (New York, 1963); Anne Moody, Coming of Age in Mississippi (New York, 1968), pp. 247, 249, 252–54; Howard Zinn, SNCC: The New Abolitionists (Boston, 1964), pp. 93, 213; James Silver, Mississippi: The Closed Society (New York: 1966, 3rd ed.), pp. 28, 30, 234–40, 283; Charles Evers, Evers (New York, 1967); James Meredith, Three Years in Mississippi (Bloomington, 1966), pp. 304–310. Reference to the Mau Mau, whom Medgar Evers admired, comes from Medgar Evers, with Francis H. Mitchell, ed., "Why I Live in Mississippi," Ebony, September, 1963, p. 143, and Myrlie Evers, For Us, the Living (New York, 1967), pp. 91 ff.

[2] The biographical sketch of Medgar Evers is from an autobiographical interview taken in November 1959 by Francis H. Mitchell and reprinted in Ebony. See Evers,

These vital statistics—birth and boyhood in the country, military service in World War II, a college education on the GI bill, matrimony and children, as well as the struggle for and achievement of gainful employment—were not characteristics possessed by Medgar Evers alone. In fact, significant numbers of his cohorts, both black and white, treaded similar paths during their lives. At his birth, most Mississippians lived in the country. Moreover, vast numbers of Mississippians of draftable age answered the call to arms during World War II. And, although relatively few embarked on college careers, numerous barracks and quanset huts built on state campuses after the war attested to a widespread and voracious appetite among black and white GIs for higher education. Medgar's and Myrlie's union occurred during a decade when most GIs were married. True enough, in the same year, employment opportunities in the state for trained blacks were few and far between; still, many other Afro-Mississippians found professional employment without leaving the state.

Historians in search of explanations for Medgar's commitment to civil rights—"even if it means," he said, "making the ultimate sacrifice"—may find several. Because he was a devoted family man, with a wife and three children to support, the economic motive comes immediately to mind. By 1955 it probably was clear to all, most especially to him, that his views of irrelationships among blacks prevented a successful career in insurance sales. For one thing, he recognized that poor blacks were exploited by black professionals, or "educated

---

"Why I Live in Mississippi," *Ebony*, 143–148; others, especially John Salter and Myrlie Evers, repeat this information, which Medgar apparently always mentioned in every review of his life; Myrlie Evers, *For Us, the Living*, passim; and John Salter, *Jackson, Mississippi*, p. 24; along with Salter, who alludes throughout his book to the problems with the NAACP and the Afro-Jacksonian middle sectors, see Meredith, *Three Years*, passim. In her book his widow provides a transcript of Beckwith's trial; see the appendix. Ann Moody has suggested that the NAACP actively pushed Medgar into national prominence; see *Coming of Age in Mississippi*, p. 90. My own recollection and Salter's book reveal the opposite to have been true; see *Jackson, Mississippi*, passim. For other indications of his national popularity read a letter (which is an excellent illustration of the chain letter as a form of social protest and action): "A Letter for Medgar Evers" in Alan Dundes and Carl R. Prayter, eds. *Urban Folklore from the Paperwork Empire* (Austin, 1975), pp. 9–10.

Negroes," in addition to whites. This class, of course, included insurance agents. Moreover, because of his desire for racial advancement, he often neglected his job in order to organize and mobilize NAACP chapters in the Delta. The post of field secretary, then, provided employment without the worry of exploiting blacks or of neglecting a career.[3]

In one respect the economic motive proves inadequate. For, although it holds for the early part of his life, this motive did not apply during his last years. Sometimes lucrative job offers came from outside of the state. On one occasion, for example, Sargeant Schriver approached Medgar during the course of an unplanned encounter on an airplane about working for the Federal Government.[4] Certainly, employment of this sort would have required that he leave the state; but one should not forget that Medgar could have remained in the state, without fear of imminent danger or of being fired, if he had compromised by focusing upon voter registration and legal remedies to racism rather than upon direct action primarily.[5] This stubborn refusal to compromise on the best method of accomplishing racial survival and uplift eloquently reveals that other factors overrode concern for the financial welfare of his family.

Psychohistorians may advance their own models to explain Ever's devotion to blacks, the state, and the South. His mother exerted considerable influence. More than anyone else she instilled Biblical precepts like the brotherhood of all men and apparently curbed his tendency after the war to accept violence as a weapon in the struggle against injustice. At the same time, a wholesome sibling rivalry held his brother Charles and him close together. In 1946, for instance, they and four others organized, registered, and tried to vote in Newton county.[6]

On a rare occasion Medgar recalled an episode involving a family member, his father, that heightened his commitment.

[3] Evers, "Why I Live in Mississippi," pp. 143, 146.

[4] Medgar Evers seriously considered the offer. Recollection of Lillian Louie, his secretary. Phone conversation, Cleveland Donald, Jr., and Lillian Louie, March 1980.

[5] Conclusion based on Salter, *Jackson, Mississippi*, pp. 35, 81, 153.

[6] Evers, "Why I Live in Mississippi," p. 144.

As the elder Evers lay dying of internal hemorrhaging in a Union, Mississippi, hospital two things became etched in the younger son's memory. The first evoked an omnipresent sense of place. Beds for blacks, Medgar would recall, were located in the uncomfortable basement of the hospital, while the better beds were upstairs and for whites only. The second elicited an equally pervasive sense of strife. Upstairs at the admissions desk a violent confrontation ensued between policemen and a black whom they had beaten and brought to the hospital. Responding to the urgent plea of a nurse, Medgar rushed upstairs and successfully ended the fracas. Later the events of the evening bubbled with symbolic meaning. "A Negro cannot live here or die here in peace," he reflected, "as long as things remain as they are." This realization led him shortly thereafter to accept the NAACP position.[7]

A problem with the pschoanalytical approach is that Medgar said little about his family—either that of origins or that of orientation. He did express, however, an intensely passionate love for the South. In pastoral imagery reminiscent of such literary giants as William Faulkner he reveled in the special quality of Mississippi's soil. He dreamed of owning land on which he would raise cattle. To those who knew of Southern oppression "it may sound funny" that he did not "choose to live anywhere else." Yet, "there's land here, where men can raise cattle. . . . There are lakes where a man can sink a hook and fight the bass. . . . There is room here for my children to play and grow, and become good citizens. . . ." When it became too dangerous to indulge his passion for fishing, Medgar drew upon these paradisiacal visions of Mississippi to relax and be sustained.[8]

Like others out of the pastoral tradition Medgar used the utilitarian quality of the soil to justify the presence of people. His goal of landownership and of making a "positive contribution

---

[7] Evers, "Why I Live in Mississippi," p. 146.

[8] Evers, "Why I Live in Mississippi," p. 146. For a discussion of Utopianism in one facet of the black experience see, John M. Reilley "The Utopian Impulse in Afro-American Fiction," *Alternative Futures: The Journal of Utopian Studies*, 1:3–4 (Fall 1978), 58–71.

to the overall productivity of the South" represented what was required of all Mississippians. People had to identify with the land. Moreover, this affection for the soil led Medgar to steps further: first, he located Southern backwardness in the unjust system of race relations and in the behavior of its supporters. Bigotry and systemic injustice spawned a detestable and pathetic creature, the parasite. No matter how much he wanted to remain in the state, "and whether whites like it or not," he declared, "I don't plan to live here as a parasite." Second, he saw that local prosperity depended upon harmonious race relations. And, as proof that race relations could be better even in Mississippi, he drew on two experiences, one of childhood recollections of happy playtimes with white children and another of his wife's hometown, Vicksburg, Mississippi, where blacks and whites lived "side by side" in some sections.[9]

The parasites identified by Medgar were whites and elements of the black middle sector. These groups hindered the development of the state by exploiting the black community through a patterned opposition to change. Two cases illustrated the dynamics of their opposition.

One case concerned Medgar's efforts to vote in 1946 and highlighted systemic resistance in all its phases. First, responsible whites politely questioned the wisdom of Medgar's actions. Second, "their Negro message bearers" tried to pursuade Medgar and his friends to take their names off the voter registration books and not to show up to vote. In the third stage the confrontation escalated, as an outsider, Bilbo, arrived to advocate that the best way to prevent blacks from voting was to "visit them the night before." When this stage (during which local leaders spoke through an outsider) passed, a fourth stage began; in 1946, "15–20 armed people [waited] at the courthouse." Then came the dramatic climax: Medgar and his group retreated, white leaders regained control of their violence prone followers, and the "Negro message bearers" falsely rumored—

[9] Evers, "Why I Live in Mississippi," pp. 143, 146.

to warn others and to reassert influence—that those who had attempted to vote had been "whipped, beatened up, and run out of town." However, the finality of the resolution rested on manifestly dysfunctional features: how well whites bridled their constituents and especially how violators of communal mores responded. For Medgar the message had rung clearly: "Well, in a way we were whipped, I guess, but I made up my mind then that it wuld not be like that again—at least not for me."[10]

The second case exemplified how he thought whites expected the system to operate. In February, 1954, Medgar applied for admission to the University of Mississippi's law school. In the first stage some whites complimented him. James P. Coleman, then attorney general for the state, interviewed the young civil rights leader, and following an extremely cordial conversation, told Evers that he would be notified of the results. Here the system operated smoothly because Coleman had discovered an irregularity in the application. Two days after the deadline the attorney general denied Medgar's petition on grounds that he had failed to obtain two recommendations from prominent members of the community. Yet, while the system had functioned perfectly, one of its dysfunctional features left the ultimate issue unsettled. The next decade found Medgar deeply involved in efforts to admit James Meredith to the University. This time, however, he watched the effort to full term, fearing only, according to John Salter, the consequences for the black community.[11]

Notwithstanding his criticism, Medgar recognized the complexity of the white community and the black bourgeosie. He often viewed whites indiscriminately; yet he relied on individual whites like John Salter and Ed King. He approached black interstitial groups cautiously and held them responsible for

[10] Evers, "Why I Live in Mississippi," p. 144.
[11] For a discussion of his application to the University see Evers, "Why I Live in Mississippi," p. 145; see also Myrlie Evers, *For Us, the Living*, p. 99, and Salter, *Jackson, Mississippi*, p. 24.

proving their relevance. However, friends and supporters like Sam Bailey, Robert Smith, and Melvin Daniels came from their ranks.[12]

Furthermore, awareness of the diversity within the two groups figured in his strategy for the improvement of Mississippi and the black community. Initially he distinguished the two groups by race. Whites deserved his love, for example, not because they were worthy but because the gift of love constituted a powerful test of his devotion to fundamental beliefs. Moreover, whites were unconverted. And love facilitated their conversion. This consideration made him eschew violence, since it did not take "much reading of the Bible though, to convince me that two wrongs would not make the situation any different, and that I couldn't hate the white man and at the same time hope to convert him."[13] On the other hand, "Negro message bearers" had always enjoyed his love. They lacked pride rather than conversion. Whereas whites were infidels who worshipped the ungodly form of race relations that had stifled local advancement, members of the black middle sectors resembled wayward or backsliding Christians only temporarily and conveniently removed from promises of the land inherent in racial progress.

Medgar devised a two-fold strategy for converting whites, corralling stray members of the black bourgeoisie, uplifting the masses, and developing the state. First, he sought "to embarrass the whites to death. For a long time, they literally got away with murder. Now, when a Negro is mistreated, we tell the world about it." This holding of injustice up for public display had represented a byproduct of voter registration programs and court litigations. But after 1958 Medgar relied increasingly upon the second feature of his strategy: namely the use of the black masses—"little men"—and youths to engage in collective and massive protest action to embarrass whites. The masses could and should participate, he believed, in their own

[12]Salter, *Jackson, Mississippi*, and Evers, "Why I Live in Mississippi," pp. 145, 146.
[13]Evers, "Why I Live in Mississippi," p. 143.

emancipation. However, although he wanted youths to help because they would be the ultimate beneficiaries of change and because he believed in their good judgment, the civil rights leader always saddened at the thought that young blacks had to make such sacrifices, when "at their ages most white boys don't have to be concerned with anything more serious than where they play."[14]

In spite of his misgivings about the involvement of youths, Medgar's analysis provided an effective base for organizing blacks. Perhaps, one must establish the setting for the major occurrences of his life to appreciate his progression from a rustic Decatur lad to a seasoned World War II veteran so attuned to the salient events of the time that in giving his first-born the middle name Kenyatta, he symbolically united the struggles of Afro-Mississippians with those of oppressed people everywhere.[15] Two major phases appear in this evolution, one rather protracted and the other far too brief. In the first, which began in 1925 and lasted until 1960, several intellectual changes and an uncounted series of incidents related to the essentially caste and racial nature of Mississippi society bombarded his conscious and unconscious thought and later conditioned his responses to experiences of the second phase. He recalled the first time a white playmate branded him a nigger, the segregation of the army, the integrationist spirit of French society, the inspirational example of the Kenyatta and Mau Mau struggle to liberate their land, the numerous lynchings, the impoverished "little men" of the Delta, and the agony he had endured to overcome hatred. The collective intensity of these events often required some form of personal response.

[14] Quoted from Evers, "Why I Live in Mississippi," p. 147; Meredith, *Three Years*, p. 92, and Salter, *Jackson, Mississippi*, passim, discuss his role with youths. Medgar's move away from legal remedies and voter registration may have resulted from the tendency among utopians to be anti-political; see Gorman Beauchamp, "The Anti-Politics of Utopia," *Alternative Futures: The Journal of Utopian Studies*, 2:1 (Winter 1979), 49–59, for this tendency.

[15] Indeed, he had wanted his son to have Kenyatta as a first name, but his wife did not like the idea and substituted, without Medgar's knowledge, the first name Daryl on the birth certificate; see, Evers, *For Us, the Living*, pp. 90 ff.

Moreover, the length of elapsed time alone was able to abate those major episodes that were of such impact that they formed his consciousness and provided appropriate explanations for subsequent encounters. In the second phase, from 1960 to his death in 1963, the number of ideological alternatives consolidated and polarized along the black-white continuum of the caste society; the number of major happenings decreased sharply and became more compacted in time and space as well as more intimately linked to immediate and important commitments. His time span came to encompass 1960–1963, his space Jackson, Mississippi, and his commitments the Jackson Boycott and the effort to mobilize Afro-Jacksonians.

Thus time and events shifted. So did the relationship between them. But more importantly, the actual process of developments became extremely significant, since the reduced time span, the frequency of events, the breath of space, and the number of options left little chance for introspection and contemplation. Expressed differently, realizing that he had lost the option of standing still and could choose only between advancing and retreating, Medgar moved forward to the quickened tempo of a polyrhythmical ritual that had been paced more slowly during the first phase of his life. Drawing upon the waltzy rhythms of the 1925–1959 period, he danced intuitively to the jazzy beat of the second. Medgar was not, however, out of control; he had known beforehand how events would transpire, and he knew that another option remained.[16] He could have retreated.

Medgar Wylie Evers lived in a "liminal" time and space, a situation in which writes Victor Turner, the anthropologist, "those being moved in accordance with a cultural script were liberated from normative demands." This civil rights leader was not caught simply between conflicting lifestyles, as Manneheim has theorized about socially and economically

---

[16] All who knew him felt that Medgar recognized the risks of his position. See, for examples, Salter, *Jackson, Mississippi*, p. 43, and quotes of a University of Mississippi professor in Silver, *Mississippi*, pp. 88–89.

mobile individuals. No Freudian or other psychoanalytical construct explains his behavior and attitude. Rather, for him "the possibility existed of standing aside not only from one's own position but from all social positions and of formulating a potentially unlimited series of social arrangements." Neither were his actions solely the result of a grand design nor of his free will. Such actions derived from the "processual nature of social action itself." Medgar was a "liminal" man.[17]

In Medgar and his circumstances the historian may recognize two "root paradigms" at work. Perceived in a racial context as far back as the epic social drama of Toussaint L'Ouverture and Napoleon Bonaparte, these root paradigms leave powerful clues to the motivation behind the more contemporary struggle of an NAACP field secretary for justice in Mississippi. A dystopian model, represented by Byron de la Beckwith, fostered segregation and a way of life that rested upon violence and the intimidation of blacks.[18] On the other hand, Medgar personified a utopian paradigm that wanted to integrate the community, to rid whites of racial hatred, and to insure justice. Beckwith's dystopia may have loved the land as much as Medgar's utopia. However, in Beckwith's the land connoted apocryphal visions of white supremacy, while in Medgar's it evoked Arcadian imagery of the equality of all men. Furthermore, an even more fundamental difference existed between the two patterns. With his Beckwith could possess the land as a right available only to whites; with his Medgar could claim the land out of duty to all men. Beckwith's prompted a selfish preoccupation with the land, exactly as Medgar's allowed great altruism. For this reason, above all else, Beckwith may have taken a life, but Medgar surely gave one for his homeland.

[17] Victor Turner, *Dramas, Fields, and Metaphors: Symbolic Action in Human Society* (Ithaca, 1974), p. 13; Karl Mannaheim, *Ideology and Utopia: An Introduction to the Sociology of Knowledge* (New York, 1959).

[18] Based upon a clipping among Medgar Evers' papers of a news article by Ted Poston; Poston examined the significance of the fact that Evers had kept a Beckwith letter which had appeared in a "comments from readers" column of the *Jackson Daily News*, April 16, 1957. Poston noted that "The letter may have been the first curious link between the two men." Date and source of the Poston article unknown.

SUGGESTED READINGS

Evers, Charles, with Grace Halsell. *Evers.* New York: World Publishing Co., 1967.

Evers, Medgar, with Francis H. Mitchell. "Why I Live in Mississippi." *Ebony,* September 1963, pp. 143–148.

Evers, Mrs. Medgar (Myrlie), with William Peters. *For Us, the Living.* Garden City, N.Y.: Doubleday, 1967.

Evers, Myrlie. "Why I Left Mississippi." *Ebony,* March 1965, pp. 25–28.

Jackson, James. *At the Funeral of Medgar Evers in Jackson: A Tribute in Tears and a Thrust for Freedom.* New York: Publisher's New Press, 1963.

Meredith, James. *Three Years in Mississippi.* Bloomington: Indiana University Press, 1966.

Mannaheim, Karl. *Ideology and Utopia: Introduction to Sociology of Knowledge.* New York: Harcourt, Brace and World, 1959.

Moody, Anne. *Coming of Age in Mississippi.* New York: Dial Press, 1968.

Salter, John. *Jackson, Mississippi: An American Chronicle of Schism and Change.* New York: Exposition Press, 1979.

Sewell, George Alexander, "Charles and Medgar Evers: Leaders in Civil Rights." In *Mississippi Black History Makers.* Jackson: University Press of Mississippi, 1977.

Silver, James. *Mississippi: The Closed Society.* New York: Harcourt, Brace and World, 1966.

Turner, Victor. *Dramas, Fields, and Metaphors: Symbolic Action in Human Society.* Ithaca: Cornell University Press, 1974.

Zinn, Howard. *SNCC: The New Abolitionists.* Boston: Beacon Press, 1964.

Contributors

John K. Bettersworth, Vice President Emeritus for Academic Affairs at Mississippi State University, is a trustee of the Department of Archives and History, is the founder of *The Mississippi Quarterly*, and is the author of several books, including *Confederate Mississippi*, *Mississippi: A History*, and *Mississippi in the Confederacy: As They Saw It*.

William Boozer of Nashville is a frequent reviewer of Faulkner studies and is the author of *William Faulkner's First Book: 'The Marble Faun' Fifty Years Later*.

Nash K. Burger, who collaborated with John K. Bettersworth in writing *South From Appomattox*, was until his retirement an editor at *The New York Times Book Review*.

William Jack Crocker lives in Memphis but is a native of the Mississippi Delta. He is a singer, song writer, and poet whose works have appeared in several journals and quarterlies.

Cleveland Donald, Jr., was the second black student to be graduated from University of Mississippi. After being awarded a Ph.D. from Cornell, he returned to the University of Mississippi to direct the black studies program there.

Louis Dollarhide, professor of English at University of Mississippi, has been a feature writer for *The Clarion Ledger—Jackson Daily News* and is the author of numerous poems and short stories.

John Carroll Eudy, a native of Chickasaw County, has been chairman of the Department of Social and Behavioral Science at North Harris County College, Houston, Texas. A portion of Dr. Eudy's study of Thomas Rodney was read at the 1968 meeting of the Southwestern Social Science Association.

Shelby Foote, who lives in Memphis, was born in Greenville, Mississippi, and is the author of the monumental study *The Civil War: A Narrative* and several novels, including *Follow Me Down, Jordan County, Tournament, Love in a Dry Season,* and *Shiloh.*

A former president of Mississippi Historical Society, Nannie Pitts McLemore was a noted state historian who contributed articles to *The Journal of Mississippi History* and *Encyclopedia Britannica.* With her husband, the late Dr. Richard A. McLemore, she wrote *The Mississippi Story,* a textbook used in elementary schools, and *The History of Mississippi College.*

Willie Morris was a Rhodes Scholar and was editor-in-chief of *Harper's.* He grew up in Yazoo City, Mississippi, and is the author of *North Toward Home, The Last of the Southern Girls,* and *James Jones: A Friendship.*

Emmie Ellen Wade is a native of Arkansas but has lived in Mississippi since childhood. She continued her career as an educator after serving in the U.S. Coast Guard in World War II. She recently retired from Northwest Junior College, where she taught history for many years.

William Winter, chairman of the board of trustees of the Department of Archives and History, is Governor of Mississippi.

Dean Faulkner Wells and Hunter Cole, the editors of this volume, are native Mississippians who live in Oxford.